MEXICAN LABOR AND WORLD WAR II

Mexican Labor and World War II:

Braceros in the Pacific Northwest, 1942–1947

Erasmo Gamboa

UNIVERSITY OF TEXAS PRESS AUSTIN

Printed in the United States of America

First edition, 1990

∞ The paper used in this publication meets the minimum requirements of American National Standard for Information Sciences—Permanence of Paper for Printed Library Materials, ANSI Z39.48-1984.

Library of Congress Cataloging-in-Publication Data

Gamboa, Erasmo.
Mexican labor and World War II : braceros in the Pacific Northwest, 1942–1947 / Erasmo Gamboa.—1st ed.
p. cm.
Includes bibliographical references.
ISBN 0-292-75117-6 (alk. paper)
1. Migrant agricultural laborers—Northwest, Pacific—History—20th century. 2. Alien labor, Mexican—Northwest, Pacific—History—20th century. 3. World War, 1939–1945—Manpower—Northwest, Pacific. I. Title.
HD1527.A19G36 1990
331.5'44'08968720795—dc20 89-37605
CIP

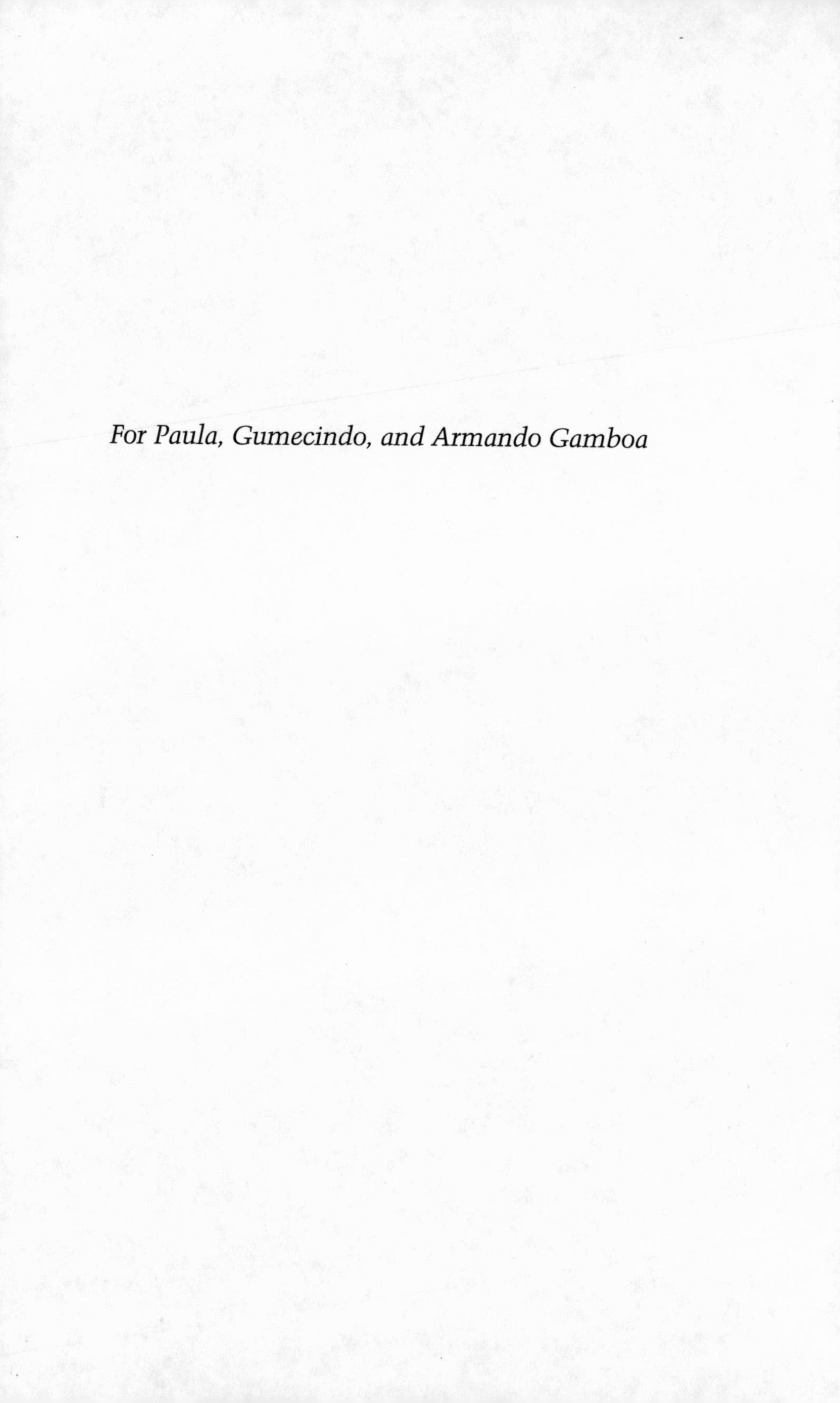

For Paula, Gumecindo, and Armando Gamboa

Contents

One of my poor countrymen had spent three months in a place where the climate made him ill. Once he was better, the rain and snow prevented him from working. In consideration of his poor health, his board, which he had not paid, was forgotten. At his request and so he would not go further in debt, the officials agreed to return him to Mexico.

He told me that during all the time he was in the United States, he only managed to send home a ten dollar money order. He was wearing all the clothes he owned. His pockets contained ten dollars.

What saddened him the most was the thought that his family had written several times telling him that they expected him to return with many of the things they wanted.

—JESÚS TOPETE, *AVENTURAS DE UN BRACERO*

Despite the occasional abuses which the Mexican workers suffer at the hands of United States farmers, one of the happiest aspects of the bracero program is the personal relationship that develops between workers and farmers. The mutual pleasure and cordiality with which the workers and their employers greet each other when the worker arrives with a new contract after a long absence in Mexico is unmistakable. It is a rewarding experience to witness the departure of braceros at the end of the season, to see a Spanish-speaking farmer say farewell to a group of his homeward-bound braceros, embracing each one individually and calling him by his first name. The well-fed, well-dressed, happy men who, wearing their inevitable new Stetson hats, depart for Mexico carrying shiny new trunks and great, clanking, canvas-wrapped bundles containing everything from plows to sewing machines, can hardly be recognized as the lean, ragged, worn-looking men who arrived in the United States in the spring with their possessions in small burlap bags.

—RICHARD H. HANCOCK, *THE ROLE OF THE BRACERO*

Acknowledgments

IN THE COURSE of writing this book, I have profited from the advice and generous assistance of colleagues, librarians, archivists, and friends. But I am especially indebted to Professors Robert E. Burke, Joan C. Ullman, and the late Carl E. Solberg from the History Department at the University of Washington. They provided warm encouragement and from them I learned the discipline. As best they could, they also tried to teach me how to avoid the pitfalls that come with the task of interpreting the past. I value their counsel, challenges, and the opportunity to benefit from their vast experience.

Historians Rodolfo Acuña, Albert Camarillo, and Mario T. García kindly read the manuscript in its early stages. I am particularly grateful to Mario T. García, who unselfishly offered written, detailed critiques and sound judgment with respect to publishing this book. My good and dear friend Angélica Hernández typed first through final drafts of the typescript. Peter Bacho gave of his time.

I appreciate the assistance of Theresa J. May and the editorial staff at the University of Texas Press in helping to prepare this book for publication. The Graduate School Research Fund at the University of Washington provided a generous grant so that I could travel to the National Archives.

The persons who told their life story to me, and the braceros themselves, are a very special part of this book. As I attempted to learn about their experiences in the Pacific Northwest, their perseverance inspired me. They have my utmost respect and are heroes in their own way.

My family, Carole, Andrea, and Adriana, provided constant warm and enduring support. They deserve more thanks than I give them here.

E.G.
MAY 30, 1989

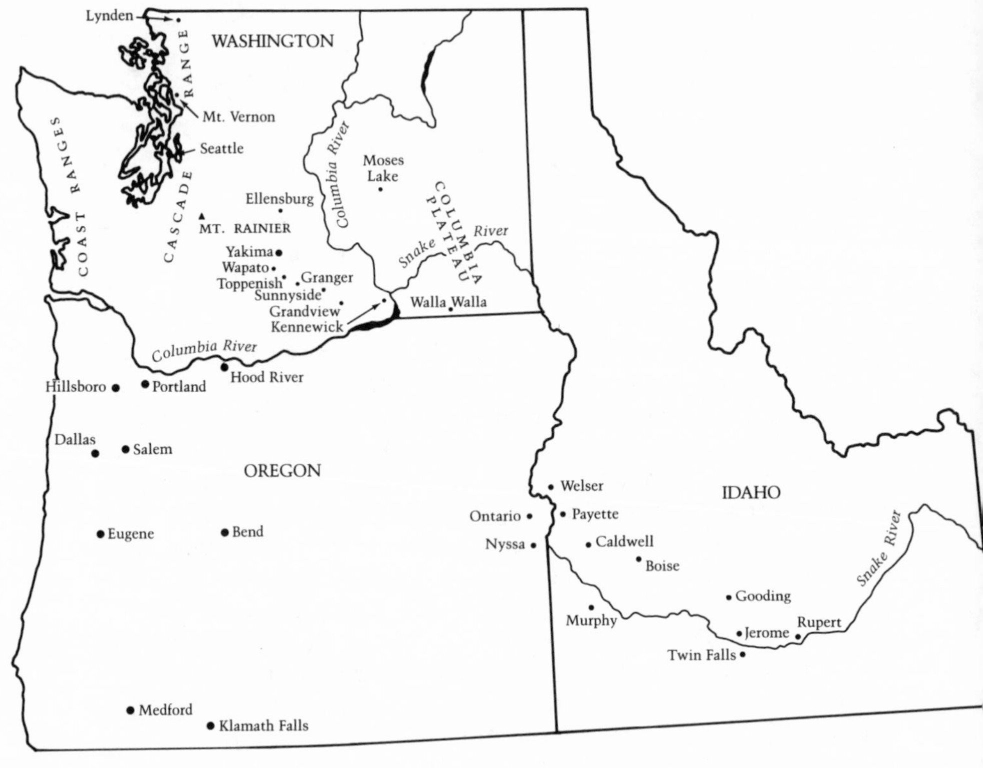

The Pacific Northwest

Introduction

MORE THAN ANY other event, World War II prompted an unprecedented effort to mobilize human resources toward the common goal of victory. Across the nation farmers faced the dual challenge: to produce food and fiber for national consumption and the armed forces as well as the Allies. That they met the goal was remarkable. However, success did not result entirely from the initiative and efforts of the farmers. Agricultural laborers were a most critical factor in farm production because the war had drained the supply of field workers. As early as 1942, critical labor shortages threatened farm production. To resolve this crisis, the U.S. government imported Mexican agricultural workers, or braceros.[1] Between 1942 and 1947, these men made the difference between lost production and harvested crops in the Pacific Northwest states of Idaho, Oregon, and Washington. This study examines the history of the bracero program in this region.

During the last few years, scholars have broken new ground by interweaving the study of Mexican immigration processes with the Chicano experience and the history of the United States. However, in exploring Mexican labor and the bracero program in particular, the bracero program in the Pacific Northwest and other regions of the country has remained essentially unexplored and poorly understood.[2] More than two decades after the bracero program ended in 1964, Ernesto Galarza's *Merchants of Labor: The Mexican Bracero Story* (1964) remains one of the definitive works on this topic despite its focus on California and the scant attention devoted to the critical period of World War II. The other seminal work, Richard Craig's *The Bracero Program: Interest Groups and Foreign Policy* (1971), likewise is limited to a discussion of the federal labor program in Texas and California.

This case study of Mexican contracted workers in the Pacific Northwest seeks to fill the gap by concentrating on the war years. By examining the bracero program in the Pacific Northwest it places this important farm labor program into a broader national context. Also, through a description of the work and social experiences of the braceros, the voice of the men comes through. While it is true that braceros in the different regions of the country shared many experiences, several factors, including the type of farms, climate, distance from Mexico, and labor strikes, set the Pacific Northwest apart. For these reasons alone, this study is important. In terms of time, the focus on World War II is significant, because while historians of the Chicano experience might disagree about the details, they agree that the war had an unsettling effect on the economic, social, and political structures of the Mexican American community.[3]

During World War II, the nation's call for record-shattering farm production exerted tremendous pressure on an already labor-starved agricultural economy. As a result, Congress, as it had during World War I, authorized the importation of contracted agricultural workers from Mexico under the auspices of Public Law 45 (PL-45). The bracero program of World War II quickly became institutionalized among most of the nation's farms.

National in scope, the wartime-contracted farm labor program reflected the experiences of Mexico and the United States with immigration prior to the war. It also exemplified the practical knowledge gained by both governments during the first bracero program of World War I. Decades after its demise, the bracero program continued to influence the course of Mexican immigration, because untold numbers of Mexican immigrants had first entered the United States as contracted workers.

The main themes of this study are familiar ones: wretched living and working conditions, prejudice, ill treatment, and poor wages. Against the backdrop of previous studies of the bracero program, it is difficult to think of the braceros in any other terms than as men who were pathetically weak, unable to control their own destiny, easily exploited, and at the mercy of an oppressive labor system. Although this conceptualization is filled with hard truths, it is nevertheless open to question.

With respect to theoretical concepts, this study is a straightforward history.[4] It is limited by the fact that much of the general course of Chicano history in this region, as in other areas outside the Southwest, is still at the basic research and data collection levels. As a consequence of this limitation, this work attempts to augment the knowledge of the broader national bracero program as well as Chicano and U.S. labor and social history of World War II.

During the first phase of Mexican immigration of the twentieth century, from 1910 to 1920, agriculture and railroads recruited workers to the Pacific Northwest. The spatial distribution of Mexican immigrants to the northwesternmost corner of the United States was conditioned by the same factors operating in the Southwest: an open immigration policy toward Mexico and economic expansion with a corresponding labor economy.

The flattened national economy during the Depression meant that large-scale Mexican immigrant labor was no longer needed. Although repatriation is a central theme in Mexican immigration history during the thirties, the partial recovery of the northwestern agricultural industry made the recruitment of Mexican and Mexican American migratory workers from the Southwest to the Northwest necessary. During this decade an insidious New Deal policy which offered Anglo farm migrants but not seasonal Mexican farm workers an opportunity for upward mobility created a permanent unskilled migratory community in the Northwest.

World War II ushered in a robust economic building cycle. As the demand for farm products expanded, the agricultural industry was forced to search for a cheap, seasonal, and productive mobile labor force. The search ended in 1942, when Mexican contract workers became the centerpiece of an emergency national farm labor supply program. Mexican workers were contracted in their homeland and brought to northwestern farms. Although the bracero program was national in scope, local, federal, and state officials tailored the federal farm labor system to meet regional labor market demands. This meant that the bracero program differed across regions and helps explain why it ended sooner in some areas like the Pacific Northwest but continued in the Southwest until 1964.

The men who came to the Northwest experienced social conditions markedly different from those in states such as California. The braceros experienced terrible living conditions and widespread racial discrimination everywhere. Yet extremely cold temperatures and the lack of a Spanish-speaking community were significant differences between the lives of men in the Northwest and the Southwest.

On the job, northwestern braceros were subject to the same dual wage system and racial oppression, which have long been features in the history of the Mexican working class in the United States. Yet these workers stood up to their employers and the federal government by striking, demanding repatriation, deserting, or employing other forms of protest. In part, their defiance was encouraged by the Mexican consuls, suggesting that the Mexican government was more active in protecting the rights of its citizens than is propounded by the literature on the braceros.

The end of the war signaled the end of the bracero program in northwestern agriculture. Mechanization, cited in other studies as a reason for discontinuing the importation of contracted workers, had little effect in this region. Instead, the strikes and administrative changes in the bracero program forced employers to reconsider the ongoing use of Mexican workers and replace them with less troublesome Chicano workers.

Looking back, these braceros had a profound influence on the Pacific Northwest. They faced legal, economic, and social adversities; still, they maintained the regional and national growth of a country at war.

1. Agribusiness and Mexican Migration

ALTHOUGH THE Pacific Northwest is culturally different and distant from the Southwest and Mexico, Mexican people have long traveled to this region. Even so, a discernible pattern of Mexican migration did not develop until the beginning of the 1900s. Agricultural growth coupled with a liberal immigration policy toward Mexico and conditions in the Mexican Republic itself were the underlying factors that account for this migration. As the pace of agricultural development quickened during the twentieth century, many newcomers, including Mexicans, were attracted to the Northwest. The latter were immigrants residing in the Southwest and then drawn north by an incipient labor-intensive farming economy. Even during the Depression, which saw many workers sent back across the U.S.-Mexican border, northwestern farms continued to pull Mexican laborers away from many southwestern communities. Their experience in this region between 1900 and 1940 is a relatively unknown chapter in the larger pattern of Mexican immigration into the United States.

Until the 1900s, economic development in the Pacific Northwest was slow for several reasons. People considered the region to be too distant from the populated areas of the eastern United States, the road along the way arduous, and the investment in time and equipment too great. Only after the last half of the nineteenth century did yeoman farmers arrive in appreciable numbers, and even then they faced the problem of reconciling their dreams of opportunity with the geographic and economic realities of the area. Optimism in the agricultural potential of the region did not begin until the completion of the northern transcontinental railroad and the subsequent development of private and public irrigation projects.[1]

Once this economic infrastructure was in place, the full agricultural capability of the Pacific Northwest became evident. West of the Cascades, farmers discovered that the bottomlands of the Willamette Valley in Oregon and the Puyallup and Skagit valleys in Washington were exceptional producers of specialty crops. Not only were yields high, but they were superior in quality and commanded attractive market prices. East of the Cascades and into eastern Oregon, southern Idaho, and south-central Washington irrigation projects opened up thousands of formerly arid but rich acres of topsoil that made possible repeated yields. In other areas such as the Palouse country, wheat farmers could produce record crops without irrigation and little more than alternate fallows and sufficient winter moisture. All this should not suggest that some farmers did not hang precariously between mere indebtedness and total loss, but once the region's agricultural potential was tapped, farm failures were few.

The Cascade Mountains determine agricultural productivity more than any other regional topographic feature. They rise abruptly from the coastal area, creating a series of fertile littoral valleys, such as the Rogue and Willamette in Oregon and the Skagit and Puyallup in Washington, and traverse Oregon and Washington in an almost true north-to-south longitude. In this coastal area, the ocean's influence prevents either extreme cold or heat and produces a temperate climate with well-defined seasons conducive to agriculture.

East of the Cascades, the geography consists of tablelands of increasing elevation extending east into the Bitter Root Mountains of Idaho. Interspersed among these plateaus are other important agricultural valleys such as the Snake River, which runs the breadth of southern Idaho, linking several small valleys into a major agricultural belt. In Washington, proportionately smaller farming valleys such as the Wenatchee and Yakima are equally significant. As a whole these valleys receive less precipitation than the coastal area, and summer temperatures exceeding 100 degrees Fahrenheit and 0 or below during the winter are not uncommon.

The limitation of the agricultural-producing areas of the Northwest was, and remains, its relatively short growing season of about 180 days. Despite this limitation, irrigation and extraordinarily fertile soils made possible extraordinarily high yields of a wide variety of crops. This cornucopia of grapes, sugar beets, hops, fruit and nut trees, wheat, strawberries, beans, onions, and many other crops has led residents to coin appropriate sobriquets such as "Magic Valley" and "Fruit Bowl of the Nation" for the Boise and Yakima valleys.

Yet in spite of its comparative advantages, the success of all northwestern farming enterprises has always pivoted on an extensive supply of farm labor. Throughout the Northwest, excepting some areas along the coast, labor shortage was the most serious obstacle encountered by farmers. A combination of factors, such as low density of population, distance between populated centers and farming areas, intense oscillation between peak demand and lull, and the often arduous nature of the work itself, exacerbated an already critical problem. For these reasons, farmers used novel ways to recruit workers onto their farms and then encourage them to leave during the long winter dormancy.

When considered together, the farmers' zeal for farming, the region's natural advantages, and labor's central role in agricultural production form an interesting trilogy. In a microcosm, the Yakima Valley illustrates this triumvirate feature of the northwestern farming economy.

Historically, Yakima's combination of public and private enterprise as well as comparative natural advantages brought it early national attention as one of the country's most important agricultural-producing areas. In 1935, Secretary of Agriculture Henry A. Wallace commented on the area's reputation "as one of the outstanding irrigated valleys in the country and a pronounced success."[2]

Yakima's production was large but from a comparatively small valley, approximately sixty miles in length and at its breadth fifteen to twenty miles. In spite of federal reclamation projects during the Depression, Yakima County contained only 1 percent of the nation's irrigated acreage in 1939.[3] Ten years earlier, it had already ranked sixth in the nation in the value of agricultural production. Only three counties in California, one in Maine, and another in Pennsylvania stood ahead of this northwestern gem.[4] Even in the midst of the Depression, Yakima Valley farms continued to rank tenth in value of production.[5]

One explanation for this remarkable productivity was farm management. Crop farms accounted for 80 percent of the total production, and the remainder was livestock-related.[6] The crop farms were highly specialized and mostly owner-operated, because crops such as hop cultivation or fruit orchards required considerable knowledge and a high investment in trees, yards, and other capital improvements. This type of highly specialized agriculture made farmers extremely reluctant to jeopardize their investment through careless or inefficient tenant or absentee management. Even in hard times, most growers preferred to sell their farms or operate at a loss before relinquishing control. As a result and through the Depression, many farms were still in the hands of the original homesteaders or farmers. This kind of personal and not too common commitment to excellent management was a cornerstone of the valley's outstanding production record.[7]

With respect to the relationship between farm labor and production, the Yakima Valley was an anomaly. In general, the farm labor needs of most agricultural economies were relative to the size of farms and the type of land tenure. Small acreage family farms, for example, generally supplied their own labor needs or called on nearby residents. Larger commercial farms, on the other hand, either absentee or family-owned, would exhaust the local work force and employ seasonal migrants. Prior to World War II, Yakima agriculture consisted primarily of small-acreage farms. Yet the demand for labor was so high and seasonal that the valley became one of the most important users of seasonal farm workers in the West. This unusual dependency on seasonal migrants had little connection with farm size and much to do with labor-intensive crops.

Hop and fruit cultivation best illustrate the shape of the labor market. In 1935, the area devoted to hop cultivation was small, approximately 5,500 acres, and required 130 man-days of labor for harvest alone.[8] Conversely, the fruit acreage was considerably larger, at 54,733 acres, and the same amount of labor was sufficient for all orchard care, including harvest.[9] Other variables associated with these two crops were also critical to the valley's labor market. Since hops reached optimum maturity suddenly, farmers tended to delay the harvest as close to the ripe stage as possible. This produced an intense harvest-related labor demand that peaked quickly during three weeks in September and was over a short time later. At the point of harvest, farmers hurried the laborers because diseases or insects could rapidly devastate an entire crop, and rain or wind could just as easily fell a heavily laden yard. Fully cognizant of potential financial losses, employers generally advertised for many more workers than were necessary as a safeguard to the highly vulnerable acreage.

Fruit was not as susceptible to ruin or total loss as hops, but it had a similar swing between low and peak demand for labor. Late winter and early spring pruning resulted in a minor spurt of labor activity that was easily met by local workers. August brought the early fruit harvest and a slight need for workers that peaked in early October. Following the autumn harvest, little if any outside help was employed by fruit growers until the work cycle was repeated the following year.

Most of the Yakima farms had similar oscillations between peak labor needs and lapses. For instance, Yakima Valley agriculture needed 33,000 hired workers at the peak of the 1935 harvest. Conversely, during the winter months, from November through January, little more than 500 workers were sufficient to meet the valley's entire labor demand.[10] In other words, Yakima farmers employed sixty-six times as many workers at the September peak as they did during winter inactivity. For this reason, each year Yakima farmers faced the critical problem of recruiting large numbers of migrant men, women, and children.

The Yakima Valley was not unique; the Willamette Valley of western Oregon had many of the same characteristics: fertile soils, specialty crops, high production, and an intensive labor economy. In 1935, Willamette hop farms accounted for over half the national hop supply.[11] Other area farmers raised substantial yields of vegetables, fruits, and nut crops. This outstanding capacity to produce placed the Willamette Valley second in the nation in green bean production by World War II.[12] Idaho's Upper and Lower Snake River Valley counties also yielded high quantities of specialty crops with strong market values such as potatoes, sugar beets, and peas. For instance, in 1938 potato farmers planted thirteen times less acreage than grain growers but received just slightly less than two and one-half times the value of wheat production.[13] Potatoes commanded such high prices that Idaho growers raised 40 percent more than Washington and Oregon combined and twice that of California.[14]

Like their Yakima counterparts, Willamette and Snake River growers were confronted with the annual task of recruiting thousands of out-of-state workers. In Idaho, the sparse state population and the distance from other populated areas made the recruitment of farm labor more troublesome and, therefore, a more critical factor in production.

Labor's role in agricultural production was critical due to other added factors. Like California, the high perishability of the area's crops heightened the need for a large pool of farm labor. The crops' high commercial value meant that growers required sufficient help in order to rush their crops to market at the optimum point of maturity and command the highest prices. In addition, as was pointed out earlier, in most areas several competitive labor markets—fruit and row crops—co-existed in time and space. For these reasons and others, farm labor was of strategic importance to successful farming.

From the onset this type of labor-intensive agriculture in the valleys of Idaho, Oregon, and Washington began to pull Mexican workers away from areas of the Southwest and Mexico. This process of recruitment, either directly through handbills and other advertisements or indirectly through word of mouth, invited countless numbers of Mexicans along with other groups into the region's farming economy. Yet for reasons that will be developed later, Mexican laborers as a group did not become essential to Northwest farming until World War II. Nevertheless, because their arrival coincided with the first wave of people from Mexico, their experiences call attention to a broader interpretation of early Mexican immigration.

The combined effects of the Díaz dictatorship, the Revolution of 1910, and the absence of any real improvement in the lives of most Mexican people after the revolution gave impetus to as well as sustained the exodus of people across the U.S.-Mexican border. Between 1875 and 1910, increasing population pressures and worsening rural poverty in Mexico began to force its citizens abroad.[15] The net effect of the Díaz dictatorship was only a forerunner of increasing emigration from Mexico. The Revolution of 1910 exacerbated conditions so that people fled to escape intolerable living conditions and also for personal safety. In the following decade of civil war, upwards of one million persons crossed into the United States.[16]

As the mayhem of the revolution subsided, the failure of the Constitution of 1917 to deliver on its promise of sweeping economic and social change encouraged an increased number of emigrants to leave. Internal conflicts between the church and state and a spent economy gave Mexicans added reasons to depart from their homeland. In point of fact, more emigrants entered the United States during the 1920s than in the preceding tumultuous decade of civil war.[17]

Too often, scholars neatly catalog Mexican emigration as a phenomenon confined to the Southwest and parts of the Midwest but not important to the Pacific Northwest.[18] Although many details of the story remain obscure, the evidence is clear that the outward ripples of Mexican immigration also carried Mexican people to the Pacific Northwest. By 1910, Oregon ranked seventh among states outside the Southwest with Mexican-born residents.[19] Juan Ramón Salinas, born on June 26, 1872, in a village near Valparaiso, Zacatecas, was typical of that generation of immigrants. Raised in poverty and limited to a third-grade education, Juan never learned to read or write in Spanish or English. Yet in spite of this tremendous disadvantage and at one hundred years of age, Juan was remarkably precise and lucid when he recorded his life experiences in 1974.[20]

As a young man, Juan left the state of Zacatecas and moved north to the mining towns of Durango, Mapimí, Torreón, and Gómez Palacios, Durango. In 1899 Juan, like countless others, boarded the Mexican central train from Torreón to Cuidad Juárez on the U.S.-Mexican border. From Juárez, Juan had no problem crossing the border to El Paso, Texas. Here and at the age of twenty-nine, he began a seventy-three-year odyssey that was to take him through much of the western United States and as far east as Nebraska. Returning only periodically to Zacatecas, Juan lived the rest of his life in the United States until his death in the Yakima Valley in 1974. As an immigrant, Juan worked when and where work was available—as a stage driver, railroad track worker, and cotton picker. In his itinerant wandering, Juan witnessed and participated in the course of Chicano history during the early 1900s. California's Mexican atmosphere reminded him of life in his native Mexico. He recalled the large Mexican crowds in Los Angeles transfixed by the anarchist oratory of Ricardo Flores Magón. Later in 1906, he experienced firsthand the terrible earthquake in San Francisco. His proudest moment was being present as President Taft's train arrived at Sacramento.

In 1907, Juan was encouraged to come to the Northwest by labor agents who were recruiting workers from Mexico and the Southwest for employment in salmon canneries in Alaska.[21] Together with several other Mexicans, he got as far as Seattle, which was a "mud hole" and lacked the atmosphere of the San Francisco–Oakland area. He was discouraged, and in Seattle Salinas hopped an eastbound train without knowing that it was bound for the Yakima Valley. The year was 1907, and sixty-five years later a local newspaper reporter dubbed this diminutive Zacatecan the valley's first Mexican.[22]

Juan R. Salinas and his companions were representative of the stream of immigrants that scholars say had crossed the Mexican border "well before the start of the Revolution of 1910."[23] Once in the United States their journey's end, like that of other immigrant groups, was determined not solely by ethnicity and other social factors but by the more important economic consideration of employment. Even as the prospect of landing a job in Alaska's salmon canneries drew Juan to Washington State, sugar beet companies from as far away as Colorado were engaged in a more systematic and aggressive recruitment of Mexicans.[24]

In 1907, the Dillingham Immigration Commission noted that 1,002 Mexican workers had traveled a "considerable distance" from their homes in Mexico to Colorado.[25] The commission's report serves to underscore the point that the diffusion of Mexicans was approaching southeastern Idaho. It would be safe to conclude that if Juan Salinas and his companions were not typical, they were at least symbolic of the widening geographical distribution of the Mexican population in the United States noted by the Dillingham commission.

Two years after the immigration commission published its report on Mexicans in northern Colorado, the immigrants entered Idaho. Geraldo Cárdenas was one of them. He was born in Monte García, Zacatecas, and emigrated to this country in 1911. Two years later he was one of several Mexican farmers cultivating sugar beets in Idaho.[26] Juanita Ramírez, who arrived in 1916, was another early Mexican resident of Idaho.[27] These two persons were not unique;

they represented the ongoing northern extension of Mexican immigration. In 1920, the federal census estimated a ninefold increase in Idaho's Mexican population from 1910. Not too surprisingly, nearly half these immigrants were in the adjoining counties of Bannock, Brigham, and Bonneville, the heart of Idaho's developing sugar beet industry.[28]

The course of Mexican immigration to the Northwest was as much the result of U.S. immigration policy as it was an opportunity for employment. Just months after the Immigration Act of 1917 had established a literacy and head tax requirement for Mexican immigrants, the secretary of labor authorized western sugar beet enterprises to recruit alien labor without enforcement of the restrictions.[29] This special waiver, which was prompted by a general wartime labor shortage, stood to benefit western growers because they were especially hard hit. Farmers took advantage of the open border policy to flood the Southwest with cheap labor, thereby accelerating the flow of Mexican workers into the Northwest. Historian Mario T. García points out that by 1918 hundreds of workers had been recruited from El Paso to Idaho's sugar beet fields. The following year the Amalgamated Sugar Company and the Utah and Idaho Sugar Company (U & I Sugar Company) established labor agents in that city.[30]

By 1920, a combination of socioeconomic and political conditions in Mexico, recruitment by growers, and lax federal immigration policy made Mexican labor commonplace in Idaho. A year earlier, an Idaho newspaper reported several thousand Mexican sugar beet workers "penniless" in Pocatello.[31] Five years later, the U & I Sugar Company adopted a policy that pledged to provide Mexican laborers for sugar beet farms of twenty-five acres or more.[32] The Amalgamated Sugar Company followed this precedent and began to supply Mexican beet workers for five thousand acres of sugar beets contracted exclusively to the company in the Twin Falls area.[33] The arrival of workers to the Twin Falls area meant that Mexican people were keeping abreast of the spread of sugar beet cultivation westward along the Snake River Valley and in the direction of Washington State.

Geraldo Cárdenas was one of several Mexican immigrants who left Idaho for Washington State during the 1920s. Prior to migrating to Washington, he farmed sugar beets near Twin Falls. While there, Geraldo was encouraged to move to the Skagit Valley in Washington by the U & I Sugar Company, which was interested in attracting farmers and labor to its new Bellingham sugar beet factory.[34]

As Geraldo Cárdenas settled in the northwestern corner of Washington, the leading edge of Mexican immigration was fixed some twenty-three miles from the U.S.-Canadian border. Many other Mexican sugar beet workers also arrived in Washington as the U & I Sugar Company replayed the recruitment process already witnessed in Idaho.

Simultaneous to their arrival in Idaho and Washington, Mexican laborers also entered Oregon. By 1924, Mexicans were contracted from the southwestern states for sugar beet work at three dollars per day.[35] The number of laborers residing in Oregon was substantial, because the Gunn Supply Company recruited Mexican workers from Portland.[36] This Oregon city, along with Denver and Los Angeles, "the great Mexican peon capital of the United States," was one of the company's principal areas of recruitment for Mexican laborers.[37]

Even as agricultural expansion gave rise to Mexican immigration, a parallel growth in the supportive economic infrastructure required still more laborers. Construction companies sought cheap and unskilled Mexican workers to develop new irrigation tracts and enlarge established projects. Outside of agriculture, the railroad companies became one of the prime employers of recent immigrants in order to construct connecting feeder and trunk lines. In 1929, six of nine western railroad companies reporting significant increases in the number of Mexicans employed as track maintenance workers were operating in the Pacific Northwest. Of the reporting railroad companies, the following operated in the Northwest: the Union Pacific, Denver and Rio Grande, Northern Pacific (west of Paradise, Montana), Oregon Short Line, Oregon Railroad and Navigation Company, and the Spokane and Cascade Divisions of the Great Northern. According to Paul S. Taylor, the number of Mexicans employed on section gangs by the nine railway systems had jumped from 17.1 percent in 1909 to 59.5 percent in 1929.[38]

Albeit small in numbers, Mexican railroad workers represented another facet of the progression of Mexican immigrants into the Pacific Northwest. Generally, employment agencies recruited in the Southwest or Mexico and railroad companies stationed the workers at key terminals or junctures. In 1924, the Union Pacific had one such group of Mexicans stationed east of Nampa, Idaho.[39] Since the job of maintaining the right-of-way in good repair offered long-term and steady employment, railroad workers were among the first of the Mexican immigrants to settle permanently in the Pacific Northwest.[40]

In less than one decade after the outbreak of the Revolution of

1910, Mexicans had pushed into the Pacific Northwest and continued as far as the salmon canneries of Alaska.[41] Their presence was the end result of two separate but not unrelated processes: economic regional expansion and Mexican immigration.

As might be expected, the market crash of 1929 sharply curtailed the entry and northwestern progression of Mexican immigrants into the United States. Beginning in that year, the State Department instructed its consulates in Mexico to enforce the literacy, head tax, and visa requirements on departing emigrants more stringently, causing legal immigration to plummet. Meanwhile, immigration officials and, on occasion, state authorities became more diligent in stopping illegal border crossings. The effects of the economic depression cut so deep that, beginning in 1930, federal and local governments in concert with local communites began to repatriate and deport Mexican people in order to provide jobs for unemployed citizens and avoid the social cost of caring for the destitute immigrants.[42] These deportations, which were carried out in communities with large Mexican populations and as far from the U.S.-Mexican border as the state of Indiana, signaled Mexican laborers to leave.[43]

The closing of the border and deportation had less to do with anti-Mexican sentiment than with the depressed economy. Mexican laborers, long characterized as cheap and easily available, were simply not needed as jobs evaporated in agriculture, industry, and the service sectors of the economy. In the Northwest, the farming economy reeled with the economic setback of 1929. As crop prices plummeted, farmers were forced to cut back sharply shipments of market commodities. Their dilemma was exacerbated by the fact that most produce was sold in markets outside of the tri-state area. These two factors, declining prices and distant markets with high shipping costs, caused some farmers to neglect their orchards or leave parts or all of their farms unattended. By 1936, however, prices for some northwestern crops started to recover due to a combination of price supports, development of new marketing strategies, tariff protection, and other factors.

Therefore, as farmers cut back production of some crops, they expanded others. The repeal of Prohibition, for example, encouraged Washington hop production to increase from 2,200 acres in 1930 to 6,300 in 1934; Oregon's hop cultivation shot up from 14,000 acres to 23,000 for the same period.[44] Similarly, in both states fruit production increased from an initial drop in 1931 as growers adopted California's use of uniform packing, shipping, pricing, and advertising.

By 1936, growers had organized the Pacific Northwest Fruits, Inc., patterned after California's successful Fruit Growers Association, to represent the combined interests of most Washington and Oregon apple producers.[45]

Idaho agriculture made its own adjustments to soften the effects of the Depression. In the Twin Falls area, the price of beans, which had sold for $5.18 in 1929, was only $1.16 per hundred pounds in 1931.[46] Faced with downward spiraling prices, farmers made the best of their situation by shifting to more stable or subsidized crops such as potatoes or sugar beets. While no complete recovery was apparent, the 1929 index of farm prices in Idaho reached a low of 45 percent in 1933, then rose to 90 percent of pre-1929 levels by 1935.[47]

In the meantime, as bread lines became longer, agriculture was often the only source of jobs. Even so, in many communities the unemployed preferred to add their names to relief rolls or try to obtain employment in the Federal Emergency Relief Administration, Civil Works Administration, or later, the Works Progress Administration to doing farm work. Many farmers were surprised that their offers of employment went begging. The hard work, the seasonal nature of agriculture, and the highly impersonal relationship between farmer and farm workers were only partial answers. More important, the average annual income of farm workers fell 51 percent, from $430 in 1929 to $210 in 1933, while factory wages slumped only 34 percent.[48] By 1939, farm workers earned $2.60 per day in Washington, $2.50 in Idaho, and a farm worker in Oregon toiled all day for $2.45.[49] In the Depression wage economy, the unemployed were much better off if they were able to secure jobs outside agriculture or in federal works projects. That same year and in contrast to farms, entry-level unskilled workers in federally funded road construction received $6.29 per day in Washington, $5.86 in Oregon, and $5.61 in Idaho.[50]

The substantial decline in farm wages was a complex issue that went beyond falling crop prices.[51] Some farmers recognized the luxury of idle labor and simply cut wages and justified the low wage scale by the minor degree of skill required for farm work. The fact that farm workers in the Northwest, as in other parts of the country, had not the slightest influence in determining wages or conditions of employment contributed further to the dismally low wage scale.[52]

Given the general unemployment, farmers did not anticipate worker shortages to worsen, but they did. Depression or not, in the major agricultural areas of the Northwest the local labor force was insufficient to meet the heavy demand for springtime and harvest workers. Of the myriad of problems that beset farmers during the early years of the Depression, the labor issue remained as serious as it had been during the preceding decade and symbolic of an imperfect farming economy.

Until midwestern farm migrants began to arrive between 1935 and 1938, farmers had a limited source of potential farm labor. The class of pre-Depression non-Mexican migratory laborers, augmented by farmers who suffered mortgage foreclosures and others who sank deep into material poverty, was still present. In spite of the reversal of immigration, scores of Mexican farm workers remained in the Southwest and were readily available. In California, their numbers declined only about 30 percent, and although they were fewer in numbers after 1930, they still represented the largest foreign group of agricultural laborers.[53] For this ethnic group of farm workers, the search for the good life in the United States had proved elusive during normal years. They had made little progress in contrast with the Italians, who became prominent in grape cultivation and wine making; the Japanese, who became excellent truck farmers; the Portuguese, who entered dairying in California; or the Volga Germans, who became beet growers in the Rocky Mountain states.[54] The Depression caught Mexicans at much the same level of social and material existence as when they had arrived earlier from Mexico. As conditions worsened in the Mexican communities, the people became willing candidates for recruitment to northwestern farms.

In the midst of the Depression, it was especially hard to obtain a sufficient supply of sugar beet workers. In normal years this type of back-breaking job did not appeal to most workers because it was demanding and poorly paid. Workers were expected to arrive in time for spring thinning and then depart and return again for the fall beet harvest. The sugar beet industry solved its labor problem by recruiting scores of destitute Mexicans from communities in California and Texas.

The demand for Mexican labor grew as the Jones-Costigan Amendment to the Agricultural Adjustment Act stabilized the long-standing problem of overproduction and low sugar prices. The amendment limited national production, while restrictions were placed on sugar imports from Cuba, Puerto Rico, Hawaii, and the Philippine Islands.[55] In exchange for restricted sugar beet cultivation, the federal government paid growers a cash subsidy based on past and present acreage. Under this type of tariff protection, ceiling on production, and cash subsidy, sugar beet cultivation in the Northwest remained steadily above the 1929 level during the Depression.[56] The Jones-Costigan Amendment also raised the average income of most sugar beet farmers by 20 percent.[57] Consequently, sugar beet cultivation increased from 61,000 acres to 105,000 acres in 1933.[58]

Since communities had insufficient local field labor, the Amalgamated and U & I Sugar companies had no other option but to continue the pre-Depression practice of recruiting Mexican labor. Soon other employers, such as pea processors and hop growers, followed the sugar companies' lead and recruited Mexican workers as well.

There is no reliable way to estimate how many Mexican people were recruited or otherwise arrived in the Northwest during the years of the Depression. They were doubtless included in the general tide of penniless workers which flowed into the three states. This is evident from the case of fifty-year-old Jesús López, who left Mexico in 1916. During his first years in the United States, he did track maintenance work on various midwestern railroads until the possibility of larger earnings with his wife and children took him to the Texas cotton fields. He then left his family and got a steady job as a section hand near Broken Bow, Nebraska. At the start of the Depression and at the age of forty-seven, Jesús López was considered "too old" for industrial work by the railroad companies. After 1932, he worked mostly as a field worker and never earned more than $75 in any one year. In 1935 he was living in Seattle's shanty town, Hooverville, selling wood and collecting junk for income.[59]

The flood tide of freewheeling migratory farm workers carried many other Mexicans to communities like Driggs, Idaho, for the annual pea harvest.[60] In 1931, a newspaper estimated that nearly two hundred pea pickers were housed in labor camps at Arco in Butte County.[61] Four years later, the potato harvest drew hundreds of Mexican and Filipino pickers from California to Bonneville County, Idaho.[62] In Washington's Yakima Valley, Mexicans searching for employment arrived like clockwork, prompting a reporter to note that many "Indians, Mexicans, and Filipinos" were present in the summer of 1933 in anticipation of the fall hop harvest.[63]

The large number of Mexican migratory workers present in the region attracted the attention of Paul S. Taylor, who noted that many of California's Mexican migrants annually migrated north to the Idaho pea fields.[64] Elsewhere, he wrote, the migrants traveled far from the Imperial Valley near the Mexican border to Oregon's Hood River and Willamette Valley as well as the Yakima Valley.[65]

The sugar beet industry, more than any other factor, brought the greatest number of Mexican laborers north. In contrast to Oregon and Washington, with one processing facility, Idaho recruited extensively in order to keep its eight sugar beet factories in operation.[66]

In 1935, the Idaho Sugar Beet Growers Association brought so many Mexicans for spring thinning that the local residents felt discriminated against in employment. The growers responded that "white workers" were amateurs who did the job poorly and were slower and less efficient than the Mexicans, who were professionals at this type of work.[67] By 1936, a Boise newspaper editor characterized the arrival of three hundred Mexican beet thinners aboard a special thirteen-car train from Sacramento, California, as a well-established practice.[68]

When they were recruited, most of the workers traveled north under the direction of Mexican farm labor contractors based in California or Texas and skilled in recruiting for farmers throughout the country, including the northwestern states. The Tolan House Select Committee to Investigate the Interstate Migration of Destitute Citizens found that the "great bulk of the contractors" operating along the western part of the country were "Mexican and Filipinos" who conducted their business with little regulation by either the state or federal government.[69] They functioned as powerful intermediaries between laborer and employer because most understood English and Spanish and were able to mediate the conditions and terms of employment such as wages, time of arrival at work site, and housing, as well as the customary kickbacks.

Although testimony before the Tolan committee disclosed that contractors in Alameda County, California, provided workers for Idaho and Texas, in all probability they also supplied most of the Mexican labor destined for the Northwest during the thirties.[70] In sheer numbers Texas had the most migrants available, estimated at 600,000 in 1937 by the Texas State Employment Service.[71] Eighty-five percent were of Mexican descent and 66,000 reportedly traveled out of the state for seasonal work.[72] In remarks before the Tolan committee the office of the Mexican consul at San Antonio stated that Oregon and Washington, along with midwestern states, received many of these workers.[73]

As agricultural stability developed and more Mexican laborers were required on northwestern farms, local white workers viewed their arrival with disdain. The latter, many recently arrived as migrants themselves, felt more deserving of employment than "foreigners" and feared that the presence of cheap labor would worsen an already marginal level of existence.

In Idaho's small communities the large numbers of Mexicans were more conspicuous than in Oregon or Washington. White workers took their protests against these apparent interlopers before the governor to complain that the Mexican workers had depressed wages to the point that $1.85 to $2.00 per day were barely possible.[74] The Idaho Beet Growers Association responded that they preferred "white labor," but since it was not available they had to advertise for help out of state. Local workers admitted that they were not taking the jobs because "white people" could not afford to accept such low wages. Confronted with the fact that wages were low, growers reiterated their earlier argument that the Mexicans were simply better workers.[75] The ongoing controversy over outside Mexican labor was a complex issue. Mexicans were recruited to take jobs that few local workers would accept even during hard times. Since relief was available, local workers could afford to be selective about the jobs they accepted. A Boise newspaper editor wrote, "Now it must be admitted that thinning beets and pulling currant bushes are not tasks designed to lure loafers from the trough. They are pure work, back busting, hand hardening work." He added, "The pay is not magnificent" either.[76] Emergency relief administrators were well aware that farm jobs went begging and had adopted a policy that the idle must "work when a job is offered or forever remain off relief rolls in Idaho."[77] With regard to Mexican laborers, they were considered deplorable "and must be avoided for the good of our own workers, who alone would be injured by such a move."[78] Two years later, too many local workers remained on relief. To put an end to the abuse of state generosity, the State Farm Placement Office began to register all transient white laborers entering Idaho and direct them to the nearest employment office. In order to discourage migratory Mexicans and Filipinos, the State Farm Placement Office declared that only white transient labor was eligible for assistance toward employment.[79] Idaho's stern policy to match white migratory workers with farm jobs did not threaten the recruitment of Mexican labor, as the interstate system was not tampered with. This being the case, Mexican workers continued to be contracted throughout the thirties to Idaho as well as the rest of the Northwest. Although commonplace on northwestern farms during the Depression, few Mexicans settled permanently because the lack of off-season employment, poor winter housing, and the expiration of work contracts convinced most that it was better to winter in the Southwest. Federal and state policies toward relief also worked to prevent migratory Mexican farm workers from establishing residency in the Northwest.

The liberal-spirited policies of Roosevelt's New Deal had little to offer farm workers but even less to seasonal migratory laborers. Before the responsibility for relief was turned back to the states in 1935, interstate farm migrants were excluded from federal relief payments under the Federal Emergency Relief Administration (FERA), although transient single men were eligible.[80] After 1935, the different state governments continued to withhold relief to seasonal workers through statutory and administrative limitations. Although policy differed greatly, all three northwestern states made continuous and long residency a condition to obtaining public assistance from county or state agencies. Oregon statutes provided that persons were eligible for general assistance if they had lived within the county for a period of one year and within the state for a period of three years. Washington's Emergency Relief Act did not contain any provision making residency a condition to obtaining relief, but the director of public welfare was empowered to adopt rules and regulations to promote "efficiency" and "effectiveness" in providing relief. Consequently, Washington made residence for a period of one year within the state and six months within the county a prerequisite to receiving assistance. Idaho was more restrictive in providing relief assistance because a person had to reside in the state for three uninterrupted years.[81]

Although the statute and administrative limitations were applicable to all needy persons, Mexicans were most affected because as seasonal migrants they never remained long enough to qualify. Disadvantaged by relief policies and short-term employment, they constituted an amorphous category of poverty-stricken persons for whom neither the state or federal government would accept responsibility. From the standpoint of local government, residency requirements were simply ways of preventing migrants from becoming a social burden. This was true of Payette, Idaho, and Ontario, Oregon, where city officials stated frankly that they would not be responsible for destitute nonresidents.[82] Elsewhere, local policy was generally the same. In the Yakima Valley, relief was withheld from agricultural migrants except in "emergency cases."[83]

The northwestern states were not unique in their disregard for interstate Mexican migrants. Migratory workers in general received little if any social uplifting from the bulk of the New Deal programs because they fell outside its scope. The northwestern regional branch of the Farm Security Administration (FSA) was particularly oblivious to the needs of destitute Mexican agricultural workers.

The FSA had evolved from the Resettlement Administration (RA) in 1937 with a charged responsibility of alleviating the plight of the rural poor as well as the rehabilitation of displaced farmers through resettlement. The administrative structure of the FSA was sufficiently decentralized to allow each state and most counties enough latitude to tailor the federal mandate to suit local circumstances. This well-intentioned but indeterminate policy led some state and county officials to observe that whoever controlled the FSA organizations might also define the farm relief program. For this reason, FSA programs differed across the nation's eleven administrative regions; in the Northwest, Oregon's policy was not necessarily that of Washington or Idaho.

FSA officials in the Northwest, although concerned with local farmers and other poverty-stricken rural individuals, were largely committed to the federal policy of rehabilitation. Its central focus was drawn to the 97,826 impoverished migrants who had arrived in the region beginning in 1930.[84] Unlike the "Okies" who entered California, 90 percent of the migrants to the Northwest originated in states north of the 37th parallel—Missouri, Kansas, or the Dakotas. Most were families which had entered the Northwest between 1935 and 1937 when the FSA itself was created.[85] In that time, 80 percent elected to settle in Oregon and Washington and two-thirds of all the incoming families chose rural communities with populations of 10,000 or less. On the whole, this migrant community was young, in the main twenty to forty-one years of age. The majority were skilled as farm owners or had some farming experience, and over 75 percent possessed at least an eighth-grade education.[86]

FSA officials in Region XI felt that, unlike other migrants, these midwestern families merited assistance and at the same time offered an unusual opportunity for rehabilitation as farmers. According to the Portland FSA office, the Midwesterners were unfortunate victims of "a recurring disastrous series of natural events leading to their economic attrition." Their resolve had not broken, a spokesperson continued; instead, "the old pioneer spirit of moving west to seek a new start after encountering adversity has been in evidence through the whole movement."[87]

There were many reasons why the FSA did not consider seasonal agricultural workers, especially Mexicans, in the same category as Midwesterners. Mexicans, although in need, had been common fixtures on the rural agricultural scene for years prior to the Depression; they had not been subject to any calamity. Moreover, they were not experienced farmers and, lacking that quality or other marketable skills, little could be done by the FSA to improve their situation. The FSA could not empathize with this group because they were "true migratory agricultural laborers of the nomadic type" and their talent was limited to "some special knack."[88] Hence, the "true migrant" was pretty much left to fend for himself.

The FSA's effort at rehabilitation of displaced farm families centered around three program activities: resettlement, a loan and grant program, and the construction of interim farm housing. Resettlement was made to order since federal projects had opened 218,000 acres of newly irrigated farm land and another 1,000,000 acres were expected to become available for resettlement.[89] The program, however, was beset with problems from the beginning. The actual supply of farms fell short of the demand, and when families received land the problem of developing farms on newly irrigated tracts was outside the experience of most individuals. These and other circumstances led some families to lose hope of obtaining a farm and eventually to return to the Midwest. However, on the whole resettlement was significant. In Oregon's Vale-Owyhee project, 1,000 migrant families settled on 90,000 acres.[90] On the average most households received 80 acres, and at no time did the FSA contemplate collectivized farms on these projects.

The resettlement process was made possible under the loan and grant program authorized by the Jones-Bankhead Farm Tenant Act of 1937. It provided low-cost mortgage loans to families who otherwise would have been unable to acquire newly developed, abandoned, or otherwise available farms.[91] Subsistence grants were also available to needy individuals without regard to state eligibility requirements for relief. Just the same, these grants were not intended to serve as substitutes for "jobs or rehabilitation" and therefore were given only after a careful review of the particular situation.[92]

The farm camp program, the third area of concern and the most controversial, demonstrated keen originality on the part of the FSA. Unlike the prototype system in California, the camp system in the Northwest was intended to furnish decent housing, stimulate employment through a centrally organized labor pool, and provide interim homes for farm families awaiting resettlement. Two types of camps were constructed, either mobile or standard, with the latter as the linchpin of the program of rehabilitation. The standard facilities, called farm family camps, were constructed at Yakima, Walla Walla, and Granger, Washington; Caldwell and Twin Falls, Idaho; and Dayton, Oregon. Each center was designed to house as many as 250 families chosen for settlement with all the amenities of a small community at affordable rents. In order to be selected, families needed experience with farm management or ownership and had to demonstrate that they were already making their way upward in the community. Under these criteria, the farm family camps became temporary homes for an exclusive group of midwestern families.[93]

By design, the mobile camps served a different purpose and population. They were not as nice or comfortable as the standard type and no extended occupancy was permitted. Since they only operated when the demand for farm labor was high, these camps served as little more than convenient labor centers and an indirect housing subsidy to farmers.

This is not to say that the FSA in the Northwest turned its back entirely on the seasonal migratory workers, but its concern was only as good as actual practice. Food, health care, and other kinds of subsistence were generally dispensed at the farm camps. Thus, residency in FSA housing, even if temporary in the mobile camps, greatly improved the chance of benefiting from the FSA's policy of providing surplus food commodities and health care to all needy persons. In truth, outside these camps the FSA did little to ameliorate the needs of the seasonal workers.

As noted already, the camp system drew the most criticism from farmers and local officials. As soon as federal officials announced plans and started preliminary surveys for the permanent camps, unsubstantiated rumors stirred the local community in opposition. Usually, growers would circulate rumors that the camp would serve as a hotbed for farm labor unionization or that it would bring in hordes of undesirables. On the other hand, devaluation of property, major police problems, and unwanted pressures on the local educational system were the major concerns of local communities. The policy of the FSA was to hold public information hearings in order to air the public's objections and assuage their fears. This approach did not satisfy some communities, and after exhausting local pressure tactics to halt construction they appealed directly to their congressional representatives. The Idaho Falls Chamber of Commerce voiced its opposition "against decent quarters for migratory labor families" to Senator William E. Borah.[94] Yamhill County residents in concert with the Oregon senate also forwarded their complaint to Congress, arguing that the FSA's plan to build a farm camp at Dayton "would reduce land values and become a sanctuary for radical agitators."[95]

These organized protests, which were generally orchestrated by large growers, turned the FSA's farm camp program into a highly political issue. At Yakima, for example, a highly charged controversy developed as soon as plans for construction of two camp facilities were announced. In order to learn more, a member of the Yakima County Welfare Advisory Board and prominent businessman traveled to Marysville and Gridley, California, to inspect several FSA labor camps similar to those proposed for Yakima County. His report, which was quite favorable and laudatory, was rejected as a misrepresentation by the Yakima farming community, headed by the Associated Farmers of Washington and seconded by the Yakima Chamber of Commerce. The FSA, encouraged by the report, circulated it widely in order to dispel local opposition to the camps. On one side of the issue were farmers who misread the purpose of the camps and distrusted the FSA meddling in their domain. Support for the FSA where it existed was for the most part disorganized and composed of inarticulate small farmers and the migrants themselves. In the end and to the credit of the FSA, the agency used its federal mandate and was able to maneuver successfully to proceed with the construction of the camps. Not surprisingly, little objection was raised against the temporary mobile camps used exclusively by Mexican and other seasonal workers.

Criticism of the farm housing complexes continued after they were ready for occupation. In a letter to Carey McWilliams, who was gathering material for his book *Ill Fares the Land* (1942), the individual who had prepared the report on the California camps stipulated that he could not afford to be quoted, for his statements might "prove quite detrimental." He answered that his report had already cost him "many so called friends as well as suffering [economic] reverses." The mere suggestion of a camp in Yakima, he pointed out, developed into bitter recriminations by the local newspapers that the camp would be "a concentration camp, breeding place of communism, a political tool, labor strife, etc., etc."[96]

All told, the decade of the Depression did little to alter the migration patterns of Mexican people to the Pacific Northwest. On the surface, it would appear that the general unemployment, the end of Mexican immigration to the United States, and the influx of many uprooted Midwesterners to the Northwest were reasons enough why Mexicans would not continue to be recruited to the northwestern states. Yet, paradoxically and in contrast to the 1920s, Mexican migratory workers came in greater numbers. This apparent contradiction of recruiting workers during high unemployment and shrinking job opportunities made possible the continued presence of Mexicans in the region. As before, the region's agricultural industry needed field workers; Mexicans were sought out because they were available, could be paid cheap wages, and would accept the laborious jobs that others turned down.

Necessity moved these migrants north from southwestern communities during a decade that witnessed major regional social and economic benefits from the New Deal. Since they were Mexican and seasonal migrants, they had no other recourse but to depart as poverty stricken as when they arrived. Federal and state relief was not extended to them, and the opportunity to escape the migratory cycle through the resettlement program was beyond their reach. Yet the lives of many of their Anglo counterparts were improved by the FSA and other New Deal programs. Paid low wages and excluded from rehabilitation, those Mexicans who became permanent residents in the Northwest and elsewhere had no significant choice but to retreat into the backwaters of the depressed rural communities of the 1930s.

2. World War II and the Farm Labor Crisis

After the fall of France in 1940 and the passage of the Lend Lease Act, much of agriculture was transformed into a booming industry by increasing U.S. involvement in the European conflict. At the same time that the Allies intensified their demand for U.S. food and fiber, the domestic need also multiplied. Northwestern farms, already beset by labor problems, quickly felt the gravity of too few workers as a result of the call for stepped-up industrial and agricultural production. In August 1939, the president appointed the War Resources Board to study the problem of war mobilization, and two months later the Department of Agriculture (USDA) called attention to the probable development of a national farm labor shortage.[1] In spite of a federal farm labor program and a patriotic pitch to the public to assist farmers, the supply of workers never came close to matching the demand. As the country was pulled toward war, farm labor shortages reached crisis levels. Two years later, agribusiness and the federal government heralded the bracero program as a solution to the labor crisis.

In general, as the region's economy expanded it was called upon to produce more. Portland, Vancouver, and the Seattle area were seemingly transformed overnight by new major shipyards and aircraft plants as well as supporting defense industries.[2] Concerning agriculture, the years immediately preceding the outbreak of the Second World War witnessed substantially greater crop output, although record-breaking production developed only after 1942. Expanding opportunity gave rise to a keen sense of optimism in recovery from the worst of the Depression. Farmers had some reservations about the hope for better times because as the manufacturing work force mushroomed so too did farm labor shortages. By 1940, the FSA pointed to "increasing labor shortages" in the Northwest and noted that farm workers were becoming more competitive with industrial laborers in their search for employment.[3]

The increased competition among farmers for labor resulted from both the pull exerted by industry and the increasing needs of agriculture. Many farm workers, including farm families who had applied for but not received settlement farms, abandoned their jobs at the first opportunity for higher wages in industry. Others left because they recognized that there were clear and inherent disadvantages in agricultural employment, such as exclusion from the Federal Wages and Hours Act, which covered industry. Worse yet, the National Industrial Recovery Act and later the National Labor Relations Act did not include or recognize that agricultural workers had a freedom of choice to establish unions for their own protection. Understandably, as more farm workers became conscious of their economic, social, and legal disadvantages, they could not turn down the benefits of defense plant employment.

A year before Pearl Harbor, the demographic shift of workers from rural to urban areas was already under way. By the spring of 1941, labor shortages had developed in Idaho, Oregon, and Washington. At Idaho Falls, farmers with beet fields ready for thinning were alarmed to find that for the first time in years virtually no labor was available. The Federal Employment Service checked the roadside from Pocatello to Sugar City and found no sign of migratory workers.[4] According to the FSA, the three to four thousand workers who were ordinarily hired to thin the beet fields "were not in evidence."[5] Oregon beet farmers in Malheur County faced a similar situation. The manager of the Amalgamated Sugar Company reported that customarily half the work force was provided by Mexican and white labor from California, but this year "very few of these transient workers" had made an appearance.[6] At Yakima, the regional office of the Federal Employment Office noted fewer migrant families in the area and many on their way to "national defense jobs."[7]

As the specter of crop losses loomed, farmers did as much as possible to prepare for the worst. The first step was to drum up all available men and women by getting officials to purge the remaining WPA rolls and close work projects. Next, business establishments were encouraged to limit their hours to generate additional workers. At the same time, the ongoing recruitment of out-of-area labor was stepped up.

One of the most threatening labor problems occurred at Yakima, where the supply of workers was characteristically inadequate. By midsummer 1941, the war industries at Portland and Seattle had exerted an unusually strong pull on Yakima's labor supply, prompting farmers to organize the Community Harvest Emergency Committee.[8] As the September hop harvest approached, the absence of workers jeopardized a $4 million hop crop at Toppenish.[9] Valley hop growers estimated that a minimum of 35,000 harvest workers was going to be necessary to bring in the crop.[10] One farm operation alone advertised for no fewer than five thousand workers.[11] Worried by the potential loss, local schools closed in order to free the students to assist with the harvest. One school superintendent tested parent opinion on school closures and, in spite of a vigorous "no" vote, the hop growers got students released for two weeks anyway.[12] Farmers applied similar pressure on the Yakima sheriff's department to do a better job of collaring all idle men in hobo areas, including the Yakima Indian Reservation, which was an alleged hangout for loafing "Negroes and Mexicans."[13] An appeal also went to businesses to close or limit their hours of operation until the crop was brought in.

Worker shortages were similar in Oregon and farmers made corresponding moves. In eastern Oregon growers called upon the Amalgamated Sugar Company "to do something to save their beets."[14] The company searched throughout the West Coast and finally located five hundred available workers, who were brought to the area.[15] When it became clear that sufficient outside labor was not available, the Ontario Chamber of Commerce suggested that all stores close one day a week. Later, the chamber ordered them to discourage shoppers by displaying cards that read, "Closed until 1 P.M. Daily except Saturday, Everyone Thinning Beets."[16] In western counties, the Oregon Employment Service set up a "harvest bee" telephone line to help direct potential workers to farm jobs.[17] Next in response to the growers' petition, WPA rolls were emptied throughout the Willamette Valley.[18]

Farm labor was as scarce in Idaho even though agriculture was probably less affected by the war industry. Through the spring of 1941, the Committee on Public Welfare was confident that enough workers were available and more concerned that an influx of needy laborers would flood the state.[19] To meet the scarcity of labor, growers and their families went into the fields. Communities closed their schools and stores and mustered every person, including those on WPA projects, to work.

As the 1941 harvest season arrived in the Northwest, it was apparent that the need for workers was the major problem facing farmers. The opening address to the December meeting of the Oregon State Horticultural Society pointed to the fact that industry had drawn heavily on the farmers' supply of farm labor. "The big problem for next year," the report stated, "is that of manpower."[20] The sugar industry, which was one of the mainstays of the region's agricultural economy, went on record that its "major problem" was the limited number of workers.[21]

Farmers had every reason to be concerned, because their spur-of-the-moment, improvised solution to the labor problem had barely pulled them through and already it was coming under criticism. Some communities were questioning some types of farm jobs, especially the proposition that "beet work was proper for white people."[22] Still other farmers stated that they would "rather not raise beets than to have to get out and thin them."[23] In addition, the use of schoolchildren under fourteen years of age on sugar beet farms, even though temporary, was prohibited by the Sugar Act of 1937. The act also applied to children fourteen to sixteen years of age and limited them to no more than eight hours of work per day. Already, the superintendent of public instruction in Idaho and Oregon had cautioned farmers concerning student workers.[24] The State of Washington went further and began to penalize districts for the days schools were in session and the students were in the fields.[25]

But even as the worker shortage increased, some farmers and other groups doubted that a real labor shortage even existed. Some farmers contended that the FSA camps were keeping persons unemployed because they preferred to remain on food stamps.[26] The Washington State Employment Service also downplayed the shortage because it was convinced that farmers tended to exaggerate the problem by requesting more workers than were necessary.[27] This opinion was shared by the federal Bureau of Agricultural Economics, which found Oregon sugar companies habitually overestimating their need for help, making matters appear worse than they were. Even FSA officials concluded that there "was much more hysteria over the shortage than was actually necessary."[28]

The sugar companies were partially responsible for the confusion because they considered the actual number of workers required for the season as "confidential" and would not release it.[29] Their policy was not to be concerned with exact numbers but to regard it as "essential" to get as many workers as possible so that the development of the beet industry would not be hindered.[30] Farmers were perplexed about the labor issue due to a dearth of official statistics on the actual severity of the shortage. Only after May 1941 did the federal Bureau of Agricultural Economics awaken to the need to compile statistics on farm labor. But even when studies were made, the labor needs were so volatile from one day to the next that the information was often unreliable. In June 1941, for example, the Idaho Employment Service in Boise County determined that enough workers were available through the peak of the season. Hardly five days later, farmers issued an urgent call that cherry pickers were needed "badly."[31] The wages paid to sugar beet workers, although established by the secretary of agriculture, were another cause of the chaos surrounding the farm labor shortage. Often workers would not thin sugar beets at the government rate, making some farmers bid the wages higher. Increased wages resulted in a stricter competition for workers by those who could not or would not follow suit. Most farmers, however, saw no correlation between higher wages and greater availability of laborers; in their view, the more they paid labor, the worse they performed the job. These unanswered questions and more were on the minds of northwestern farmers in 1941. To most, the only certainty was that laborers were much more difficult to obtain than in prior years and that the shortage would probably continue into 1942.[32] Yet the scarcity of labor on Northwest farms and elsewhere, while real, was but a harbinger of events to come.

The transition from a peacetime to a war economy produced abrupt and profound alterations in the social and economic course of daily life on northwestern farms. One immediate consequence was that the area under cultivation expanded dramatically as irrigation projects, initiated by the Reclamation Service, were brought to completion through the New Deal. In Idaho and Oregon, 2,895,000 acres of formerly desolate and arid land were cleared of sagebrush and brought under irrigation by 1940.[33] Irrigation projects in Washington were also completed a few months before the war.[34] In all, the New Deal probably conferred more permanent benefits that translated into socioeconomic change on the Northwest than on many other areas of the nation. Rural electrification, for one, combined with newly irrigated areas set the stage for enhanced comforts on the farm and agricultural development to follow.[35]

Many depressed rural towns, where a restaurant and one or two other businesses made up the central commercial section, experienced sharp new activity with the war. The quietude in these small communities, broken by the anxiety and emotionalism surrounding the world crisis, often translated into increased racial intolerance. The hardest blow was dealt to Japanese American residents in the Northwest. Although their incarceration is not described here, it is important to note that the relocation of the Japanese American communities, especially from key agricultural places like Puget Sound and the Yakima Valley, only served to exacerbate an already strained labor supply.[36] Moreover, the passage of the Alien Registration Act of 1940 encouraged the hostility directed against the Japanese Americans to spread later to other groups, including Mexican nationals and Mexican Americans.

With respect to the nagging farm labor problem, northwestern farmers had little cause to celebrate the start of the new year in 1942. Earlier in August 1941, the secretary of agriculture had lifted the controls on most crops, resulting in the highest demand for farm labor on record since 1920.[37] Now he was preparing to call for the highest farm output in history for 1942. This gave farmers a clear but grim forecast of the labor problem because the manpower drain to industry was also increasing.

In January, the federal government's announcement that it would purchase greater quantities of canned fruit and vegetables from northwestern farms was seen as a mixed blessing. Some Washington farmers, fearing insufficient labor, were reluctant to sign contracts committing themselves to deliver a crop to canneries.[38] Their apprehension was hardly eased when the Washington State Farm Labor Committee announced it would no longer help to secure labor for the growers.[39] Moved by a "food for victory" campaign but concerned about the availability of labor, farmers moved ahead with their crops.

The only contingency plan of Washington farming communities was to do as they had done in 1941, so their first appeal was to school districts. In January, some schools went on a six-day-week schedule in order to shorten the academic year and release the youngsters for farm work.[40] The Seattle Chamber of Commerce cooperated by urging schoolchildren to go into the fields.[41] In May, the state moved to register all schoolchildren eligible for work.[42] Weeks later, the Washington State Grange reported that some sugar beets were being plowed under for lack of field help.[43] The alarming news prompted the governor to proclaim May 31 through June 6 as Farm Labor Week, when all citizens were urged to register for farm work.[44] The following month, the Associated Farmers of Washington proposed that workers be drafted into the fields during critical periods. At the same time, the Washington Selective Service Board suggested that local draft boards begin to defer all farm laborers from military duty.[45] By mid-year and in spite of an earlier promise from the federal government of "rapid, efficient and adequate labor placement," farm help had not materialized.[46] Then, as if Washington farmers did not know from their own firsthand experience, the USDA reported that farm labor shortages were "more critical in the Pacific Northwest than any other region."[47]

As the crucial harvest season approached in August, the worst fears of some growers were realized when they were unable to find any workers. In desperation, farmers recruited patients from the Northern State Hospital for the mentally ill, who went to work ten-hour days.[48] In the fruit-producing communities all taverns and other businesses were closed in order to bolster the work force.[49] In Seattle, the Chamber of Commerce now proposed that to avoid a further deterioration of the labor situation, all remaining workers on farms be prevented from leaving. Two weeks later, Seattle's King County jail began to release its prisoners on the condition that they agree to work in the apple harvest.[50] These ideas were not unusual to the Northwest. Similar proposals from other areas of the nation had been criticized by Senator Robert LaFollette as "self defeating and a source of shame . . . Indeed, in many low-wage sections it would approach 'involuntary servitude,' if not achieve it."[51]

Too few workers kept Idaho farmers scrambling as well. An insufficient number of sugar beet thinners had meant that some fields had to be plowed under. By July, other farms began to consider cutting crops as much as 50 percent in order to avert the same losses as sugar beet farmers.[52]

A partial but controversial solution to the woes of Idaho farmers came with the arrival of Japanese Americans to local relocation camps. Growers and businessmen supported the idea of bringing Japanese American evacuees into the state on the grounds that experienced pickers and packers had "all gone to war jobs."[53] Farmers also argued that since California was trying to prevent Mexican migrants from leaving that state and traveling to the Northwest, the Japanese Americans could make up the loss.[54] They were correct about California; in fact, the San Joaquin Valley Fruit and Vegetable Growers Association had requested a suspension of removal of the Japanese Americans from the state in order to avoid the loss of critical farm production workers.[55]

The proposal to obtain Japanese Americans was opposed by Idaho's governor, who was vehemently anti-Japanese and led the opposition to Japanese Americans in his state.[56] By mid-1942, however, the mounting labor crisis had worked to change his mind, and by September the governor had appealed directly to the USDA for funds to transport Japanese American laborers to Idaho.[57] In all, it was estimated that Japanese American labor, if available, could provide up to 50 percent of the state's labor needs.[58] Regardless of the actual amount of labor that was contributed, the Japanese made the crucial difference between lost and harvested crops by their impressive dedication to hard work. Probably this was the very reason that Secretary of Agriculture Claude R. Wickard wrote to the city of Hunt, Idaho, where 2,400 Japanese Americans were held, seeking a Japanese family to work on his own farm back in Indiana.[59]

Even with the help of Japanese American labor, extraordinary measures were required to bring the crops in. The city of Idaho Falls closed all pool halls during daytime hours and ordered violators to be arrested on vagrancy charges.[60] Stores were closed in other localities and civic services came to a halt as city employees were pressed onto the farms.[61]

Sometimes the efforts to cope with the labor crisis were more dramatic than effective. For instance, at one point Idaho's governor led a group of three hundred businessmen to labor in the beet fields. By the end of the first day, the inexperienced volunteers admitted that thinning beets was "really tough."[62] Across the state line in Washington, the Spokane Chamber of Commerce described the governor's actions as little more than a "spectacle" and no solution to the problem.[63] On another occasion, a minister organized thirty to thirty-five young children to thin the beets. The local newspaper wrote that the children, driven by religious exuberance, were ineffective and earned more of a reputation than they did money.[64]

The Oregon farm labor situation was much the same as in the neighboring states of Idaho and Washington. To a large extent, similar improvisations and measures enabled Oregon's farmers to complete the year without serious losses. In one community, the local Farm Labor Committee canvassed every family to determine the availability of labor. Nearby, a local bakery set up a community blackboard to update the serious day-to-day labor shortages. Elsewhere, businessmen agreed to close their stores during the peak labor shortages.[65]

Oregon, however, was far ahead of Washington and Idaho as well as the federal government in developing concrete plans to cope with the labor situation. As early as 1941, Oregon was first to use public monies to acquire out-of-state strawberry pickers to fill specific shortages.[66] Later, state authorities estimated that there were 100,000 women who could be organized into a potential women's land army of farm workers.[67] In Marion County, public school teachers developed a system of work platoons and enlisted 10,000 students.[68] This kind of strategy focused national attention on Oregon, and later, in a radio address to the country, the secretary of agriculture urged women in other states to follow this lead and help alleviate the "manpower" crisis.[69]

The success of any plan to get men, women, and children interested in farm jobs hinged on instilling in them a feeling of patriotism and personal satisfaction as well as the idea that field work was healthy. They also had to be paid a decent wage. Through 1942, the routine nature and sacrifice of the war had yet to settle in, so this type of exhortation went far. Later, as the war went on and the volunteers became acquainted with the drudgery of farm work, they were much less enthusiastic and effective workers.

Realistically, some counties in Idaho and eastern Oregon were so sparsely populated—fewer than two persons per mile—that a women's land army or the mobilization of schoolchildren was impossible. In areas such as Malheur County, Oregon, farmers had no other choice but to rely extensively on Japanese American labor in order to cope with worker shortages. Yet, as in Idaho, labor shortages were not enough to convince most people to allow Japanese Americans in their communities.

At the start of the war, there were only a small number of Japanese Americans living in Malheur County. Soon after December 1941 and as additional families from coastal communities began to filter into the area, the Chambers of Commerce at Nyssa and Vale, Oregon, passed resolutions opposing the ownership or leasing of land by Japanese Americans. The Malheur County Agricultural Labor Sub-Committee adopted a similar position but urged that Japanese Americans be allowed into the area as laborers. In March 1942, the Vale Chamber of Commerce telegraphed Governor C. A. Sprague that it would not allow Japanese Americans in its community unless colonized or concentrated in groups under the surveillance and supervision of the U.S. Army. They would not be permitted to buy or lease lands, the chamber continued, and would be removed at the end of the emergency. The Vale chamber added a stern threat that unless the state took immediate action, they would "take matters into their own hands."[70] The Oregon governor's reply was straightforward; Japanese American citizens could not be prevented from owning or leasing land either by state or federal government.

In the meantime, the Amalgamated Sugar Company at Nyssa sold the Chamber of Commerce on the idea that it would be responsible for transportation costs, housing, and safety involving the Japanese Americans. Even so, this proposal was not widely accepted by the community and rejected outright by the military because the latter had ultimate charge. Eventually, the Amalgamated Sugar Company's recommendation was referred to President Franklin D. Roosevelt, who gave the final authorization, and the Nyssa community ended its holdout.[71]

In May, the first group of Japanese American farm workers arrived in eastern Oregon and, like others that followed, were most eager to prove their loyalty to the country. After the thinning of sugar beets was completed, they went to work on other crops, providing a much-needed boost to the labor supply. Because they were good workers, the Japanese Americans soon gained acceptance by some people, but because of the war many Oregonians were nonetheless loath to accept them under any circumstances. In an eastern Oregon town, a Japanese American shopping in a hardware store was attacked with a pitchfork by a farmer who was distraught over the recent loss of a son in the Pacific.[72] This incident did illustrate that, in spite of their excellent work and loyalty, the Japanese Americans were far from an ideal solution to the labor crisis.

For the remainder of 1942, farmers in the Northwest contended as best they could with the worsening worker deficit. Back in the nation's capital, the president declared that farm labor was now the most serious wartime manpower problem and signed into effect legislation that provided automatic draft deferments to certain farm workers.[73] The federal government also took steps to ensure a continued supply of gasoline and tires, which were imperative to the mobility of seasonal laborer.[74]

In spite of these encouraging signs, farmers in the Pacific Northwest still felt helpless about the lack of workers because at the same time the president was asking them to produce more. Across the Northwest, as well as in other parts of the nation, farmers responded with record production levels. Washington State, for example, produced a record-breaking crop of sugar beets in 1942.[75] As the nation was forced to give up meat, Oregon produced a bumper yield of potatoes, which surpassed all other crops in value.[76]

Farmers, plainly frustrated by a request for larger production with the same or fewer resources, complained directly to Washington, D.C. One Washington farmer wrote to federal authorities that during 1942 nearly one-half of his 250-acre farm had "produced nothing for lack of labor." Even so, the secretary of agriculture was urging farmers to plant more.[77] A farmer's wife from Minnesota wrote to Secretary of Agriculture Claude R. Wickard to stress that on top of the absence of help and lack of machinery and gasoline there was also this "dawn until dusk stuff."

> All fall we've been running around the pasture with flashlights rounding up the cows. Now we have to wait two to three hours in the morning for daylight before we can start the days work. Does Washington expect the farmers to win this war alone, and feed the world besides? Who's going to dish out the good crop growing weather, the President, Secretary Wickard, Madame

> Perkins [Labor Secretary Frances Perkins], or Harold Ickes [interior secretary]? If an intelligence test was conducted, I have no doubt proportionately more nit wits would be found in Washington than on the farms. It gripes my soul and I think I speak for the majority of the farmers.[78]

If the writer did not speak for the majority of the farmers, she did echo the sentiments of many, including those in the Northwest.

It was against this background of crisis between the fall of 1942 and the middle of 1943 that the federal government developed its basic wartime farm labor program and policy. Although Lend Lease had defined agricultural commodities as munitions of war, the president, the secretary of agriculture, and the chairman of the War Manpower Commission (WMC) had delayed the formulation of a comprehensive and effective approach to farm labor shortages until the start of 1943. Once the basic federal program was outlined and agreed upon it remained unchanged until 1947, and even then much of the war farm labor policy was carried over into the postwar period. Therefore, these months were seminal and saw farmers moving visibly farther away from their Jeffersonian credo of self-reliance. They became less reluctant to oppose government management of the farm labor question and eventually came to expect that the federal government should procure labor. With respect to the social and economic welfare of field workers, however, farmers remained unbending in their opposition to government intervention.

There were several reasons for the lack of a thorough solution to the farm labor problem. In part, it stemmed from the relationship between agriculture and the federal government. Through the thirties, the main problem on the nation's farms was surplus production. For that reason, the federal government directed very little attention to farm labor and categorized it as a nether sector of agriculture and the country's work force. Farmers, of course, wanted it that way. They were glad to be left alone to manage their own labor problems without the interference of the federal government.

Another reason for the lack of a national farm labor policy rested with the president. On the one hand, Roosevelt identified food production as a first-line war munitions, but he never conceded that agriculture was a defense industry.,[79] Harold Ickes noted that unlike the industrial labor shortages which preoccupied the president, Roosevelt approached the farm labor problem in a "romanticized" fashion.[80] Seemingly, he felt that a voluntary crop of women and youth could solve the problem. Having failed to recognize the pivotal role of an adequate labor supply in agricultural production, the president then erred again by concluding that farmers were simply not willing to work to their capacity of previous years.[81] Obviously, in the case of labor-intensive crops, such as those in the Northwest, no amount of will to produce could substitute for a worker shortage. In defense of the president, he had very poor statistical information to use in measuring the actual severity of the farm crisis. Also, agriculture did meet food production goals through 1942, although barely.

To a large degree, the president reflected the views of his advisors on farm labor. Theoretically and from an organizational standpoint, the secretary of agriculture, as food production chief, had first-line responsibility for ensuring a full supply of labor after December 1942. All the while, the WMC was also responsible, but it had not given much thought to farm worker shortages.[82] Like the president, the WMC treated the issue lightly and thought that idle women together with higher wages could fill the shortages and control the drain from the farms. In fact, there were few idle women. In Seattle, the Puget Sound Naval Ship Yard employed virtually no women in 1940. By the summer of 1943, one out of five construction workers was female.[83] Under these circumstances, the shortage of workers was hardly that simple to resolve. Moreover, until the fall of 1942, the military drafted as many farmers and farm workers as left to work in industry. Also, the government's determination to hold the line on inflationary farm prices through low agricultural wages turned workers away.

The matter was clouded further by the antagonism and dogged determination of the American Farm Bureau Federation to control the secretary of agriculture and the FSA. As early as 1935, the Farm Bureau had opposed the social programs of the FSA under the New Deal.[84] It rejected social rehabilitation of impoverished small and part-time farmers because they were a source of low-cost labor to larger growers. In February 1942, the Farm Bureau's powerful congressional farm lobby used the Agricultural Appropriations Bill to slash nearly 30 percent from the FSA's budget, strip the secretary of agriculture of the federal farm leadership, and dismantle the FSA. Hardest hit in the FSA were the Migratory Farm Labor Camp and Tenant Purchase budgets. Ironically, at a time of increasing labor shortages, the Farm Bureau had rendered ineffective the sole government agency concerned with farm labor.

Unknown to many farmers, the FSA was crucial. At the start of the war, the FSA and the U.S. Employment Service (USES) were the only agencies that dealt with farm labor on a national scale. The FSA's primary function had been to provide housing, sanitation, and health service to displaced and stranded migratory farm families through the Migratory Farm Labor Camps. Then, when the signs of increasing labor shortages became evident, the FSA began to use its permanent and temporary camp facilities for housing and distributing out-of-area workers to farms. The USES's role in farm labor was largely to recruit and systematically find jobs for farm workers who applied through the agency. Additional administrative support to the USES and the FSA came from other areas within the USDA. For example, the Sugar Section established minimum wages for sugar beet and sugarcane workers, and the Bureau of Economics provided some statistical information.

However, no central authority existed for farm labor, in spite of the fact that Secretary of Labor Frances Perkins had recommended the establishment of a Bureau of Farm Labor to the USDA as early as 1937.[85] Now with a weakened FSA, the secretary of agriculture assumed full operational responsibility for recruitment, placement, transfer, and maximum utilization of farm labor. More time passed until a War Food Administration (WFA) was designated in the Department of Agriculture. Even then, the WFA was not entrusted to the authority of the secretary; instead, the WFA administrator reported directly to the president.

Under these circumstances, the problem of insufficient labor on the nation's farms was as much a political issue as it was a manpower shortage. This was evident in a sequence of conflicting reports on available manpower issued by the USDA, the WMC, and the Farm Bureau in early 1943. In January, the WMC optimistically reported before a Senate subcommittee on appropriations that labor needs could be met for 1943. Immediately after, the USDA addressed the same committee and warned that more labor would be necessary.[86] The following month, the Farm Bureau presented an independent survey, which concluded that food production would decline 20 to 30 percent due to labor scarcity. Three months later, Wickard refuted the Farm Bureau by indicating that food production had increased in all areas except sugar beets, potatoes, and peanuts.[87] Yet within a matter of days the secretary reversed himself by testifying that labor shortages were indeed a problem and sufficient funds should be made available to solve the crisis.[88]

When Secretary Wickard assumed control of the farm labor supply program, the responsibility had already been partially assigned to the USDA through a series of directives. In June 1942, the WMC had directed the secretary to institute a program for the movement of agricultural laborers from surplus areas to localities in need of workers and to assure that transportation, health, and welfare services be provided. Under this arrangement, the FSA began to move surplus workers to areas in short supply. In order to encourage prospective workers to relocate at great distances from their homes, the FSA developed contracts between workers, farmers, and the government guaranteeing transportation, employment over a specific period of time at prevailing wages, adequate housing, and medical care. Under this plan, the first six hundred workers were recruited in Illinois and brought to work in the 1942 Washington apple harvest.[89] A second mandate, in November 1942, instructed the secretary of agriculture and the Selective Service to cooperate closely in determining the necessary number and type of farm deferments.

From the start of the labor shortage, the powerful farm lobby in Congress had pushed for blanket deferments for all agricultural workers.[90] Notwithstanding the fact that such a request was prohibited by the Selective Service Act, the farm lobby continued to pressure for a waiver from the draft until the WMC issued a reclassification plan to retain essential workers on dairy, livestock, and poultry farms. In order to determine when a worker was essential to farm production, a table converted jobs into war units with sixteen units necessary for deferment.[91] The passage of the Tydings Amendment to the Selective Service Act provided additional deferments for agricultural workers. It read in part that a worker was eligible for reclassification if "necessary to and regularly engaged in an agricultural occupation or endeavor essential to the war effort."[92] Later, all crop activities were assigned war units to determine when a worker could be deferred, and local boards were given discretionary powers to exempt a worker for as little as eight units. In effect, this amounted to a freeze on the drain of labor to the military and came as close to a blanket exemption as was possible under the Selective Service Act. As far as the draft was concerned, no other sector of the economy received such preferential treatment as did agricultural employers.

As the national farm labor program took shape, the Office of Economic Stabilization delegated its authority to regulate farm wages to the USDA. The secretary of agriculture's plan to stabilize farm wages was intended to retain workers on farms by allowing annual income to rise to a $2,400 ceiling. At the same time, the secretary expected to control inflation, since wage limits would protect farm income and leave little reason for farmers to request increased crop prices. Finally, in January 1943 the WMC transferred all the responsibility for recruitment, placement, and transportation of farm labor from the USES to the Department of Agriculture.

As it stood in January 1943, this was the basic administrative and legislative outline of the federal farm labor program. Once the congressional appropriation hearings got under way, the program was amended and resulted in Public Law 45 (PL-45), signed into effect in April 1943. Amendments placed the administration of the farm labor program jointly in the War Food Administration and the Agricultural Extension Service of the USDA and trimmed the annual appropriation request from $65,075,000 to $26,000,000. More important, Representative Stephan Page from Georgia introduced an amendment that effectively thwarted the interstate movement of workers unless they were released by their local county authorities.[93] The intent was to protect against the raiding of local labor supplies, but inadvertently it also raised the probability of labor hoarding and weakened the transfer of labor to much-needed areas. Another change stipulated that no funds could be used to directly or indirectly fix, regulate, or control hours of employment, impose minimum wages or housing standards, or impose or enforce collective bargaining requirements on agricultural workers with the exception of imported foreign labor.[94] This prohibited further use of contracts that spelled out wage and housing standards between employers and interstate workers. Since the FSA had used minimum guarantees as a means to encourage domestic labor to relocate, this amendment did much to weaken this aspect of the farm labor program.

As a whole, the federal farm labor program, as defined by PL-45, was symbolic of the political power and interest of the congressional farm lobby as well as northwestern agriculture. The amendments were the result of critical testimony provided by various farmer organizations, including the American Farm Bureau Federation and the National Grange. Their most stringent criticism was directed at the FSA's social programs and, second, at the central authority of the secretary of agriculture. As an alternative, the Farm Bureau wanted all the responsibility for farm labor activities to be transferred to the more conservative and decentralized Extension Service. Northwestern farmers delivered their own testimony and aggressively lobbied Senator Rufus C. Holman from Oregon, the only representative from the Northwest on either the House or Senate subcommittee on appropriations for farm labor. Their testimony and approval or opposition to the congressional proceedings said much about the concerns of the region's farmers.

On the whole, farmers in the Northwest felt that the secretary of agriculture, who was a farmer himself, had little sympathy for their problems. These sentiments reflected the regional jealousies and differences in agriculture. According to the *Northwest Farm News,* the "Indiana Gang," composed of the secretary, Clifford Townsend, former governor of Indiana, and the head of the WMC, was being purposefully deceptive about farm production.[95] Also, some of the USDA's activities, whether they benefited agriculture or not, were out of harmony with the farmers' conservative mentality. For example, the president of the Oregon State Horticulture Society felt that the use of farm labor camps to relocate workers was sound and could go far in saving production. But, he cautioned, they could only be as good as "the men who head them. They must not be set up and operated as relief agencies with schools of social thought."[96]

The contracts entered into between the FSA, employers, and out-of-state transported labor were also a point of conflict between the Department of Agriculture and northwestern farmers. A potato grower from Twin Falls, Idaho, testified in Congress that the contracts were "so ridiculous that we had to guarantee the Japs a bath every night before we could get them on our farms . . . so, if we didn't have sufficient facilities on our farms, we had to take them into town to the barbershops,then bring them back at night so they could have their bath."[97]

When the federal farm labor program was placed in the USDA, the *Northwest Farm News* warned that the FSA would now have more of an opportunity to attempt to write wage, hour, living, and housing conditions into seasonal labor contracts. It also encouraged farmers to write to Congress and voice opposition to placing the farm labor program in the hands of the Indiana Gang, which backed the "radical FSA policies from behind the scenes."[98] On the matter of drafting farm labor, the Northwest members of the Western Farm Bureau Federation petitioned the national headquarters to urge that all farmers be deferred.[99] At the same time, the Associated Farmers of Washington proposed that men be drafted onto the farms as well as into the military.[100] If complete exemption was not possible, Governor C. R. Bottolfsen of Idaho recommended that the military furlough Idaho servicemen back to the farms during the critical periods of labor shortages.[101] The *Northwest Farm News* also opposed the wage stabilization program because it felt that the secretary of agriculture had given in to the president's concern with inflation at the expense of farm prices.[102] The Washington State Farm Bureau suggested that at the very least industry be placed under similar wage and price controls as agriculture.[103]

In essence, northwestern growers, like their counterparts in other parts of the country, wanted the federal government to help them secure workers as long as it did not impose conditions of employment. This was a peculiar position to take in the midst of such a widespread manpower shortage. Farmers failed to realize that the competition for workers from all sources would require some concession in the terms of employment. Hampered by this tunnel vision, they did not anticipate the consequences of their position on the new farm labor program under PL-45.

The most telling example of agriculture's steadfast position on farm labor came in 1943 with the near total failure of the interstate worker transportation program. At the start of the year, a number of workers were relocated to Washington from Little Rock, Arkansas.[104] During March, forty additional families went to live in Oregon and fifty-two more went to live at the former FSA farm family camp at Granger, Washington.[105] However, unlike the workers transported to the Northwest from Illinois at the end of 1942, these laborers did not have contracts guaranteeing any conditions of employment.[106] Although they had promised, in exchange for transportation, to stay on the job for at least three months, no sooner did they arrive than they left for the more attractive national defense employment. Except to farmers, this hopscotchlike movement of labor was not surprising, because earlier the *Oregonian* had reported that "fabulous wages" in industry tended to pull transient workers from the farms.[107] This same springboarding of workers through Idaho and in the direction of better jobs was noted by the *Idaho Daily Statesman.*[108]

The difference in the success or failure of the recruitment of interstate agricultural workers between the previous years and 1943 was a matter of expectations. In 1943, these workers had a well-grounded hope for a chance to better themselves through rising employment opportunities; when agriculture did not provide this, they found that the industrial sector would. Since the federal government had already provided transportation to the site of this employment, farm families entered national defense jobs without much effort on their part. This explains part of the frustration of a farmer near Richland, Washington, the site chosen by the U.S. Atomic Energy Commission for the Hanford Atomic Works project. In July he had obtained a crew of workers, recently arrived from Missouri, from the farm labor supply camp at Granger. By the end of the month, all except two had left farm employment.[109] The same thing occurred with the families from Oklahoma that arrived to farms near Carnation, Washington, a few miles from the magnetic pull of Seattle's aircraft and shipbuilding plants.[110] The level of industrial growth was evident in expanding job opportunities at the Boeing Company in Seattle. In 1939, it employed four thousand; by 1944, more than fifty thousand men and women worked in the Seattle plant.[111] The families transported to Oregon's Willamette Valley also left agriculture at the first opportunity for the Kaiser shipyards in Portland.

Farmers had inadvertently placed themselves in an unenviable position. Under no circumstances could they compete with wages and the burgeoning job opportunities in the region's defense industry. At the same time, farmers had rendered the transportation of additional workers under PL-45 ineffective because there was no way to keep the labor on the farms without contracts. On top of this, the Page amendment also hampered their ability to replace lost labor from surplus but competing rural areas.

Against this background and for more than a year, the secretary of agriculture had been bombarded by requests from different states to import workers from Mexico. The first request arrived in July 1941 from the Arizona Farm Bureau in support of cotton growers, followed by urgent petitions from Texas, New Mexico, and California.[112] It was clear from these appeals that the nation's commercial agriculture interests, inclusive of northwestern farmers, had made a decision to import Mexican labor in order to cope with the manpower crisis. Well before negotiations between the governments of Mexico and the United States were completed on the issue, the forthcoming availability of Mexican contract workers for the Northwest was common knowledge. As early as May 1942, the *Northwest Farm News* reported that plans were being drawn by county and state farm placement centers for bringing Mexicans to Washington.[113] One month later, the Idaho State Farm Bureau Federation announced that it was also taking steps to obtain one thousand Mexican workers.[114] This move was underscored by the U & I Sugar Company's request for an immediate supply of contract workers.[115]

Throughout 1941, the USDA was reluctant to approve the requests for Mexican workers. Since the mid-thirties, the FSA had worked to ameliorate the wretched conditions of farm workers and now the entry of Mexican labor could conceivably undermine many years of effort. The agency and others concerned with agriculture also feared that the importation of such workers could obstruct the effort to raise farm wages for domestic labor. The WMC took a similar position and remained convinced that the cause of the farm labor shortage was chiefly a matter of wages, which were too low.[116]

The USDA hesitated to certify the requests because they were reminiscent of a similar program for admission of Mexican workers during the labor shortages of World War I. This previous experience with contracted Mexican workers had been plagued by many problems and was a tragic failure long before the program was terminated in 1919. Most often, employers did not honor the workers' contracts and exploited them ruthlessly. In general, the end result of the first bracero program was so shocking that both Mexico and the

United States were only too happy to put it behind them.[117] Twenty-two years later, this experience made the USDA and the Mexican government reluctant to enter into a similar agreement without strict controls.[118]

Another reason for the secretary's reservations about imported labor was the federal government's concern with the manner in which the Mexicans would be received. Anti-Mexican sentiment, which was a carry-over from the Mexican American War and before, was a factor. On top of that, the systematic repatriation of Mexican people from Los Angeles and Chicago during the 1930s was still too fresh in the minds of many people. Now the war itself had ushered in a new era of anti-Mexican riots accompanied by gross miscarriages of justice, especially in some California and Texas communities.[119] This xenophobia of people of Mexican descent prompted the federal government to view the bracero program as a "ticklish experiment in racial relations."[120]

In the Northwest, where anti-Mexican prejudice was not as strong, public opinion was against the admission of Mexican nationals. Months before the secretary of agriculture departed for Mexico to secure an agreement, a farm labor conference in Yakima went on record opposing the employment of contracted Mexicans as a solution to the labor shortage.[121] Idaho farmers also echoed a resistance against the use of imported Mexican laborers.[122]

In spite of his reservations and other concerns surrounding the possible effect of foreign labor, the secretary of agriculture departed for Mexico City in June 1942 to address the Inter-American Conference on Agriculture. A month earlier, the basic terms of a bilateral farm labor program had been agreed upon by Mexico and the United States, so the secretary's trip to the Mexican capital was to finalize the negotiations. This trip, at a time when the powerful Farm Bureau was attempting to slash FSA appropriations in Congress, indicated that at last the secretary was responding to the pressures from agricultural interests. By now, the labor crisis had reached unprecedented levels and angry letters spelling out the frustrations of farmers were flooding the USDA. In Idaho alone, the USES had certified the farmers' need for fifteen hundred Mexican workers as accurate and pressing.[123]

Wickard concluded the negotiations successfully, although the agreement was not ratified by both countries until August 4. Briefly stated, the general provisions of this agreement between Mexico and the United States stated that Mexican contract workers would not be expected to serve in the U.S. military or be subjected to discriminatory acts of any kind. The federal government guaranteed round-trip transportation expenses from Mexico and agreed to provide adequate living arrangements while in this country. Additionally, Mexican nationals would not be used to displace local workers or to lower their wages.[124]

In order to implement these general guidelines, the agreement outlined specific conditions. Employment was exclusively in agriculture and on the basis of a written contract (in English and Spanish) between the worker and his employer. Employment was guaranteed at wages equal to those prevailing in the area of employment, but in any case not less than thirty cents per hour, for a minimum of three-quarters of the duration of the contract. Workers were guaranteed the right to organize among themselves. Each laborer would have 10 percent of his earnings deducted and deposited in a savings fund payable upon his return to Mexico. Finally, workers would be provided adequate housing and sanitary conditions and were free to purchase merchandise where they pleased.[125]

For the remainder of the war, no significant changes were made in the basic agreement reached in 1942. In 1943, the agreement provided the right of the Mexican consul and Mexican labor inspectors to intervene in disputes on behalf of the workers. Another modification stipulated that each worker would receive subsistence without cost for each day (except Sundays) when he was willing to work and was not provided employment in excess of four hours.[126]

Two months after the agreement was ratified, the first group of Mexican workers entered the United States at El Paso en route to Stockton, California.[127] As if by design, the announcement of the agreement with Mexico coincided with the start of the fall harvest in the Pacific Northwest. The *Northwest Farm News* was first to report that Mexican workers were indeed available.[128] In October, the U & I Sugar Company followed by announcing that five hundred workers were scheduled to arrive and be allotted to Washington sugar beet farmers.[129] Between October and the end of 1942, 4,189 Mexicans had been certified for work in the United States.[130]

The Office of Labor within the USDA's War Food Administration had the responsibility for implementing the Mexican Farm Labor Program (MFLP), or bracero (referring to arms, *brazos,* helping hands) program, as it was called. The administration was organized by regions, and the Pacific Northwest Division, with headquarters in Portland, consisted of Washington, Oregon, Idaho, Montana, Wyoming, and Utah.[131] The Portland divisional office was subdivided into health, transportation, shelter and feeding, and engineering, finance, and business operations.

In addition to the Office of Labor, the Extension Service was also partially responsible for the MFLP. As far as farm labor was concerned, it handled all matters pertaining to migrant interstate labor (except housing) and job placement (including foreign workers). The Extension Service was also organized by regions, except that state administrations were independent of each other. Each state had a state director of extension who appointed a farm labor supervisor to analyze all farm labor needs, develop an annual farm labor plan, mobilize existing labor resources, and operate the various farm placement centers. The state director reported directly to the federal offices of extension and the input was used to plan the manpower needs of the MFLP. The administration personnel of the farm labor program were under the state Extension Service of the respective land grant colleges in each of the northwestern states. Generally, the key administrative personnel for the Extension Service's farm labor program were appointed directly from the ranks of the faculty at the University of Idaho, Oregon State College, and Washington State College.

The county extension agent, along with a farm labor advisory committee, made up of local farmers and different state agencies concerned with agriculture, was responsible for the day-to-day farm labor operations at the local level. At first glance, it appeared that the Extension Service had little to do with the MFLP. But although it was limited to farm placement, it actually determined the place and conditions of employment for the Mexican workers. This meant that the MFLP, except for transportation and housing accommodations, was actually in the hands of the county agents and local farmers.

Several other federal agencies also worked in close cooperation with the Extension Service and the Office of Labor. The most important of these was the State Department, responsible for negotiations with Mexico, and the USDA War Boards, which cooperated with the local selective service on farm deferments.

The MFLP appeared to be detrimental to the best interests and the traditional independence of most farmers. Written contracts covering conditions of employment, adequate housing, and subsistence without cost during times of unemployment were not at all harmonious with the farmers' deep-seated attitudes toward labor. They were prone to reject the idea of providing such concessions to labor in general but in particular to imported sweat-of-the-brow workers because it was a radical departure from past practices. If left to their own devices, most farmers would have preferred a return to an open border policy in place of the MFLP.

In the Pacific Northwest, the *Northwest Farm News* led the opposition toward the MFLP when it printed the views of a critical "anti–New Dealer":

> Somebody in our government with a lot of high ideals went to the Mexican government and made an agreement to send laborers to the United States. They arranged to have a contract which would deal with each laborer as a free agent and put in all sorts of conditions which the farmer who had to hire him had to agree to, including housing, transportation, and a minimum per diem rate. But instead of sending over experienced farm laborers, the Mexican government gathered a lot of ne'er-do-wells and hobos. It didn't work. In fact the farmers got less help than usual. The trouble was that before, the American farmers had been making contracts with patrones [bosses] who got the money and the workers, established the working conditions and paid the workers as they saw fit. They brought in trained workers and made them work. But the starry-eyed members of the Mexican and American governments wouldn't hear of making use of the patrón system.[132]

Basically, farmers wanted the federal government to provide Mexican nationals in order to provide relief from the labor crisis, but they wanted it on their own terms. As the president of the American Farm Bureau Federation testified in Congress, the growers desired the right to deal with Mexicans in a simple, "common, horse-sense business" manner.[133] The *Idaho Daily Statesman* cautioned against such a freethinking attitude and said that, while it favored the importation of foreign labor, some safeguards were necessary.[134]

In spite of these initial reservations, once the Mexican nationals arrived in the Northwest farmers found little need to worry. From the beginning, the men performed admirably and their numbers helped ease the labor shortage. More important, employers quickly realized that decentralization in the Office of Labor and the autonomy of the state Extension Service, in which they exercised some influence, made it possible to easily circumvent or simply abrogate the provisions and strict language of the workers' contracts. Moreover, unlike the braceros in the Southwest, the men on northwestern farms were distanced from Mexico. In the Southwest the braceros had access to the Mexican consul, while the nearest consular office for the Northwest was in Salt Lake City, Utah (a full consular office was established in Portland, Oregon, in 1947).[135] This meant that braceros lacked the immediate protection of their consulates against violations of their contracts. For these reasons and others, the MFLP provided the best immediate replacements for some of the thousands of other workers who had been swept away to the various activities of the war.

Even as the federal farm labor program moved from an experimental basis to the MFLP under PL-45, growers were worried by reports that shortages would be more serious during 1943. In January, the USDA predicted that the demand for food commodities was so great that no conceivable amount of production could satisfy it.[136] In a national appeal to assist farmers, President Roosevelt proclaimed January 12, 1943, national Farm Mobilization Day.[137] Two days later, the WMC expressed the growing level of concern with the matter of farm labor shortages by calling for development of a new agricultural manpower program for 1943.[138] The WMC's anxiety grew from dire forecasts that agriculture would lose an additional one million workers by mid-year and another quarter-million would leave farm employment by fall.[139] The MFLP notwithstanding, farmers in some areas of the country were contemplating a shift to less labor-intensive agriculture as a partial solution to the crisis.[140]

In the Northwest, the 1943 production goals were also at odds with the deteriorating labor situation. Oregon's agricultural industry stood poised to produce the largest volume of food products in the state's history.[141] In Idaho, crop production, without considering sugar beets, was estimated at about $20 million in value.[142] Washington sugar beet growers indicated that in spite of the demand for more tonnage and adequate processing facilities, a 30 percent reduction in acreage was probable due to insufficient labor.[143] In conflict with the call for record crop production, during February the *Northwest Farm News* alarmed its readership with the headline "Lowest Number of Farm Labor since 1925."[144] Matters only worsened in March with a report that the annual migration of Canadian Indian berry pickers to western Washington was not expected.[145] To call attention to the severity of the crisis in the state of Washington, the governor's office estimated that 80,000 was the "absolute minimum" number of additional workers required for summer and fall work.[146]

Before the Extension Service, in cooperation with other state agencies, could justify acquiring Mexican workers for 1943, it had to exhaust all available local labor, including schoolchildren.[147] This started with a telegram from the secretary of agriculture to the three Northwest governors suggesting a state proclamation to dismiss school for harvest work.[148] As soon as the wire arrived, Idaho complied and drafted its proclamation. Oregon's governor was well ahead of the secretary, having already published a similar statewide decree in the *Oregon Journal.* Washington requested similar school closures but also submitted a measure in the legislature to continue payment to districts while they remained closed.[149]

Colleges and universities also revised their school calendars in order to free students for agriculture work.[150] At the University of Washington, the dean of students excused students from their classes for six to nine days and generally encouraged the absences as patriotism.[151] Other northwestern state and community colleges, including private institutions such as Gonzaga, Whitman, and the College of Puget Sound, also ordered classes suspended during critical times. As a result of such widespread closures, some Idaho counties reported that the students accounted for as much as 50 percent of agricultural labor.[152]

However laudatory its effect on the labor shortage, the employment of youths was not free of controversy. Some farmers supported the school closures because they were convinced that the children's physical dexterity made them the best workers.[153] Others argued, and correctly, that as crops were being saved the educational development of the students was being sacrificed. The specter of lawsuits arising from the fact that employers were legally liable for any injury to the youngsters also discouraged some farmers. But even when the students were not in school, the USDA continued to limit the number of hours that children could work in crops such as sugar beets. Beyond that, the closure of schools and patriotic persuasion did not in itself guarantee that children could or would work. Some were not physically fit for the rigorous farm jobs and did little more than go through the motions. Other students used the opportunity of the dismissal of classes to take an early vacation, until school authorities began to double-check that the youths were indeed on farms working. To make certain, some adopted a strict policy of "no job, no vacation."[154]

Next, a Women's Land Army was also organized but with mixed success, especially in rural areas that had sparse populations. The areas around Seattle and Portland also had difficulty establishing a Women's Land Army given the lure of national defense jobs at the Kaiser Shipyards, the Boeing Company, and the Puget Sound Naval Yards, as well as the physical demands of some farm work that was considered unsuitable for females. The mixed success of the Women's Land Army was self-evident. In 1943, Oregon placed 15,284 women in seasonal agricultural jobs, but Idaho placed only 3,344.[155] Washington's Women's Land Army was so ineffective that by October 1943 all future plans for a large-scale Women's Land Army were dropped.[156]

As in 1942, the business community also contributed to alleviating the problem of farm labor shortages. Most businesses, particularly those that depended on farm orders for their own economic well-being, were quick to respond and displayed help-wanted notices or consented to close their businesses as requested. In Oregon, the Sears Roebuck Company took extraordinary steps and produced two instructional films on how to pick apples. Not only did the company provide the films, but it also provided a mobile projection trailer so that the films could be used in rural areas.[157] Other business establishments rented billboards at their own expense to call attention to the urgent need for laborers.

In spite of the campaign to mobilize all available persons, a few individuals were not stirred to work by simple appeals and preferred to spend their time in pool halls, beer parlors, and the like. Grange members at Jerome, Idaho, found this lack of patriotism so damaging to the war effort that they passed the following resolution. They recommended that "all gambling devices, including specifically pinochle and poker tables, slot machines and punch boards, in public places be banned for the duration of the war." Moreover, "all social clubs selling liquor by the drink and operating any and all of the above nature should [also] be closed for the war."[158]

In 1943, the search for any and all under-utilized workers was extended in other ways. The WFA requested that states consider the use of state prisoners as farm laborers.[159] As it turned out, Idaho had too few men in its state institutions to make the proposal realistic, and Oregon delayed acting on the idea altogether. Only Washington elected to advance the release dates of selected offenders at the state's penitentiary and reformatory. By this means, several hundred men were paroled early and placed in honor camps in eastern Washington counties or on some Skagit Valley farms.[160] Prisoners of war were also authorized to do farm work in the Northwest, but these men were limited primarily to the heavy work in sugar beets and only when no other source of labor was available.[161] The War Relocation Authority continued to provide Japanese American laborers to farmers in eastern Oregon and Idaho, but the number of available workers did not increase significantly from 1942. As the search for workers widened, various fraternal organizations, including the Fraternal Order of Eagles, made good use of their membership to roust out additional workers.[162]

As a whole, the federal and state farm labor program to mobilize domestic workers functioned well under the circumstances. Most persons understood the grave nature of the manpower shortage and contributed as they could. The public's response stemmed from a clear understanding that the labor shortage not only threatened the farmers but was a grave state and national economic and military problem. Yet in spite of all the energy devoted to finding a solution, the fact remained that the supply of local workers in the Northwest and in other regions as well was insufficient to meet the expanding wartime needs of agriculture. As this fact became clear, some farmers felt helpless and panicked by cutting back on production or plowing crops under for lack of labor. Others started to hoard workers, which only served to worsen the crisis by depriving others of labor.[163] For these same reasons, the federal government, at the farmers' insistence, had engaged with Mexico to secure the use of Mexican contract workers. It is to the experiences of the contracted men that this study now turns.

At work in Idaho hop field. National Archives, Washington, D.C.

Twin Falls Standard Farm Labor Camp, Twin Falls, Idaho. Mexican workers on their way to work on back of truck. National Archives, Washington, D.C.

Twin Falls Standard Farm Labor Camp with view of tent shelters where braceros were housed. Twin Falls, Idaho. National Archives, Washington, D.C.

Braceros pitching pea vines into combines near Lewiston, Idaho. National Archives, Washington, D.C.

Prisoner of War camp near Toppenish, Washington. Braceros were housed here after the war. Historical Photograph Collections, Washington State University Libraries.

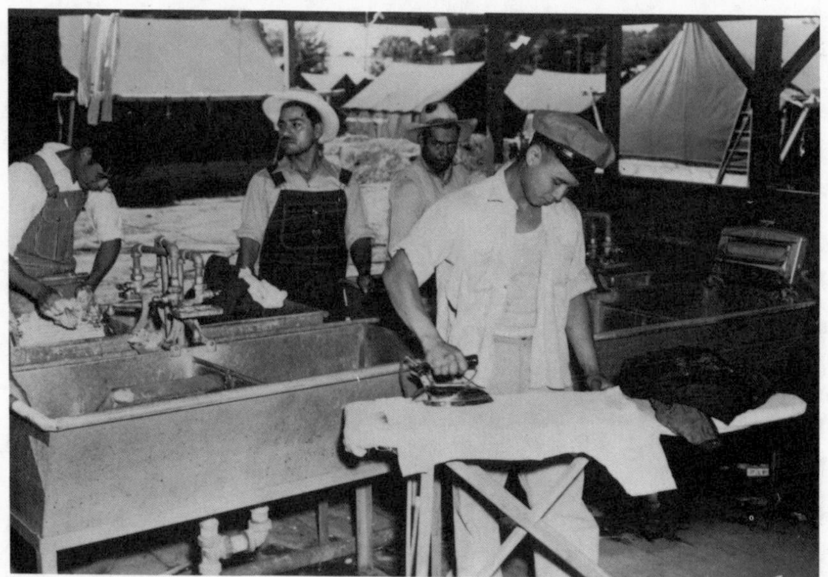

Workers doing laundry on their day off. Note the structure of the temporary camp facility. Photo, courtesy of Oregon State University Archives, P20:1069.

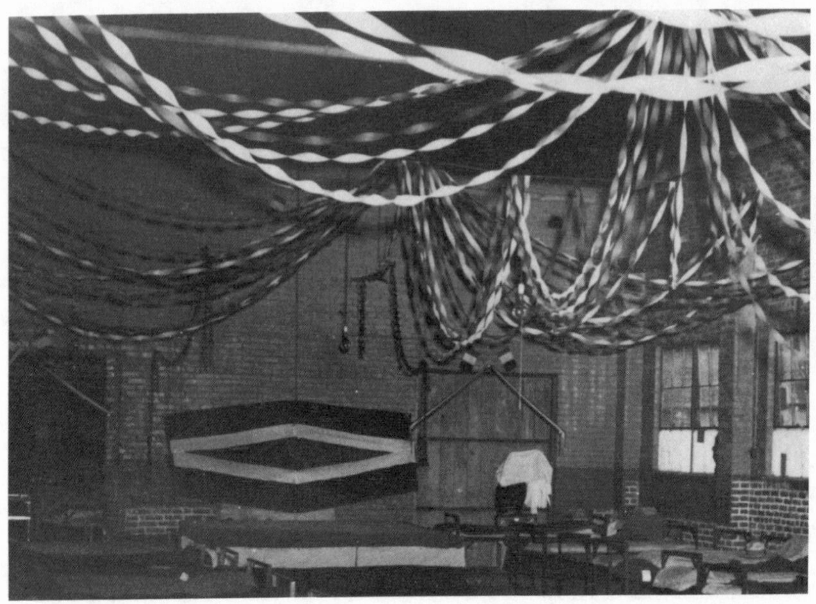

Fruit warehouse, in Wenatchee, Washington, decorated in celebration of either Cinco de Mayo (May 5th) or the 16th of September. Historical Photograph Collections, Washington State University Libraries.

Tent camp in Wenatchee. Lack of trees or other forms of windbreaks made these camps exceedingly hot in the summer and cold during the winter months. Historical Photograph Collections, Washington State University Libraries.

Mexicans harvesting cucumbers in Columbia County, Oregon. Note the workers' hats and the farm labor official standing posed in the middle of the workers. Photo, courtesy of Oregon State University Archives, P20:518, photo by Maurice Hodge.

Braceros preparing the following day's "sack lunches." Jam jar is on the table. Grandview, Washington. Historical Photograph Collections, Washington State University Libraries.

Interior of newly constructed, but not completed, bracero sleeping quarters. The electrical wiring is visible, but there are no lights. Photo, courtesy of Oregon State University Archives, P120:2744.

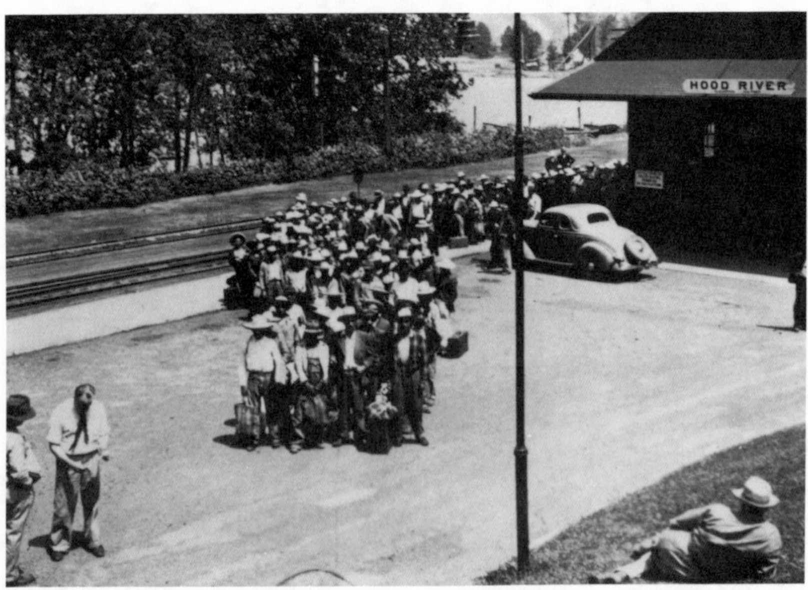

Braceros fresh from Mexico arriving at the Hood River train station. The men carry their personal belongings, while the farm labor program officials check the passenger list. Photo, courtesy of Oregon State University Archives, P20:790.

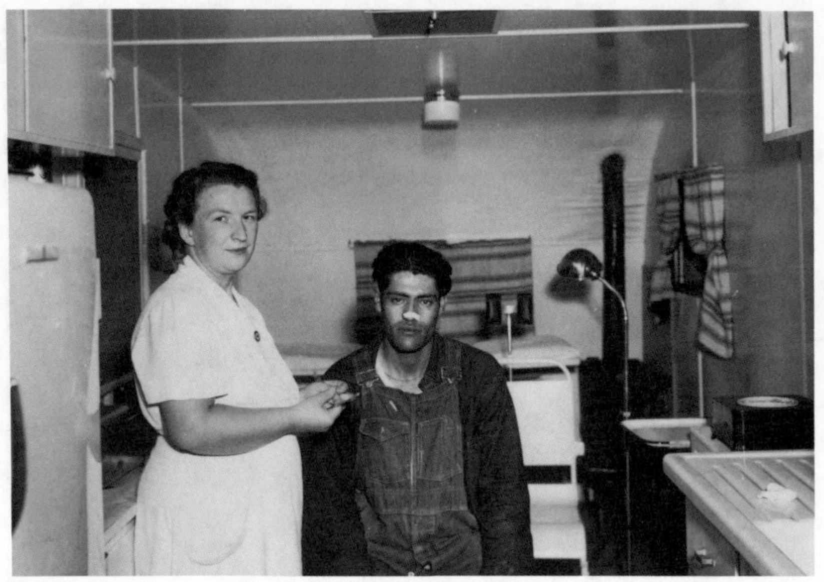

Nurse at Athena, Milton-Freewater Farm Labor camp treating bracero in trailer dispensary. Photo, courtesy of Oregon State University Archives, P120:2806.

Morning and off to the orchards to pick fruit. Men are boarding an already crowded truck. This was the cause of many accidents. Photo, courtesy of Oregon State University Archives, P120:2789.

Typical leisure time activity. Inside of tent has picture of woman, possibly a loved one. Photo, courtesy of Oregon State University Archives, P120:2781.

"Mail wall." The sign on the lower right reads "muchachos colocar leche botellas aqui" (boys leave milk bottles here). Photo, courtesy of Oregon State University Archives, P120:2778.

Flag-raising ceremony during Mexican Independence Day at an Oregon camp. Mexican flag is visible. A trumpeter to the left of the flag calls the men to attention. Photo, courtesy of Oregon State University Archives, P20:519.

Picking potatoes in Oregon's Klamath County area. Oregon Historical Society, Portland.

Ahtanum Standard Farm Labor Camp located in Yakima County. At least eighty cabins, indicative of the size of the camp, are visible in this partial view. Photo © Irwin Nash, 1974.

Staging center for braceros in Mexico. U.S. Department of Labor.

Recruitment center in Mexico for braceros bound for the U.S. U.S. Department of Labor.

Final check before U.S. immigration officials and before departing from Mexico. U.S. Department of Labor.

Sugar beet worker. U.S. Department of Labor.

Braceros being processed in Mexico. U.S. Department of Labor.

Hands are checked for evidence of physical labor. U.S. Department of Labor.

Interior of mess hall. Note empty soft drink bottles in center and tortillas on the plates. U.S. Department of Labor.

Health inspection for venereal disease, tuberculosis, and other infectious conditions. U.S. Department of Labor.

3. The Bracero Worker

THE DRIVE to maximize agricultural production as the resident labor supply diminished exerted tremendous pressure on farmers to introduce thousands of contracted Mexican workers into the northwestern agricultural economy. As disconcerting as the idea of admitting more Mexicans into the country and signing work contracts with them seemed, the crisis was enough to convince agribusiness that foreign labor was essential to full production. By entering into an agreement with the Mexican workers and the federal government in 1943, agriculture took the first step toward an institutionalized dependency on braceros that would last beyond the end of the war. Within a year, Mexican nationals became a vital mainstay in farm production in many areas, especially the Pacific Northwest. Of the 220,640 laborers who entered the United States under PL-45, approximately 21 percent were contracted by northwestern farmers; only California recruited more workers.[1]

The need for Mexican laborers was one thing. But bringing the workers from deep in Mexico required complicated preconditions, including a system of recruitment, transportation, and housing. The task was not simple, especially in the face of federal government supervision, wartime scarcity of materials, and the farmers' penchant for violating the spirit of the binational agreement and doing as they pleased.

Beginning in 1943, the procedure to obtain the braceros required that farmers organize into farm labor associations, which functioned explicitly to enter into contracts for Mexican workers. The federal government required that interested farmers pool their labor needs and make one request for braceros through the association. This was a change in policy from 1942, when individual farmers contracted for workers, producing a mass of paperwork and labor hoarding.

Although the farm labor associations were legal entities, their administrative structure was kept simple. Growers were required to pay a nominal membership fee of five to ten dollars to cover general operating costs and a flat fee or a one-time assessment based on crop acreage for each worker delivered by the association. Other than that, membership implied that growers would agree to abide by the rules of the organization and to comply with the Mexican work agreement. The facility with which the associations and their membership could be established led to a proliferation throughout the region until most counties had one or more of these bracero-sponsoring groups. The Twin Falls County Labor Committee in Idaho, which had 630 member farms, was one of the largest farm labor organizations in the Northwest.[2]

The farm labor association quickly moved beyond its function as an intermediary and began to set the pattern of life for the contracted Mexicans. This power developed from its many possible activities, such as the operation of feeding services, handling of employee payroll for the members, employment, and, at times, ownership of labor camps. Beyond this, the main function of the farmers' associations was to act as procurers of Mexican labor. In this capacity they provided their greatest service to northwestern agriculture because the labor needs of farmers were so varied. Unlike the Southwest's large-scale and near year-round growing season, only hop and large sugar beet growers could employ scores of workers from early spring through the October harvest. Most average farms required only a small number of workers during certain parts of the year and even then they were employed intermittently. Smaller growers, on the other hand, sometimes required one or two workers for little more than two weeks' employment, as is illustrated by a sample of typical labor requirements from the Whatcom County Farm Labor Association.

> H. M. Monsen, 4 Mexican workers wanted from May 1 to June 1; from May 20 to June 6.
>
> Clarence W. Jones, 2 Mexican workers from March 1 to May 1.
>
> Henry Elsasser, 1 Mexican worker from May 15 to June 15; 1 worker August to September.
>
> Carl Hansen, 6 or 8 Mexican workers, last part of May to first part of June; same number April 15.
>
> Johnny Schultz, 26 Mexican workers from July 5 to July 12.
>
> H. K. Russell, 1 Mexican worker form May 1 to August 31.
>
> Mrs. A. F. Gutzman, 1 Mexican worker form June to July; 1 August to September.[3]

The wide range of labor requirements common to northwestern agriculture made it unreasonable to expect that the federal government would authorize the braceros to travel to the Northwest for such a short period of employment. On the other hand, the farm labor association could pool the labor needs of a number of individuals and then allot the workers as they were required. For this reason alone, the region's many farm labor associations proved to be essential.

In order for an association to determine the actual labor needs of the membership, each farmer estimated the number of workers required and the period of employment. This information was then compiled and forwarded to the Extension Service for approval through certification. The Extension Service compared the association's request with its own manpower projections and approved or rejected it. The Extension Service empathized with the associations but was aware that most farmers operated on the assumption that it was better to have a surplus than to be caught short. Once an inflated request was added to that of the other employer groups, the state's total order for contract labor mushroomed quickly. Therefore, the Extension Service held back certification as an effective means of forcing farm labor associations to scale down their requests to more realistic levels.[4]

Once the Extension Service certified the total number of workers required in the state, an order was forwarded to the WFA for further review by the Office of Labor. If the number of workers was determined to be excessive, it was returned and ordered scaled down. This paring down of a state's request was common because the Office of Labor was well aware that the federal government was ultimately responsible for the care of the foreign workers. A dramatic illustration of the final say of the Office of Labor occurred in 1943, when Washington, Oregon, and Idaho sugar beet farmers submitted a combined request for 21,291 braceros but received only 7,686 laborers.[5] If the Extension Service's order was approved outright, it was forwarded to the State Department for transmittal to the WPA representatives in Mexico. In all, four to six weeks elapsed from the time the order was initiated by the northwestern labor associations until it was processed in Mexico City and the workers arrived.[6]

Across the border, the search for the men was carried out through newspapers, radio, and word of mouth and originated in the small towns and villages of Mexico's central plateau. Once alerted to the need of U.S. agriculture, prospective workers enlisted at a selection center located at the National Stadium in Mexico City. Theoretically, workers were required to obtain a permit from their town or village mayor prior to departing for Mexico City. In practice, however, countless individuals rushed to the assembly center on their own initiative with the expectation of obtaining one of a limited number of contracts. In addition to the plain fact that many individuals were desperate for employment, several reasons account for this hurried dash to the contracting centers. In many cases, the returning 1942 braceros had exaggerated the benefits of the program and at the same time underplayed the requirements for obtaining a contract. Sometimes the men did not even understand that permission from the local mayor was necessary prior to departing for the assembly center. In other instances, the men felt compelled to leave without permission because provincial mayors issued the permits in return for favors. In 1943, a multitude of men rushed to enlist in the bracero program, causing severe problems for the city, the government, and the applicants themselves.

At the assembly center, the workers were interviewed by the WFA about their qualifications and experience in agriculture. If qualified, they were required to pass through comprehensive health and physical examinations, including chest X-rays and serological tests for venereal disease. Those that were acceptable were then photographed and vaccinated against smallpox and had the contract and working conditions explained for their signature. If the men accepted, the U.S. immigration authorities then issued the necessary entry permits and the Office of Labor dispersed individual ration books.

Although the men came from throughout Mexico, the greater number were from the rural, least developed, and more isolated regions. Furthermore, they were of the lower socioeconomic classes with life experiences limited to their own localities. This meant that in spite of the fact that the contract was explained to them before they affixed their signatures, most of the men did not have a rudimentary understanding of the terms and conditions. The whole idea that a young person from a tiny community in Michoacán could comprehend the meaning of being away from his family for the first time, a strange language, the work ethic of farmers, and related factors was farfetched. In reality, the workers understood little beyond the fact that they were going to work in the United States.

The braceros traveled from the assembly center to the border via the Mexican National Railroad. At the border, a representative of the WFA met the braceros and organized them into groups according to area of employment. As the men crossed the U.S.-Mexican border, they did so waving flags of both countries amidst a joyful but serious patriotic atmosphere.[7] The men traveling to points in the Southwest usually traveled by bus, while those contracted to northwestern destinations made the trip by train.

By the time they arrived in the Northwest, the braceros had begun to experience the effects of culture shock and lack of foresight on the part of the WFA. Their initial exultation in crossing the border turned sour for a number of reasons, but the change in weather was particularly unsettling. In April 1943, the first group of 250 braceros arrived by train at Yakima attired in clothes more suited to the semitropical climate of Michoacán and not the cold weather of the Northwest. The *Yakima Daily Republic* featured a picture of the men on its front page, noting that "many of them wore their native broad-brimmed hats which will stand them in good stead later on."[8] The point was that these hats, light clothes, and huaraches were appropriate for summer but not April, a month when cool mornings and freezing nights are not unusual.

The men arrived in a state of semibewilderment from their long trip across the country. They were met at the train depot by the labor association that had requested them and then taken immediately by truck to a labor camp. As stipulated in their work contract, the men were not afforded time to orient themselves to their surroundings but were required to report for work the following day.

The emergency nature of the bracero program, coupled with enough local administrative control, gave growers the flexibility to shape it into a model that best served their own interests. From the moment the workers arrived and were turned over to the employers and the camp managers, the bracero program in the Northwest began to take form.

As a whole, the laborers that came to the Northwest were a choice lot because of the method used to recruit the workers in Mexico. In 1943, the secretary of agriculture permitted grower representatives to travel to Mexico to assist the WFA in the selection of workers.[9] This practice, together with the WFA's own screening process, ensured that only able, experienced, and healthy individuals received contracts. This kind of uncommon cooperation of growers with federal and state agencies was so perfectly planned that few adjustments were necessary in the next five years. Even when the Mexican government shifted the recruitment areas among the states of Nayarit, Guanajuato, Aguascalientes, or Veracruz, the growers and WFA officials experienced few difficulties in selecting good candidates.[10] Still, the growers were always mindful of refining the contracting process to ensure excellent workers. In 1945, for instance, the sugar beet industry produced a descriptive thirty-two-minute sound film to use in Mexico as an aid in recruitment.[11]

In addition to the selection process, the farmers and the WFA worked to limit the role of the Mexican inspectors, who were supposed to be permitted to examine working and housing conditions, arbitrate contract disputes, and, in general, serve as official spokespersons for the braceros. Well before these officials had departed from Mexico, the U.S. embassy warned: "I do not think we should expect too much of them [the inspectors] and I only hope that they will not be more of a nuisance than of help. Brown [the WFA representative in Mexico City] tells me that they were largely chosen because they are personal friends of the Minister of Labor and not because of any previous experience as labor inspectors."[12] The ambassador's view encouraged WFA officials to adopt a paternalistic and distrustful attitude toward the Mexican labor officials. Recommending "great patience" and tact, the WFA in turn pointed out to the regional offices that these "inspectors must realize that this journey of theirs is not just a great adventure but a difficult complicated task."[13] As a result, the Mexican officials could not travel into the employment areas without close supervision by the WFA.[14] The WFA's position quickly filtered down to the growers, reinforcing an already negative view of the bracero program. In short, the role of the Mexican inspectors, as protectors of the workers, was rendered ineffective before it even had a chance to develop. Yet, even if the Mexican labor inspectors had been given the time to prove themselves, they were too few in number to be of much value to the workers, who were scattered throughout the nation. In 1943, two inspectors, headquartered at Portland, were responsible for all the braceros working in Utah, Idaho, Oregon, Washington, and Montana.[15]

Until the federal government actually turned the workers over to the farmers, the spirit of the binational agreement was followed. However, once the men were consigned to their employers the best intentions of the Mexican and U.S. negotiators went astray because the farmers exercised so much control over the Extension Service and the Mexican labor inspectors were so few. At this point, the employers had full say and could do literally as they pleased with the workers and their contracts.

Technically, the grower associations employed the braceros and in most cases handled all bookkeeping duties from information supplied by farmers concerning hours worked, deductions, and other payroll matters. This system was far from ideal. Workers complained constantly because most of the farmers were terrible record keepers and simply detested the chore of preparing daily employment records in triplicate for each employee as required by the Extension Service. On the other hand, the braceros did not always understand the completed employment forms because they were printed in English and filled out by the employer, yet they had to sign it, attesting to its accuracy. Not only was the daily routine unfair to the braceros and time-consuming for the farmers, but carelessness at the end of the day and a desire to return home caused both parties to overlook errors.

Proper identification of each worker and credit for hours worked was another problem for the men. Growers seldom got to know the workers on a first-name basis due to the sheer numbers of braceros as well as the difficulty of pronouncing Spanish. Instead, farmers generally relied on the worker's six-digit contract number to credit each man, but this number was not always recorded correctly. Employers made other errors because they were also expected to fill out worker absentee reports that included the person's name, contract number, and a coded explanation for the absence. Finally, and in spite of the fact that each man received a daily copy of his work record, the payroll clerks ultimately calculated all wages at a later date and another place. Days later, upon receipt of his wages, the bracero got the first real opportunity to judge whether his work record was correct. By that time, it was generally too late for corrections.

To cope with this problem, experienced braceros soon learned to double-check the daily work slips for accuracy. Some employers also recognized the problems inherent in the record-keeping system and devised alternate procedures, such as issuing each worker a numbered pin badge with his first and last name and contract number.[16] This simple idea made correct identification easier and nearly foolproof so that workers were properly credited for their work.

Beyond basic record-keeping problems, the bracero program was structured so that the imported workers served as emergency workers that could be deployed rapidly to crop operations in distressed areas. As laborers under contract, they were expected to adapt and stay on the job under adverse conditions that would turn others away. The Extension Service was quick to recognize the intrinsic value of the bracero work force in a low-paying job market and reserved the Mexicans for the "heavy" and worst paid tasks.[17] This meant that the bulk of the imported work force was fixed largely in the production and harvesting of crops requiring large amounts of seasonal hard stoop work. The farmers were in agreement, and in their eyes the braceros were a welcome blessing because even during the years of labor surpluses local workers shunned stoop labor.

The contracted workers were ideal, declared a representative of the growers, because "the cutting of weeds is done with [short] hoes and the Mexicans are declared to be adept to that class of work."[18] Other farmers were of the opinion that "whites" did not make good sugar beet thinners because it was "back breaking work for taller persons, and those of shorter stature work best."[19]

Tied to the claim that Mexicans were better suited for back-bending labor, farmers began to insist that they could not continue to operate without braceros because others steered clear of this type of work. The Washington State Extension Service backed up the claim by reporting that contract laborers were essential "for work in areas . . . which local labor will not accept."[20] Oregon State Extension Service officials reiterated that almost all Mexicans were allotted specifically to the least desirable sugar beet work.[21] In Idaho, federal employment officials stated that the farmers' calls for "stoop labor" went unanswered, forcing a dependency on braceros.[22]

The farmers' preference for contracted men as stoop laborers had more to do with the way the bracero program grouped the workers into an organized and tractable work force and less with the Mexicans' innate physical ability. It was to be expected that growers would quickly recognize the advantages of hiring this seemingly compliant group and seek to control the bracero program locally. In time, some farmers who had an interest in or were owners of food-processing operations argued for permission to employ the workers at will in jobs outside of field labor and without regard to the work agreement.[23] Washington farmers were so pleased with the men's adaptability to different farm jobs that they attempted to use them on wheat combines during the harvest.[24] But in the first few months of the bracero program, the Extension Service refused to certify contracted laborers for food-processing or cannery operations on the grounds that local workers would be displaced. Nevertheless, labor shortages were so widespread and the bracero program was so new that growers hired the Mexicans in canneries and similar jobs without the Extension Service's prior approval and in violation of the workers' contracts.[25] By employing the braceros at their own discretion, growers set their own precedent and forced the Extension Service to grant certification for nonfield employment in 1943. The Extension Service's authorization only served to heighten the demand of food processors so that two years later labor officials reported that "many Mexican nationals were being used in canneries."[26] At Walla Walla alone, the Libby McNeil and Libby Corporation, the Walla Walla Canning Company, and the Bozeman Canning Company all took advantage of the availability of Mexican contracted labor for food-processing jobs.[27] Oregon employers placed braceros in seed treatment plants and otherwise made extensive use of this work force.[28] Idaho was no different; at Payette, the Idaho Cannery Company relied on Mexican nationals to handle the annual pea crop, and near Twin Falls, the Bozeman Canning Company hired many braceros to help pack the sweet corn harvest.[29]

As the number of contracted workers placed in these jobs increased, the earlier worries of the Extension Service were realized. In August 1943, the residents of Kittitas, Washington, were up in arms against the Bozeman Canning Company because it hired Mexicans over local workers.[30] Federal labor officials in Washington State were likewise "embarrassed" by community discontent at Mt. Vernon, Sumner, Puyallup, Seattle, Wenatchee, Prosser, Kennewick, and Walla Walla.[31] Not only were local residents angry, but the farmers' plan to get the Extension Service to certify braceros for work outside of field labor began to backfire against them. For instance, when growers near Seattle tried to obtain workers from a nearby bracero camp, they learned that the men were not available because they were certified exclusively for employment by the Bozeman Canning Company.[32]

Mindful of the mounting controversy, the WFA expressly banned braceros from employment in food-processing plants after 1945 except when the imported men were idle and other workers were not available. In order to determine when Mexican nationals could be employed in canneries, the WFA gave local workers first priority, followed by transported interstate labor, prisoners of war, and finally braceros. According to the WFA's guidelines, all workers in each category had to be exhausted before hiring from the next group was permitted.[33] The WFA's directive seemed to work well to assuage the farmers' concern that too many contracted laborers were going to canneries, but the competition for the braceros did not end here. Frequently food processors were permitted to hire the braceros on the condition that they would release them immediately to farmers. This was disruptive to food production and brought complaints that "in some instances the Mexicans were needed in the fields and young girls replaced them in the plant"[34] Finally in July 1945, Secretary of Agriculture Clinton P. Anderson moved to end the strained relations between the canners, farmers, and local workers. Hereafter, he ordered, braceros were prohibited from employment, under any pretext, outside of field work.[35] Actually, the overwhelming majority of the workers were employed in stoop labor and similar jobs all along. But the USDA's decision inextricably locked the Mexican men into the least desirable types of agricultural employment with little opportunity to improve their skills.

Although the jobs reserved for the braceros were generally despised, they were nonetheless essential first links in the robust war food production chain. In this capacity, the Mexican workers made a most vital and measurable contribution to the total war effort. The WFA estimated that during the war the composite of all categories of workers recruited from elsewhere to the Northwest Division provided significant amounts of labor. In Idaho, they thinned 14 percent and harvested 31 percent of the sugar beet crop, thinned and harvested 22 percent of the lettuce crop, and harvested 60 percent of the sweet corn acreage and 15 percent of the onion production. Oregon workers thinned 25 percent and harvested 40 percent of the sugar beets, thinned 50 percent and picked 10 percent of the apples, and thinned 60 percent and picked 30 percent of the pear crop. They also harvested 25 percent of the asparagus, 20 percent of the onion crop, 60 percent of all cucumbers, and 60 percent of the peas. In Washington, nonlocal labor thinned and harvested 13 percent of the sugar beets as well as harvesting 29 percent of the asparagus, 31 percent of the canning peas, 90 percent of the sweet corn production, 2 percent of the apples, and 17 percent of the grape crop.[36] This category of workers provided substantial inputs of labor to other crops as well.

Braceros made up the largest group of workers transported from all areas to the Pacific Northwest by the Extension Service and labor branch. In 1946, they accounted for 70 percent of all nonlocal workers in the Northwest Division, including Utah, Montana, and Wyoming. In contrast, interstate migrant labor, Japanese American evacuees, and native Americans constituted 19 percent, while Jamaican contracted workers made up the remaining work force.[37] For several reasons, Mexican nationals were largely employed in Idaho, Oregon, and Washington, so the percentages relative to other categories of workers were even higher. Jamaican laborers, which amounted to 11 percent of the Northwest Division total, were not contracted to Oregon and Washington and very few were employed in Idaho. Japanese American evacuees were ordered relocated away from the Washington and Oregon coasts and defense industries so they were concentrated mainly in southern Idaho with a few in Oregon. Table 1 indicates the total number of braceros by state under PL-45.

The importance of the braceros to crop operations in Oregon, Washington, and Idaho can be examined in other ways. They were distributed in mobile camps throughout a broad geographical area in

Table 1. *Total Number of Braceros Employed by State, 1943–1947*

State	1943	1944	1945	1946	1947
Idaho	1,779	4,434	3,728	3,241	2,434
Oregon	3,138	4,651	3,782	2,504	1,061
Washington	2,379	4,351	5,393	2,788	1,271
Total	7,296	13,436	12,903	8,533	4,766

Source: Compiled from *Farm Labor Report,* Bureau of Agricultural Economics, U.S. Department of Agriculture (Washington, D.C.: U.S. Government Printing Office, 1943–1947).

the three states, underscoring their significance. Mexicans were found in the cranberry bogs at Ilwaco, Long Beach, and other coastal communities.[38] Near Seattle and Tacoma, the workers were trained as skillful pruners by blueberry growers in the Puyallup Valley and Cowlitz County and recruited to do this chore.[39] In Oregon, the braceros gathered record-setting potato harvests in Klamath County and, to the east, they were the "main source of labor" in the pea fields near Pendleton and Umatilla.[40] In southern Idaho they were literally everywhere.

In emergencies, the men went into temporary service in areas outside of farm work. Idaho's pool of contracted workers repeatedly helped out the National Forest Service. Although the lumber industry was an essential war resource, forestry service jobs, like farm openings, went unfilled because they were hard, dangerous, and not well paid. These characteristics were enough to suggest that braceros would be drawn to these jobs. The men were loaned by the WFA to the National Forest Service provided that the workers were willing to transfer temporarily.[41] In practice, the National Forest Service disregarded the WFA's precondition, and in time Mexicans were among the first to be placed on forest fire duty.[42] In 1945, braceros labored long and hard constructing fire lanes to halt a five thousand–acre conflagration that threatened the Coeur d'Alene National Forest.[43] By the end of the war, a clear pattern was well established: as soon as fires broke out, the Mexicans were called regardless of the existing regulations and their willingness to go.[44] When on loan to the National Forest Service, the braceros were sometimes instructed to perform other important jobs such as planting pine seedlings in reforestation projects. Still others were involved in critical insect and blister rust control as well as other related duties.[45]

As more and more braceros were transferred from field work to forestry, local workers began to object to the practice, especially after the war. In March 1946, a dejected resident wrote to Oregon Senator Wayne L. Morse expressing the concern of many residents affected by the Forest Service's actions. The letter called attention to the fact that Mexican aliens were employed with the Forest Service while 63,000 Oregonians were without jobs. It also alleged that the Forest Service was purposely depressing wages by underpaying the Mexican workers a mere $.90 a day.[46]

Their need to improve their financial condition and that of their dependents in Mexico made the braceros excellent and dependable workers for the growers and the Forest Service. They became even more valuable employees when trained to do a job properly. Raising worker productivity through training was no easy task because the majority of the growers lacked the most basic managerial skills to use the men effectively. Often they simply pushed them constantly or used intimidation and outright violence. Some farmers were certain that the braceros performed better only after they were threatened or warned that contract renewals were dependent on satisfactory work records.[47]

The WFA and the Extension Service, because they were attached to the state colleges, recognized that men unfamiliar with northwestern agriculture could not simply be pushed through the door and called farm workers. For this reason, they approached the training of the men more intelligently. Still, it took two years after the start of the bracero program for the Extension Service to finally convince employers of the need to train the inexperienced workers. The Extension Service's basic training philosophy was patterned after that in use in industry and intended to make use of the resources at the state colleges. In an address to farmers, the Extension Service expressed the need for training of the Mexican men:

> We must try this year to increase the efficiency of these workers. We have and should use a lot of people in this State College who are adapted to training and teaching; these people can assist us greatly in developing methods of training workers to increase their efficiency. I have been told you cannot do much with a Mexican—if he knows one way to do a job you cannot change him. I know of Mexicans who have worked a whole season and yet when retrained have shown a remarkable increase in their output. There is something in training. If there were not I am sure industry would not have put the thousands of dollars they have into training of workers for industry; they are very far ahead of us. The application of that principle to agriculture is proving to be very worthwhile.[48]

After 1945, all but the most recalcitrant farmers accepted the concept of training the braceros, but other problems remained.[49] For the benefit of employers, the Extension Service printed easy to understand illustrated bilingual training brochures in Spanish and English for the various crops and jobs,[50] but their effectiveness as instructional aids was limited because most braceros were unable to read. During the period under consideration, illiteracy was high in Mexico; in 1940, only 41 percent of all students over six years of age were literate. Ten years later, in spite of educational reform, literacy was barely 55 percent.[51] Without doubt, the lack of education among the bracero age group was even higher than the national rate since most of the workers came from the rural areas where education was most lacking. In addition, since the push for educational reform was so recent in Mexico, it had probably missed this generation of workers entirely.

To enhance the instruction of the braceros, films that had proven effective with interstate workers in the early years of the war were also used as training aids. In 1945, the U & I Sugar Company translated a German-language film, which described sugar beet cultivation for the German prisoner of war workers, into Spanish for the braceros.[52] After viewing the twenty-minute program the Extension Service was unconvinced of the worth of the film as an instructional medium. The officials wrote:

> Although we couldn't understand what the narrator was saying, it was plain that the picture was just another publicity picture, publicizing the great importance of the sugar and sugar-beet industry. Out of the 20-minute run of the film, less than five minutes were devoted to actual training techniques which might be helpful to a new worker . . . if he is able to get the sugar beets thinned, blocked and topped after carrying out no more of a training program than just seeing the picture, he is a better man than I think he is.[53]

Although many farmers accepted that training was important to increased worker productivity, they had neither the time nor the real desire to be instructors. They found it too difficult to explain the bilingual brochures to the unschooled men. The paper pamphlets were also troublesome because they did not stand up to the wear and tear in the open field. Worse yet, the Extension Service provided the materials but little assistance to the growers in the instruction of the men because it was not permitted to take part in the actual training. In the end, farmers tended to disregard the training aids and the ad-

Table 2. *Relative Performance of Various Types of Workers in Idaho*

Potato Harvest		Beet Harvest	
Worker Category	Performance Indexed at 100	Worker Category	Performance Indexed at 100
Migrants	108.00	Japanese evacuees	122.24
Mexican nationals	100.00	Migrants	114.35
Japanese evacuees	98.90	Nonfarm men	112.9
Nonfarm men	95.20	Jamaicans	109.33
Jamaicans	87.71	Onfarm workers*	102.63
Onfarm workers*	86.46	Mexican nationals	100.00
Nonfarm women	73.83	Nonfarm women	71.80
Nonfarm youth	50.92	Conscientious objectors	71.80
Prisoners of war	49.63	Nonfarm youth	61.72
Conscientious objectors	49.39	Prisoners of war	43.54

*Onfarm workers were largely family workers, youth, and elderly persons.
Source: "Farm Labor Supervisor Annual Report 1944," Box B, Idaho-Iowa, File: Idaho, p. 18a, RG33, NA.

vice of the Extension Service and resorted to teaching by example, with much sign language and liberal doses of broken Spanish and English. To most growers, many who were unschooled themselves, this latter approach was more practical, convenient, and probably more effective too.

Thus taught and with experience, the contracted men became better workers, but it is exceedingly difficult to compare objectively the performance of the braceros to that of other workers involved in the war farm labor program. In 1944, before farmers accepted the concept of training, the Idaho State Extension Service did make an attempt to calculate the output of the different category of workers. Table 2 lists the Extension Service's findings.

According to this ranking, the Mexican nationals were neither the best nor the least productive workers. However, in all probability, their work performance was higher than indicated here since job training was not initiated until after 1944. In 1944, braceros across the nation harvested crops with an estimated value of $432,010,000. Of this total, $383,600,000 was in California, Michigan, Montana, North Dakota, Idaho, Oregon, and Washington.[54] Just the same, social discrimination, language handicap, cultural dislocation, and the farmers' method of supervision and training cut into their work capacity.

From the lavish praise bestowed by farmers on the braceros, one is led to believe that they were exceptional workers. From the start, farmers, WFA officials, and others lauded the character and adeptness of the Mexicans. In 1943, federal labor officials in Idaho wrote, "We continue to receive many good reports about their adeptness in learning quickly and doing a good job."[55] "They're all right, good workers," offered a farmer at Burlington, Washington. "I only hope I can get them again."[56] A nearby cannery spokesman told the Extension Service that his company preferred the braceros "over local help."[57] Walla Walla pea farmers agreed: "We wouldn't trade one of these Mexicans for ten of the kind of help we have had on this job before."[58] "These new Mexicans are as good as any help I ever had," said another.[59] The *Northwest Farm News* wrote authoritatively that the men were very "industrious," so much so that they were "being sought in numbers more than can be supplied."[60]

Oregon pea growers at Umatilla credited the braceros with rescuing the 1943 crop from loss.[61] Hood River apple orchardists were gratified that the Mexican workers had arrived to fill "jobs requiring grown men rather than women and children."[62] Following the first full year of the bracero program in Oregon, Governor Earl Snell addressed a letter to the Mexican Republic expressing a sincere appreciation from Oregonians for the contribution of the Mexican men.[63] He had every reason to do so. Earlier the Oregon State Extension Service had concluded: "The utilization of Mexican Nationals from early June throughout the remainder of the year provided the greatest single contribution to the production and harvesting of Oregon crops in 1943 of any single special group."[64] Perhaps the comments of a farmer's wife best expressed the view that the braceros were unexpectedly ideal. "We sure like these new Mexicans," she said. "They want to work all the time. Only trouble is when it rains or something and they have to lay off." She considered the braceros to be more virtuous than the earlier Mexican American migrants. In her view, "The new Mexicans go or send to town for only one purpose . . . for their groceries and needed clothing. They are eager to get their money to send it back to Mexico where an American dollar exchanges for $1.50 in Mexican money."[65]

This litany of praise soon became a familiar refrain. As soon as the braceros arrived for the second year, the accolades started again. An employer was emphatic: "The men are good workers. They want to work and they do work, there is an absolute minimum of shirking."[66] The farm labor supervisor for the Washington State Extension Service described the Mexican workers as extraordinary because they could double the output of local help.[67] Oregon's Extension Service was no less direct: "We have had far and away the best results from the Mexican Nationals. They are doing a good job."[68] The Washington Farm Bureau summed it all up. The braceros, it wrote, were "a God-send to farmers."[69]

Growers denigrated the ability of POW and Jamaican workers, underscoring the ranking of worker productivity found in Table 2. Idaho farmers complained, to some extent justifiably, that the German prisoner work force produced about 50 to 60 percent as much as other workers.[70] In spite of the fact that the Extension Service considered Jamaicans better workers than POWs, it had worse misgivings about the Caribbean men and felt that they would just as soon go AWOL as work in the sugar beet harvest.[71]

For as long as PL-45 was in effect the Mexican contracted workers were publicly commended and seldom criticized. Agriculture maintained this constant chorus of praise because it had come upon a suitable replacement labor force for the thousands swallowed by the war and wished to make it a standing institution. Of course, some farmers were sincerely grateful for the contribution of the Mexicans. For the rest, the constant praise was a deliberate attempt to stem local objection against the presence of foreign labor and to ensure a permanent resupply of Mexican workers.

The intention to make the bracero program a permanent institution of cheap labor was apparent from the start. Following 1943, the Washington State Extension Service was convinced that farmers would scheme in order to satisfy an insatiable craving for braceros.[72] Idaho State Farm Labor Committee officials refused Jamaican contracted workers in lieu of Mexicans because they were too much trouble. In their opinion, "it would be best to bring colored labor into [the] state only for short seasonal labor peaks in cases of emergency, and if that were done, some type of supervision should be provided."[73] According to the Extension Service, the contriving attitude of some growers to hoard the bulk of the Mexican nationals by bringing "considerable pressure to bear" was a major problem in the success of the overall farm labor program.[74] It noted that in some instances, farmers "refused to utilize local labor by insisting on having Mexican Nationals."[75] At other times, some employers went so far as to attempt to exchange prisoner of war workers for the more coveted braceros.[76]

Two years after the first men arrived, farmers did little to mask their preference for the braceros over other types of workers. In May, the Washington State Extension Service was dismayed to learn that orchardists and farmers had refused six hundred Jamaicans in spite of a shortage of Mexican nationals.[77] The racist implication of the farmers' unwillingness to accept the black workers was evident to the Extension Service officials. "This office," they noted, "has the impression that everybody wants more Mexicans but if they are not available counties feel that they can squeeze by someway. If this is true certainly they cannot be very short."[78]

To some extent, employers simply resisted the Jamaicans because they were black and their very presence among other workers led to disruptive racial problems and jealousies over jobs.[79] In October 1945, a serious half-hour fist and club melee erupted between some Jamaicans and other workers at Idaho's Twin Falls labor camp.[80] The incident was significant because the following day white laborers began to leave the camp in protest against the Jamaicans.[81] This and other outbreaks of violence gave farmers enough reason to label the Caribbean men as troublemakers and simply not worthwhile.

Despite the farmers' ongoing favorable public commentary and as much as employers tried to idealize the braceros, the Mexican farm labor program was hardly tailor-made for northwestern agriculture. Local residents saw the Mexicans as different and protested the fact that farmers had brought these foreigners into their midst. One of the most serious problems associated with the bracero program was the indignation of the local farm workers over the practice of hiring the Mexicans ahead of residents. Unlike the limited protests against the canneries, this displeasure was widespread because farmers openly discriminated against white agricultural workers on the basis that the braceros were twice as effective. Oregon employers considered the Mexicans as superior "to the jalopy brigade of white migrants that followed the crops in the pre-war days."[82] Idaho farmers were convinced that only 60 percent of the nonbracero workers made any real effort at all.[83] In addition to the "low quality" and "poor performance" of white farm workers, growers were equally displeased with their "rapid turn over."[84]

Although victimized by discrimination, most white farm workers could manage to find alternative employment outside of agriculture during the war. But when the war ended and the economy temporarily slowed, returning veterans and out-of-work Anglo workers felt the cutting effects of job discrimination. When this happened, the protests against the Mexicans escalated and became more serious. In 1946, public demonstrations against the Mexican nationals were evident in many northwestern communities. At the Dayton Farm Labor Camp in Oregon, nineteen Anglo families circulated a petition urging that Mexican contract workers be excluded from the camp on the grounds that whites remained unemployed while farmers hired the braceros.[85] In Snohomish County, Washington, local workers, the American Federation of Labor, and the American Legion challenged the employment of braceros.[86]

In general, farmers responded that Mexican labor was necessary as long as the labor shortages continued but would remove them when and if domestic unemployment became a factor.[87] In truth, most farmers were skeptical about charges of job discrimination and pointed out that there was a difference between unemployment and a plain refusal to work. Nevertheless, as long as farmers could use the bracero program to maintain low wage scales, they could dispute charges of unemployment if local workers would chose not to accept agricultural jobs.

After the war and the easing of labor shortages, some employers hoarded the Mexicans rather than release them to other states or return them to Mexico. Idaho in particular contracted as many braceros in 1946 as in 1945, while Oregon and Washington ordered fewer. In June 1946, Mexican government inspectors concluded that Idaho had so many contracted workers that they were simply loafing.[88] Growers, of course, were well aware of the fact and resorted to advertisements in the *Idaho Daily Statesman* in order to get jobs for the idle workers.[89] Washington pea growers also kept unemployed braceros in reserve without releasing them for work elsewhere.[90] The stockpiling of braceros was one thing during the war. Now farmers had few legitimate justifications to continue the practice because more local workers were reportedly available than at any time since the start of the war.[91] To counteract public pressure against the bracero program, employers wrote to the secretary of agriculture that many thousands of dollars' worth of valuable food crops would be left in the fields without the braceros.[92]

In other ways, the Mexican nationals were the most troublesome of all the farm workers. As illiterate and young as they were, the braceros were far from passive and were capable of bringing pressure to bear over unfavorable working and living conditions. In the first year of the program, the workers signed contracts for a six-month period beginning as early as April and returning by September. This meant that some farmers were left shorthanded because the apple harvest ended after November and sugar beets even later, and some workers insisted that they be repatriated at the expiration of their contracts.[93] Unless the bracero willingly renewed his contract while still in the Northwest, farmers had little recourse but to release the worker at the end of the contract period. More often than not, employers had difficulty convincing the braceros to stay longer because job conditions, the farmers' incessant pressure, and cold weather made workers reluctant to stay longer than necessary.

Common sense told the farmers to try to hold onto their workers and attempt to keep them in the country. Beyond the fact that labor was scarce, employers had no guarantee that workers, once trained, would return the following year. Some workers returned to the Northwest, but most went to states where contracts were available regardless of location. In addition, farmers contracted the workers sight unseen. Sometimes the braceros who arrived, although physically fit, were just too light to do the heavy work involved in northwestern agriculture.[94]

There were exceptions to this situation, as some workers were fortunate to find good employers and remained for years without returning to Mexico. Some employees found that farmers would take extraordinary steps to keep them in the country permanently as well as provide assistance in bringing their wives from Mexico.[95] If these bracero families had children, permanent residency and employment on the same farm were almost always guaranteed.[96] For the majority of the braceros, however, finding someone to intercede on their behalf was difficult because farmers were very selective in whom they helped remain in the United States. Some men appealed to Congress "to be freed" to do work "without restriction" but were denied permission to remain in the country on a permanent basis.[97]

Yet even if the braceros attempted to remain past the termination of their contracts, others felt strongly that the Mexican work force should be changed yearly. Otherwise, they argued, the men became too familiar with life in the Northwest or too lonesome for home to the point of becoming unmanageable and insolent. According to a camp manager, if the braceros were kept in the country too long they developed a propensity to get drunk and absent themselves from camp and work.[98] Another camp manager categorized the attitudes of the braceros according to their length of stay in the Northwest:

> The First Year—*Very Cooperative*
> The Second Year—*Too Smart for Their Own Good*
> The Third Year—*They Begin to Think They are Running Things*
> The Fourth Year—*They Expect [to] Take Over.*[99]

As an example, the manager cited his own experience. During the winter and for reasons of economy, he had been compelled to reassign a reduced population of braceros into two barracks. When he ordered a group of men who had been in the country three years or more to move, they refused. The following morning, the braceros still would not relocate. Finally, by the third day the manager had had enough and "ousted them bag and baggage" from the barracks. He wrote, "In the main, I conscientiously believe, we would have a better working condition if we had a yearly change."[100] "However," he added, "by the same type of thinking, we have those Mexican Nationals who improve with age and training."[101]

Undoubtedly, some of the braceros became defiant the longer they were in the country and as they became conscious of the demand for their labor. When this happened a few men could influence an entire camp. In one case, Jesús Hernández Martínez was removed from the camp population and ordered returned to Mexico. Earlier, he had been placed on "probation" and warned about leaving "work without permission," adding gravel to bean sacks in order to increase their weight, and talking back "to the point of being contemptuous."[102] At Wenatchee, a group of seasoned braceros were so eager to return to their homeland that they insisted on repatriation and refused to work.[103] At the Dixie camp near Walla Walla, in July 1946 446 men were in the camp but only 29 were employed. To protest their idleness, the entire camp refused to accept any work unless farmers could provide a minimum of 200 jobs.[104] At this same camp, men became so familiar with the area that they would eat their meals and then walk into town on their own to obtain jobs in the canneries. The problem became so serious that at one point it was impossible to get over 30 percent of the men out on farm work.[105]

Theoretically, only those members of the contracting group had the right to employ the foreign workers, but in practice, noncertified farmers or canneries could not resist the pool of cheap contracted workers and would offer them employment at slightly higher wages. This was bootlegging, since growers who had not joined the association or provided facilities nonetheless took advantage of the supply of workers.[106] The unofficial system operated in the following manner at Milton-Freewater, Oregon. Mexican nationals after working all night in the pea harvest would return to camp, eat breakfast, and then wander out where growers, not members of the Milton-Freewater Labor Committee, would take them to pick cherries. At the end of the day, the bootlegging farmer would pay in cash and the bracero would be ahead of his fellow worker who had remained in camp.[107]

To end the raiding of labor from this particular camp, the growers, assisted by the camp manager, started looking for all braceros working in orchards outside their contracts. The first day, "18 Mexican Nationals bootlegging, along with five growers guilty of the same charge," were netted. The braceros were penalized by having their payment for any work done withheld, and the farmers were exonerated with a warning that future bootlegging would not be handled with "Kid Gloves."[108]

Desertions, or otherwise unauthorized absences from the camps or job site, were another source of annoyance to the farmers.[109] The workers found it relatively simple to absent themselves from the contracting employer or association because they were not fingerprinted or subject to the Alien Registration Act of 1940.[110] Camp managers reported that men missing or skipping from camps in Idaho, Washington, and Oregon was a widespread problem.[111] Problems with food services, housing facilities, wage disputes, and a hardening attitude of growers toward the men accounted for an increased number of missing laborers within one year of the start of the program.[112] By itself the fact that the workers deserted did not really irritate the growers. The WFA's policy on absentees was not to replace the missing men but to charge the number to future allocations. Most farmers, therefore, made a strong effort to find the men and notify the WFA or prevent them from working outside the contract. The WFA regarded all braceros who were working in agriculture or elsewhere "with a non-contract employer, as being illegally in the country."[113] Therefore, when farmers identified missing workers to the WFA, it instructed the immigration authorities to make "no distinction" and apprehend the violators when possible.[114] The problem became worse as the men became better acquainted with the Northwest and as Chicano enclaves, which also grew during the war, began to provide easy places for the deserting braceros to hide. By 1945, the chief of operations at the WFA office in Portland considered the problem of desertions as serious and estimated that no less than 10 percent of all braceros had abandoned their contracts or returned to Mexico.[115] Outside the Northwest and for the country as a whole, the rate of desertion was higher, at 13 percent.[116] Still, to northwestern farmers any level of absenteeism was critical because it was nearly impossible to replace the men.

Inasmuch as the farmers capitalized on their control of the bracero program, the work experiences of the braceros were unpleasant in other ways. Some farmers lacked any concern for the welfare of the men by insisting that the workers stay in the field in spite of unbearably cold temperatures.[117] For instance, in southeast Idaho the ground generally froze between the second and third weeks of November, but in 1946 freezing temperatures hit the area very early. The braceros were unprepared for the winter and on the very day that they arrived from California a strong blizzard hit Idaho Falls. In the days that followed, some of the men refused to work digging beets in the cold weather and those that tried labored in the rock-hard ground for as long as eight hours "for as little as $2.50."[118] Yet the sugar beet growers demanded that the men continue to work or be penalized. This incident prompted the camp manager to comment that in his judgment this "was not right."[119] He wrote: "I noticed on some of these days the local help was not in the fields. In general I believe the Nationals were not treated as they should have been. The loss of work was not entirely their fault. Other things entered in for which they were given the blame."[120]

At other times, the administrative weaknesses of the bracero program and the farmers' reckless self-interests also put the men's lives in jeopardy. In spite of the fact that the men were selected in Mexico for their good health, they soon developed illnesses, such as appendicitis, tuberculosis, arthritis, jaundice, or meningitis, and suffered serious accidents while in the Pacific Northwest.[121] The official government policy with regard to incapacitated workers was to treat the individual and, if he was ambulatory, to initiate repatriation as soon as possible.[122] Illnesses such as pneumonia during the winter months were common, while other equally serious diseases resulted from potentially hazardous conditions. At one camp where the water supply came directly from the Columbia River, typhoid was prevalent and all residents had to be inoculated.[123]

Lead poisoning from orchard work was another critical threat to the braceros' health. Since the federal government had long been concerned with consumers receiving a residue of arsenate of lead from orchards, growers took steps to ensure that their crops would not be rejected. Some orchardists attempted to remove the noxious chemical by washing the fruit or installing felt flaps over apple-grader belts in packing houses.[124] Yet neither the federal government nor growers demonstrated much concern over the exposure of the workers except to keep them out of orchards recently sprayed with the chemical. Either Mexican workers did not comprehend the seriousness of lead poisoning or employers and WFA officials simply disregarded the danger. But in any case, in a period of four months during 1945, health authorities in the Office of Labor reported seventy-eight cases of lead poisoning in the Northwest.[125] Once contaminated, the men exhibited severe symptoms of constipation, colic, anorexia, and vomiting. The chemical had entered the bodies of the braceros through their respiratory tracts and prolonged contact with their skin. In other cases, the men were poisoned when they drank water from contaminated irrigation ditches or directly from puddles laced with lead around the trees.[126]

The farmers' lack of attention to the safety of the braceros in the work place resulted in senseless disabling and sometimes fatal accidents. In part, these mishaps stemmed from the fact that braceros had little experience with the types of agriculture and machinery found in the Northwest. When they arrived, the men received little or no training or caution about the hazards of powerful moving equipment. Not knowing any better, the braceros were careless around machinery, and accidents were bound to happen. One man working on a seed harvester lost a finger when he accidently put his hand in the machine.[127] Another bracero got his head pinned between two pieces of equipment, causing injuries to the temporal region, lacerations, and a fractured skull.[128] The camp manager reported that "a portion of an end of a bolt" had pierced down into the man's "skull to an unbelievable distance."[129] In another instance, a group of workers, including Raymundo López Camacho, were having lunch when a tractor came too close to where the men were sitting and ran over a milk bottle, sending glass flying. One piece landed in Camacho's lunch; he accidently lodged the glass fragment in his throat, sending him to the hospital for three days.[130] At the Kennewick camp, Pedro Correa Armenta lost his eyesight, and following an unsuccessful eye operation to restore his vision he was repatriated.[131]

Farmers were also at fault for these job-related injuries since they were well aware of the danger of farm employment. During the "National Farm and Home Hour" broadcast in May 1943, the secretary of agriculture called the farmers' attention to the need for safety precautions and recommended educating the uninitiated men.[132] One year later, President Roosevelt designated National Safety Week in an attempt to curb farm accidents.[133] Still, many farmers simply refused to heed the call for safety. One grower when told to take safety precautions told a WFA representative to "leave the farmers alone as the committee [the farmers' association] has insurance which covers all cases of accidents."[134] This farmer seemingly felt that insurance coverage alone excused the employers from negligence. However, the insurance protection afforded to the braceros was paltry, and sometimes workers received nothing. When a man lost his little finger in a farm accident, he was offered a $200 settlement.[135] Actually, until 1949, a glaring oversight existed in the workers' agreement; the contracts had no provision for occupational insurance. After 1949, insurance coverage, at no cost to the worker, was made mandatory, but even then the benefit for loss of life was scheduled at just $1,000. In contrast, the Victory Farm Volunteer Corp coverage for the loss of sight or both hands or feet was valued at $1,000 in 1943.[136]

Before it became mandatory for the employers of braceros to provide coverage to the workers, the matter was left to the farmers' discretion. If they obtained insurance, fine, but if not and an employee was involved in a work-related accident, the question of liability was generally resolved between the worker, the employer, and the Mexican consul.

Employers were also clearly to blame for the large number of disconcerting transportation accidents. When the braceros arrived, farmers were confronted with the problem of their transportation to and from work. In the past, most farm workers, especially migrants, had owned their own means of transportation. The braceros, on the other hand, were delivered directly by the federal government to the work area. After that, individual growers or the employing associations were responsible for taking the men to the worksite and returning them to the camps. To do this, employers used any means available with little thought to the passengers' safety. Open flatbed trucks were commonly used because they could carry a large number of men. The senseless mentality of the farmers was matched by the playful but dangerous actions of the men. They rode with their legs dangling over the sides or stood upright without the benefit of safety rails. Often when the truck hit a bump or went into a curve at high speed, the riders were thrown off. At the end of the day, farmers were loath to make more than one trip so workers were made to ride atop dangerously loose loads of potatoes, sugar beets, or lightly secured asparagus and fruit boxes. In this way, many braceros were seriously and some fatally injured. This was a critical problem in October 1943. That year more than one bracero lost his life while being transported by truck, and the Oregon State supervisor for farm labor urged county extension agents to enforce safeguards in transportation.[137]

It is impossible to know just how many similar accidents occurred in 1943 because they were not always reported. But in 1944 and the years that followed, the camp managers were ordered to make more careful note of mishaps involving transportation. The following are examples from among the litany of accidents. In July 1944, Agustine Pérez Luna was thrown from the back of a truck, striking his head and seriously injuring his spine.[138] At Nampa, a bracero employed by the Amalgamated Sugar Company jumped off a moving vehicle, breaking his shoulder blade and fracturing his skull in two places.[139] Nearby, several men were struck by an automobile, and at another camp a worker was seriously injured when he fell off the rear of a moving truck.[140] It was a serious problem that went unresolved, because in 1945 the Office of Labor reported that more laborers were killed in the Northwest in accidents involving moving vehicles than lost their lives for any other cause.[141] It noted that most accidents involved workers riding on loaded potato trucks, so a safety poster campaign was developed to stop this hazardous practice. Still, one farmer responded to the initiative with an "it can't be done" attitude.[142] The following spring, two more Mexican workers were struck by a car, sending one to the hospital with a fractured skull.[143]

Camp managers, who were responsible for the welfare of the men, became frustrated with their inability to cope with the safety issue. A troubled but safety-conscious camp manager wrote to the Portland office that growers continued to haul the men on top of trucks loaded with potatoes. He wanted the "practice stopped," because "no consideration to the safety of the men involved is given."[144] Three months earlier he had filed a similar protest describing how farmers rebuked him when he tried to instill some concern about safety.[145] The camp manager's persistence paid off; in August 1946, the Portland office sent a sharp memorandum to area representatives ordering a halt to the "practice of transporting workers on flat-bed trucks and on the top of loads."[146] The memorandum was directed specifically to the Boise and Weiser areas, where the practice was the most flagrant. Unfortunately, the directive did not arrive in Idaho in time to save the life of José Guerrero Rodríguez; he was killed when a truck overturned while carrying twenty-two men to fight a forest fire.[147] After the directive was received, its effect on the safety issue was questionable because a similar accident involving Mexican forest fire fighters occurred. This time seven men en route to the Payette National Forest were injured and hospitalized when the truck in which they were riding overturned.

Not only were the open flatbed trucks unsafe, but careless drivers compounded the problem. At one Washington camp, a concerned manager invited the state highway patrol to make a weekly safety visit to his camp. Later, in a spot check of the drivers taking the braceros to work, the camp manager was dismayed to find that "not one single truck hauling our men made a stop before crossing the tracks."[148]

After 1946, labor officials stressed greater emphasis on the safety of the braceros being transported to and from work. Nevertheless, the farmers' habit of indifference to caution was too ingrained to change, and life-threatening accidents continued on northwestern roads and highways. In June 1947, a worker in Idaho went into shock after he fell off a truck.[149] In Washington, another bracero was similarly injured. Out of concern over the numerous accidents, the Mexican consul eventually retained an attorney to sue the Eastern

Washington Co-op Beet Growers Association in cases involving braceros.[150]

In theory, the bracero agreement attempted to establish a contract labor program which balanced the needs of workers for adequate housing and conditions of employment. In practice, the binational agreement was a worthless promise between two nations because it allowed employers ultimate say over the imported men. The abuses of the first bracero program stood to be repeated, but this time on a much larger scale, because more Mexican men were involved over much of the country and for a longer period of time.

Perhaps worse, few individuals in the Northwest, outside of the officials in the bracero program, camp managers, and farmers, ever knew about the experiences and hardships of the Mexican men. Farm labor in the Northwest, in contrast with that in California, was not politicized or publicized. This region lacked a Carey McWilliams, Ernesto Galarza, Paul S. Taylor, or John Steinbeck. In this respect, the braceros were truly dehumanized. Most persons remain ignorant of the vital contribution of these Mexican men.

4. *Huelgas:* Bracero Strikes

NO SOONER had the Mexicans begun to arrive in the Northwest than the farmers began to disregard their contracts. This made the work experience of the great majority of the braceros only slightly better than that of servile labor. With some exceptions, farmers treated the workers so badly that their actions defied all logic and almost put an end to their very source of labor. This underscored the fact that farmers were not willing to allow foreign labor any say over employment conditions when they stubbornly withheld similar concessions to native-born workers.

Because both farmers and workers sought to maximize their gain during the war, the relationship between the two was bitter from the beginning. The farmers were displeased with the terms of PL-45 and could not understand why the United States had failed to convince Mexico to permit its workers to enter the country unconditionally. Most felt that they were saddled with an unnecessary and cumbersome contract, even though the United States was in need of labor and Mexico had a surplus.

But in reality, the farmers were needlessly concerned, because the workers' contract did not guarantee the braceros the right to choose employers or hours and conditions of employment. Moreover, the hierarchical supervisory system, which included the growers associations, camp managers, farmers, and crew leaders on larger farms, wielded tremendous power over the workers. They transported the men to and from work, gave instructions and supervision in the fields, maintained the payroll, and, when necessary, maintained worker discipline.

The braceros, on the other hand, contracted for employment with the thought of bettering their condition of life in Mexico. They were completely powerless to make good their intention because their contract prohibited them from striking for better conditions and they were rarely asked to provide input to advisory committees or similar supportive agencies concerned with farm labor. Certainly, no Mexican worker was asked to serve on these committees, agencies, or boards. Yet, when their treatment on the job and return for their labor fell short of their aspirations and expectations, the braceros, aided by the Mexican consul, asserted themselves against their employers through strikes and protests.

Of all the problems associated with the bracero program in the Pacific Northwest, work stoppages or strikes were the most alarming to farmers. Unlike their counterparts in other parts of the country, braceros in the Northwest exhibited little reluctance to stop work. In 1944, Ernesto Galarza wrote that workers in Illinois, Colorado, New Mexico, Michigan, and California would rarely speak critically in the presence of camp managers or labor officials. He noted also that the absence of any grievance machinery to settle employment disputes left the men with but two alternatives—"shut up or go back."[1] Other braceros probably staged labor protests (there was a serious disturbance near Fullerton, California, in 1943), but no general pattern of strikes emerged.[2] This prevailing stereotype of braceros as docile, undemanding, and incapable of organizing themselves to press for better working conditions does not hold true in the Northwest, where braceros were constantly on strike, and this made the region unique among other parts of the country. Several lessons emerge from an attempt to answer why the Northwest was such a hotbed for labor unrest for over four years.

In one instance alone, four hundred Mexicans from three Nampa area labor camps went on strike on June 17, 1946. They were joined by over six hundred other workers at Marsing, Franklin, Upper Deer Flat, and Amalgamated Sugar Company camps. The next day, the *Idaho Daily Statesman* reported that the braceros had taken to the streets of Nampa instead of reporting for work. The strike over wages continued until June 26, when Mexican Consul Carlos Grimm at Salt Lake City persuaded the men to return to work pending a hearing.[3] This particular strike put great fear into the farmers because even as the walkout continued POW workers were being removed from Idaho.[4]

The absence of Mexican government labor inspectors, farmers' attitudes toward labor, and an inelastic labor supply were factors leading to the work stoppages. In 1943, ten Mexican labor inspectors were assigned to ensure contract compliance throughout the United States; most were assigned to the Southwest and two were responsible for the northwestern area.[5] Not only were two inspectors insufficient for this region, but they were hampered by insufficient travel funds, vast territories to cover, and the close supervision of the WFA officials. Under these circumstances, the Mexican inspectors found it impossible to head off disputes or other controversies before they developed into strikes. In brief, without the tempering influence of the labor inspectors, braceros in the Northwest had little choice but to strike in order to resolve grievances.

The absence of arbitration through the labor inspectors was made worse by the uncompromising attitude of farmers toward labor. For decades, northwestern farmers had followed the lead of California in keeping workers powerless.[6] Like its counterpart in California, the Associated Farmers Incorporated of Washington was formed in 1938 in response to disturbances that had tended to prevent the harvesting of crops and their shipment to market. Member farmers believed strongly that a campaign of education could counter and obliterate "communists and other radical agitators" who were responsible for the disruptions. They were guided by the principle that those who wanted to work should be permitted and protected in their right to employment under terms suitable to them. As farmers, they also had a fundamental right to protection under the law in the growing of their crops and their movement along public highways to market.[7]

When the Associated Farmers spoke of creating and maintaining conditions under which men could work, they meant stamping out any attempt at organization by farm workers. To do so they used any means at their disposal without regard to civil rights. Even in the privacy of their own homes farm workers had to contend with private law enforcement officers deputized to maintain order. In the case of farm labor strikes, the full power of the farmers—assisted by the state highway patrol, National Guard, or other law enforcement officials—was often brought to bear on the unfortunate and defenseless workers.[8]

In essence, the federal government delivered the braceros to farmers who had long harbored strong antialien sentiments and opposed the right to collective bargaining in agriculture. In fact, concurrent with the arrival of the braceros, in 1943 Idaho approved a stringent antiunion law. The statute prohibited labor representatives from entering without the consent of the owner onto "any ranch, farm, feed and shearing plant or other agricultural premise" to solicit members, collect dues, or promote a strike. Under the terms of the law, picketing of such premises or boycotting agricultural products was also prohibited.[9] In the minds of the growers, many who were founding members of the Associated Farmers, these legal sanctions applied to the Mexican contracted labor force.[10]

However, wartime labor shortages meant that any strike was disruptive and had to be handled carefully; otherwise, production would be imperiled. When braceros refused to work, growers could do little except try to get the men to return to their jobs as soon as possible. In contrast, southwestern employers could make good on the threat of deportation because the proximity of the Mexican border guaranteed a constant resupply of legal or illegal workers. Northwestern growers had no such luxury. They understood too well that if they deported the strikers it would only exacerbate the already strained farm labor economy.

The Mexican consulate at Salt Lake City was well aware that farmers were hesitant to deport troublesome workers so it encouraged workers to protest living or working conditions. From the start of the bracero program, the consulate played a major role in trying to eliminate the worst features of the bracero program. In the Southwest, the role of the Mexican consulates was different. One study of the Mexican consular office at Los Angeles contends that officials ceased to work on behalf of the Mexican community after 1936. Thereafter, it argues, Mexico never sent "consuls who worry about Mexicans."[11] This is not altogether correct, because Consul General Miguel Calderón pushed for Texas' Good Neighbor Commission, which worked for better treatment of Mexican citizens and Mexican Americans as well.[12] According to Galarza, Mexican consuls pleaded the case of California's braceros before farmers and farm labor officials only in "exceptional cases."[13] In the Northwest, the Mexican consul was a significant advocate for braceros for several reasons. At the time, the braceros were the dominant group of Mexican nationals in Oregon, Idaho, and Washington. There were few established Chicano communities where the braceros could turn for help. Also, Carlos Grimm, consul at Salt Lake City between 1941 and 1947, and Ignacio Pesqueira, consul at Portland during 1947 and 1948, had previously served at various posts in California, including Los Angeles.[14] Both these men were quite familiar with and experienced in coping with the pernicious treatment of persons of Mexican descent. Their backgrounds, especially Pesqueira's, made them quick to act on behalf of their countrymen over matters of food services, discrimination, and employment. Perhaps this was the reason why Consul Pesqueira was reassigned to New Orleans after one year in the Pacific Northwest.[15]

Between 1943 and 1947, the most frequent root cause of strikes was wages, excepting those work stoppages related to food services. Farm labor wages were volatile and disruptive because of the arbitrary manner in which they were determined. In 1943, the passage of PL-45 required that county wage boards, under the direction of the state Extension Service and with WFA approval, determine prevailing wage rates in counties contracting for braceros. This was a tall order given the history of farm wages in the Northwest.

Prior to 1943, farm wages had been set by statewide boards under the direction of the Department of Agriculture. The purpose of the prevailing wage was to establish acceptable minimums that would aid in the recruitment of local as well as interstate labor. Wage boards, it was also felt, would prevent growers from depressing the wage economy unfairly. The wage boards, however, never functioned adequately and fell well short of their intent. The wage boards defined their function as supervisory and assumed that farmers and workers were equal and able to bargain to obtain a fair wage. This open and free competition between labor supply and demand would produce the actual prevailing wage.

In practice, the farm labor economy never operated under such near-perfect conditions. Growers were in such a dominant position, individually or through their associations, that they could literally establish any prevailing wage they saw fit. Moreover, their definition of the prevailing wage generally meant a minimum wage. By prior agreement farmers determined the prevailing wage and then took it before the state boards. On the other hand, the testimony of workers carried little weight and rarely altered the farmers' decision. Also, in the different sugar beet activities, the minimum or prevailing entrance rates were already established by the Sugar Act, rendering the workers' input to the board meaningless. Finally, an added problem resulted from the fact that prevailing wages in crops were rarely established for an entire state, and differential rates existed across county lines and in different crop activities.

Not only did the state boards fail to establish a true prevailing wage but farmers often applied it only to experienced workers. As long as this was so, new or inexperienced persons were paid less or were incapable of earning that wage. Weather and crop conditions were added variables that determined whether workers ever received the wage set by the board. In effect, by the time the braceros arrived, the substandard wages of the thirties had not been eliminated. This was the very reason that local workers could not be kept on the farms, and no sooner did out-of-area workers arrive than they gravitated toward industry.

Because the prevailing wages in each county had to be determined before any braceros could be contracted, local county wage boards also had to be established. To provide input to the county boards, the state Extension Service then organized county farm labor advisory committees. In contrast to the state wage boards, the county farm labor advisory committees and the wage boards at the county level were not strictly government bodies but consisted of local representatives and farmers. When organized, most county wage boards in the Pacific Northwest consisted entirely of farmers because the county representatives were also the farmers.

The prevailing wage for braceros was as meaningless as it had been for earlier workers because new county wage boards were controlled largely by farm labor associations or growers groups.[16] They fixed the labor rates beforehand and then received approval from the Extension Service. At times, the Extension Service agents did not even bother with the county wage boards. Instead, they circumvented them completely and held unofficial meetings with farmers to set the going rate.

Because of the collusion of the Extension Service and growers, the county wage boards had no significance as a vehicle for setting an equitable or fair wage. The Oregon State farm labor supervisor admitted as much when he said, "In general, the plan for holding hearings has been a failure."[17] Washington's farm labor supervisor placed "little value" on the farmers' testimony at the public wage hearings.[18] Idaho county wage boards were no different. Officials reported that "despite the best efforts of the county farm labor program personnel to secure broad representation at prevailing wage hearings, such hearings are attended largely by association members who, after all, are the employers primarily interested and affected by the determination of prevailing wages."[19]

An attempt by the Office of Economic Stabilization to allow pay scales to rise in order to stabilize the supply of workers and full farm production while simultaneously keeping labor costs from skyrocketing was yet another factor related to work stoppages by the braceros. Under this program, the WFA was given the authority to control farm wage rates by setting a minimum level below which wages and salaries of agricultural laborers could not be reduced. Agricultural wages and salaries at or above the level of $2,400 per annum would be maintained and specific maximum wage rates for particular crops and areas would also be set.[20]

As in the case of the prevailing wage boards, the state WFA wage stabilization boards were under the influence of growers. The federal stabilization board could only set specific wage ceilings and adjustments at the request of the local advisory committee and a petition of over 50 percent of all local growers representing specific crops and geographical areas. Still, many farmers disagreed that wage ceilings were necessary. The federal government, in their opinion, was interfering with their individual rights as farmers, and they opposed the idea as a matter of principle. In reality, these employers were needlessly concerned because they could still pay any rate below the ceiling as long as it was above the prevailing rate set by the Extension Service. Furthermore, a possible $1,000 fine or one-year imprisonment for farmers who offered wages above the ceiling guaranteed that wages would be kept low.[21]

Nonetheless, the wage controls did not meet unanimous approval, since not all farmers cooperated or followed the WFA wage board's determinations. The Washington State Peach Council rejected the program because it feared that wage ceilings would bring wages down and discourage much-needed labor away from Washington.[22] A defiant farmer told a wage stabilization officer that he "would not sign anything" or give any "information." As a matter of principle, "he would pay dollars per hour or any wage he saw fit and . . . there was not a thing the Wage Board could do about it."[23] An Oregon pear grower refused to go along because he did not feel that it was "necessary for the Government to come in and run his business for him."[24] The *Northwest Farms News* quoted the president of the American Farm Bureau: "Who in the hell makes $2,400 on a farm?" The Farm Bureau objected, particularly to mere mentioning of the ceiling, because it feared it would cause confusion and dangerous ideas to develop among workers that earned less than $2,400.[25] To a large degree, he was being prophetic and amazingly correct. Confusion did result, especially among the Mexican workers. It came in the form of numerous strikes between 1943 and 1947, the majority of which were due to questions surrounding the prevailing wage, county wage rates for specific crops, or wage ceilings.

Just months after the braceros arrived in the Northwest, they initiated the first strike and established a pattern that continued until PL-45 expired in 1947. At Burlington, Washington, a local Mexican American, with the help of a priest, convinced the braceros to halt work because farmers were paying higher wages to Anglos doing similar work. The growers ended the work stoppage by reminding the Mexicans that strikes were prohibited under the terms of the contract and by giving the Mexican American a "friendly warning against inciting a riot in a government camp."[26] The "instigator" at once left and the workers returned to their jobs.

During the first two years of the bracero program, the workers' protests over wages were so disruptive that at the close of 1943 the Idaho State Farm Labor Advisory Committee met to discuss ways of eliminating strikes during the upcoming 1944 season. It concluded that the use of different county wage rates for similar tasks was the "disturbing factor" among the Mexican workers.[27] For this reason, the committee urged wholehearted support for the wage stabilization program and recommended that employers house the braceros in private camps where they could cause less trouble.[28]

Even so, regionally the wage issue was not so easily resolved. Washington considered its wages high, so county wage boards were not even organized or prevailing wage rates established.[29] When the Idaho Agriculture Wage Board held hearings, it determined that the prevailing wages for thinning sugar beet fields planted with segmented seed that produced fewer plants was one dollar less per acre than for nonsegmented. According to the WFA, the lower rate averaged out to $.45 per hour, which was less than the prevailing hourly wages for less demanding general farm work.[30] Moreover, the Idaho State Farm Labor Advisory Committee recommended that experienced farm laborers be paid one wage and the inexperienced Mexican nationals another.[31]

Farmers learned little from their experiences with strikes and the wage issue in 1943. The next year they continued to violate their own prevailing rates, used a dual wage system, or set wages so low that braceros refused to work. By the middle of 1944, growers asked the Extension Service to help arbitrate a "serious wage dispute" at one bracero camp. The men walked off the job because one employer paid noncontract workers ten cents an hour more than the braceros were paid for identical work.[32] In this and similar situations, the Extension Service could do little more than try to persuade the farmers to follow the set wage scale. Without success, the investigating officials decided to let things go and the strikers eventually returned to work.[33]

Most bracero strikes were not so easy to put down. Idaho, which had the lowest wage scales and the most recalcitrant farmers, experienced many serious labor disturbances despite its strong state legislation to curb labor unrest. In May 1944, braceros at Preston, Idaho, went on strike over wages.[34] The growers refused to grant any increase but did offer to recheck each worker's pay for any miscalculations. "Those breaking their contracts," warned the growers, "would be taken out to the road where they would be out on their own, the proper immigration authorities would be notified, they would be picked up by these authorities, placed in jail to await court action: in the meantime while awaiting for court would have to work for 90 days without compensation, except board and room."[35] Under this threat, the men resumed work. Nevertheless, this was only the beginning of a long period of strikes throughout the summer. In July and September, the braceros struck again but did not win a wage increase.[36] In October, other workers at Sugar City and Lincoln, Idaho, refused to harvest beets after earning higher wages picking potatoes.[37]

The majority of the bracero strikes were easily broken by the patience of the growers. Even so, this does not mean that the work stoppages did not have an effect. In one instance, the braceros chose to strike in an attempt to break the prevailing wage at the same time that the sugar beet harvest was scheduled to begin. The strike was unsuccessful, but it did succeed in idling the sugar-processing facilities for three days.[38] The workers probably did not realize the full implication of their strike, but it was a clear demonstration to employers that the braceros could bring agricultural production to a standstill.

Anxiety over the threat of lost crops due to strikes and the constant disruption of work led growers to use intimidation and physical attacks against the braceros. Five months after the strike at Preston, the same braceros struck again over wages, and this time they sought the Mexican consul's assistance. The farmers responded with violence and ended the strike. "Last Friday," noted the camp manager, "one of the farmers in the area assaulted one of the Mexicans and gave him a right good mauling." The worker required medical attention after the physical attack, but, in this and similar cases, investigations followed but no one was charged. The camp manager also warned that the matter might have "repercussions and be far reaching in its effects if not properly dealt with."[39] Yet the lack of repercussions made growers aware that they would not be held accountable by the federal government or local authorities. They also understood that once the braceros were in the United States, the workers and the Mexican government officials had little to say about the conditions of employment or wages short of blacklisting an entire state.

The threat of violence or intimidation did not end the work stoppages, and labor unrest ran into 1945. That year, Klamath Falls, Oregon, potato growers faced a critical situation when braceros, together with transient workers from California, refused to pick potatoes at the established wage.[40] Knowing that potatoes could remain in the ground for some time, the potato growers stood fast against the workers and eventually succeeded in harvesting the crop at the low wage ceiling. At the end of 1945, the state supervisor of the Emergency Farm Labor Program wrote that the majority of Oregon's Mexican labor camps had been plagued with labor unrest and stoppages.[41]

Although affected by the strikes, Oregon farmers did not yield in their determination to maintain low wage levels. After the potato harvest, the growers encouraged the secretary of agriculture to continue to regulate wages and maintain ceilings because it was their only means of keeping costs down.[42] As the war shifted to the Pacific and labor became even more scarce along the West Coast, farm strikes and real labor shortages should have moved farmers to pay a bit extra. They did not, even after Governor Earl Snell described the lack of farm help as "desperate" in his state.[43] The *Northwest Farm News* tried to give Oregon a boost with the following editorial: "Contrary to the morbid story told by John Steinbeck in 'Grapes of Wrath,' harvesting the vegetables and fruits of Oregon is an aspiring industry. There's the job of being in the out-of-doors; working at top efficiency in the cool of the morning and slowing to a more languid pace as the noon sun warms the back and relaxes the spirit. There's joy in handling the ripe round fruit either picking or packing pears, apples and prunes."[44] The real issue behind the labor shortages was low wages, and clearly braceros and low wages went hand in hand. The Oregon State Wage Board plainly confessed "that the presence of Mexican Nationals in an area does help to stabilize wage rates."[45]

In Washington, agriculturalists also used the wage stabilization mandate as a guise to keep wages down. The State Farm Labor Committee went one step further and set a $.75-an-hour ceiling for all common farm labor and a higher rate for more skilled labor. The purpose of the dual wage system was to "avoid a scramble for help at ceiling wages with no differential left for skilled labor."[46] Growers quickly followed the committee's example and adopted the differential wage system to manipulate rates down. The Skagit County Pea Growers Association and Puget Sound Growers Association set the wage scale for field work at $.75 for men and women and $.60 for youths under sixteen. As members they pledged not to use "any other scale for the purpose of pirating labor from our neighbors."[47] At other times, arbitrary wage ceilings continued to be set in meaningless wage board hearings where no workers or representatives of labor were present.[48] As if by prior design, low wage ceilings and prevailing wage rates became one and the same. The Washington State Extension Service concluded that prevailing wage hearings were of "little value," and only one hearing was held during all of 1945.[49] The executive officer of the Idaho State Wage Board was certain that employers used the wage stabilization program in order to avoid "unrest among workers during harvest caused by trying to find higher wages in other areas."[50]

For these reasons, into 1945 the braceros struck throughout Idaho and Washington. Near the end of the spring harvest when yield was low, bracero asparagus cutters at Walla Walla went on strike because over a twelve-day period they had grossed between $4.16 and $8.33. The men worked ten-hours days, cutting asparagus on a piece-rate basis for three or four hours each morning and spending the rest of the day clearing ditches at $.75 an hour.[51] The braceros objected that they earned little if nothing cutting asparagus because six hours cleaning ditches yielded $4.50. The camp manager criticized the men because as far as he was concerned "there was really little reason for the boys to strike."[52] This strike, like the others, failed for lack of support outside the camp, leaving the workers little recourse but to desert or return to work.[53]

As in the previous years, the braceros' strikes in Idaho were more serious and prolonged. The first protest developed in June when Caldwell-Boise sugar beet farmers set hourly wages at twenty cents less than the rate established by the county Extension Service. This strike did win an increase in wages and a warning from the county agent that the first worker who violated the settlement would be returned to Mexico.[54] Three weeks later, braceros at Emmett also struck for higher wages. Their strike was quickly broken when farmers got federal officials to transfer the "agitators" out of the area.[55] Later in July, 170 Mexicans organized a week-long sit-down strike at the Idaho Falls camp. The strike started when fifty braceros who were new to the camp refused to pick cherries at the prevailing rate. When the strike started, it involved only the newly arrived workers. However, one day later farmers were surprised that no one was willing to work. Three days into the strike, the farmers responded by ordering the camp kitchen closed in an effort to end the strike. Several times some of the men attempted to leave the camp but they were turned back by the boss and harassment of the more militant men. This gave the Bonneville County sheriff and the Idaho State Highway Patrol the pretext to enter the camp in order to prevent a "riot." They offered to escort any bracero willing to cross the picket line. Still, no one left the camp for nine days until the lack of food ended the strike.[56]

As Idaho's critical fall harvest approached, the braceros' work stoppages became more grave in light of increasing cold weather and labor shortages.[57] In an effort to prepare for the harvest, Governor Charles C. Gossett tried unsuccessfully to obtain a seventy-five-day furlough for all Idaho men in uniform.[58] As freezing temperatures approached, anxious farmers panicked and began to violate the wage ceilings in order to secure workers. Once the growers broke the line on the wage ceilings, spot labor shortages worsened because workers sought out the higher-paying farms or areas.[59] The braceros would communicate between camps or learn by word of mouth about higher wage rates in other areas, then strike to demand the same.[60] By October, Idaho wage stabilization officials admitted "an extraordinary critical threat from Mexican Nationals in Idaho."[61] In order to bring the rash of strikes under control, state officials printed bilingual English and Spanish posters explaining the ceiling regulation and warning that violators would be prosecuted.[62]

Freezing temperatures in November delayed the harvest and brought more chaos to the farm labor economy of southern Idaho. The wage stabilization representative in the area braced for the worst to develop as the braceros asked to be returned to Mexico. "I am positive," he warned, "that the Mexicans and Jamaicans will attempt to jump the gun on beet topping and loading. . . . They don't [like] the weather, and they have earned a nice sum of money up to this time," he added.[63]

Aware that farmers were in a pinch for lack of labor and impending winter temperatures, the braceros pressed their demands for higher pay. Some camp managers emphasized with the workers and encouraged them to violate the stabilization program. One manager in particular advised the Mexican nationals to disregard the warnings about prosecution for violation of the stabilization program because the "law had no teeth in it."[64] The braceros themselves learned that although strikes during the rest of the year were not always successful, a combination of work stoppages, cold weather, and the critical harvest period was effective. A federal wage official declared that the situation in his area was out of control since the men were "demanding wages above ceiling and defying persons in control to do anything about it."[65] To try and end the chaos, area supervisors of the stabilization program asked for identification and names of all the Mexican violators for prosecution. Although the camp managers complied, there were so many violators that no arraignments followed.[66]

The experience of Idaho farmers during the winter of 1945 was a lesson to employers that although wage ceilings could serve to keep labor costs low, there was no effective way to make workers accept such wage scales. The wage stabilization program was impractical because no two fields or fruit orchards were the same. Some young orchards with small trees yielded only two or three boxes of fruit per tree, whereas more mature trees could produce as many as thirty boxes. At other times, orchards, because of improper pruning, had trees that were too bushy and tall, making picking light and slow.

Sometimes orchards were planted on steep hillsides that made the moving of ladders slow, extremely difficult, and dangerous.[67] When all or any one of these conditions were present, workers refused to work because they did not earn the same or enough under the wage ceiling. Row crops provide a graphic example. The Idaho Wage Stabilization Board set the ceiling for picking potatoes at $.10 per sack in fields yielding two hundred sacks per acre and $.22 per sack in fields with a sixty-nine-sack yield.[68] This piece rate was quite arbitrary, since neither the board nor the farmers had any accurate means of estimating crop yield until after the harvest was completed. This meant that workers expecting to earn $.22 per sack of potatoes would be upset to learn that they would be paid at the lower rate. For this reason, the Office of Wage Stabilization eventually acknowledged that some of the Mexicans' strikes during the potato harvest of 1945 were justified.[69] Stabilization program officials added that the use of uniform wage ceilings was questionable because some potato fields were much too weedy and cloddy or the potatoes were so small and low in yield that it took a considerable time and distance to fill one sack.[70]

Despite the problems associated with wage ceilings, farmers clamored that the wage stabilization program be continued into 1946. The Central Oregon Potato Growers Association termed the program "vital." Without it, they argued, farmers would return to the practice of raiding each other's labor with offers of higher wages.[71] The rationalization that ceilings meant a stable work force made little sense, because as long as growers kept wages at rock-bottom levels, disruptive strikes were bound to take place. Continued disputes over low wages eventually involved the Mexican consul.

In 1946, Mexican Consul Carlos Grimm in Salt Lake City began to share the responsibility over the Northwest with Ignacio Pesqueira, newly appointed to Portland, Oregon. Their experiences, especially in other consular posts in California, were touched by the pattern of strikes and discriminatory practices against the braceros in the Northwest. Hereafter, the Mexican consuls began to play a more central role in seeking redress for braceros.

The consuls' participation and the braceros' determination produced one of the longest and best-organized work stoppages, involving more than six hundred braceros from four camps near Nampa, Idaho, in June 1946.[72] The timing of the walkout was critical to the growers because their lettuce and pea crops were ready for harvest and because prisoners of war, who had earlier been used as agricultural workers, were no longer available.[73] In case they needed his help, the braceros notified Consul Carlos Grimm of the protest before it was announced to the growers.[74] The strike was in protest of a higher wage scale in the western part of Canyon County, where growers had to compete with Oregon farmers.[75] Government officials described the walkout as a "general strike" because it included the four camps and the men were demonstrating in the streets of Nampa in open defiance of the growers.[76] When the strike began, the farm labor associations met at Caldwell and voted to stand pat on the wage issue.[77] Later, in an attempt to control the strike and avoid crop losses, a Spanish-speaking farm labor supervisor tried to negotiate with the braceros, but each time the workers voted to stay out.[78] Nine days later, the workers called off the strike on the promise that the Mexican consul would represent them before the county wage stabilization board.[79] Twelve days later, the workers and growers got an opportunity to testify before the wage board. The braceros presented their case for a uniform wage of $.70 an hour.[80] The growers responded that some workers were paid as much as $.75 because they were skilled "American laborers" employed year-round, but as for the braceros, they were paid adequately at a $.60 rate.[81] In the end, the growers convinced the hearing examiners to rule "there was no evidence presented that warranted a change, either increase or decrease in the existing scale."[82]

The Mexican consul, in a move to force an increase in wages, threatened the growers: "Considering that ample opportunity has been given Farmers Associations [of the] Nampa District to revise discriminatory attitude toward contracted Mexican Nationals. Please proceed to remove workers at your earliest convenience unless seventy cents an hour prevailing wage in nearby areas is recognized before Monday July 22nd."[83] This threat was reinforced by Carl G. Izett of the Federal Production and Marketing Administration offices in Portland, who argued that a solution to the worker's protest was "critical to the continuation of the bracero program."[84] The labor dispute ended, however, without either an increase in wages or repatriation. Although made uneasy by the consul's threat and the braceros' "extremely rebellious attitude," the growers persuaded local law enforcement officials to break the strike by arresting the strikers ostensibly on spurious felony charges.[85]

The failure of the Nampa strike did not deter the braceros' determination. The following month, braceros at Caldwell struck to challenge a racially motivated dual wage scale. The braceros did not succeed, despite the support of the camp manager. He wrote, "There was no secret over the fact that Domestics [local workers] were receiving much higher rates of pay, sometimes in the same field." The strike, he noted, "served to bring out the fact . . . that the Nationals haven't been given a fair treatment in many cases."[86]

Like their counterparts in Idaho, braceros in Washington stopped work over the same wage issues. At Walla Walla, workers threatened pea growers with a strike unless the wage scale was increased. The growers issued their own warning: "If the Mexicans caused any trouble they would close the kitchen and let their peas dry rather than bargain with them."[87] Demoralized over the growers' response and the prospect of going without food, the strikers had little choice but to resume the harvest and make the best of their situation.

Unlike Idaho, Washington farmers, if faced with a strike, were more amicable and willing to negotiate over wages. When braceros in Whatcom County demanded a wage increase or a hearing to determine an adequate prevailing rate, farmers agreed to the increase in order to settle the dispute quickly.[88] In another case, employers also agreed that the braceros would receive the same rate as local workers.[89] These examples suggest that the braceros' demands were not always unreasonable or unwarranted and that conciliation was a far better assurance of labor stability than lengthy walkouts over low wages.

In general, braceros in Washington and Oregon were better paid, but it was no paradise for Mexican workers. Growers paid higher farm wages in these two states because they had to compete with industry for workers. Sometimes better wages simply meant that the men worked harder and longer hours. In 1946, for example, Washington pea farmers boasted that their workers averaged $90.00 a week.[90] This was true, but in order to do so, braceros had to work fifteen-hour days, seven days a week at $.85 an hour.[91]

In November 1946, President Harry S. Truman lifted all wage controls from agriculture. The return to a free wage economy had little effect on the farmers' ability to keep labor costs down. As the farm labor supervisor of the Washington State Extension Service noted, the prevailing wage structure had been meaningless, since "few farmers, and less workers attend the sessions and little satisfaction was obtained from them." Moreover, he continued, the testimony provided at the hearings had been "of little value" in determining actual pay rates.[92] Wage ceilings were likewise useless. Not only did farmers have a free hand (except in certain crops like sugar beets) to define the wage ceilings but, when necessary, they also violated their own edicts with little fear of prosecution. In the last year of wage controls, fifty-nine farmers were charged with wage infractions and two-thirds of them were dismissed without sanctions.[93]

Minus federal wage controls, farmers reverted to pre–World War II practices in order to establish 1947 farm wages for braceros. Nothing complicated, proposed a grower; "farmers of the area should agree on a uniform wage rate and then stick to it."[94] In fact, he continued, the wartime wage levels were adequate because braceros could not be expected to earn "more than the President of Mexico makes."[95] In accordance, the Walla Walla Pea Growers' Association set the contracted workers' wages at $.75 per hour, which was $.05 less than local farm hands received.[96] In Idaho, some sugar beet growers paid as much as $1.00 less per acre for thinning beets than was customary in other areas.[97]

As the braceros began to arrive in the spring, they faced a different set of circumstances surrounding wage issues. Henceforth, employers could determine farm wages. The federal government had no say in determining minimum or maximum wage levels and could not intervene in wage disputes. When this was explained to the Mexican workers and their representatives, it was obvious that they had no other recourse but to accept the wage offered to them as long as it was not below the thirty-cent minimum stipulated in their contracts.[98] The braceros' wages dropped to the point that local residents blatantly resented the Mexicans for accepting such low rates. Yet this was the first year since the start of the bracero program that Mexican nationals did not strike or demonstrate for higher pay.[99]

Looked at from any angle, the Mexican men's work contract was little more than a paper agreement that was not enforced. Several lessons emerge from an attempt to answer what went wrong with the program that was intended to protect against the abuse of the braceros.

Without question many farmers rationalized that agricultural production, by whatever means, was critical to the war and nothing less than the fulfillment of a patriotic responsibility. "Wars are largely won by farmers," wrote the *Northwest Farm News.*[100] But growers during World War II, although no less patriotic, were unlike their Revolutionary predecessors, who had left their farms and actually went to war at Lexington. Colonial farmers were yeomen; World War II farmers, both large and small, were commercial growers that stayed home. To the latter-day farm owner, the war's call for record-shattering production was a clear opportunity to escape the economic doldrums dating back to the 1920s.

As businessmen, farmers knew that labor, among agriculture's many variables, was one cost that could be controlled. Their ability to minimize labor expenses was critical because agriculture, unlike industry, did not receive cost-plus contracts from the federal government. In order to do so, farmers convinced the federal government that they required a near free gift of cheap labor in the form of the bracero program. Given the opportunity to keep labor costs down and increase net profits, farmers evaded the responsibility to the braceros and simply disregarded their contracts. All farmers were not necessarily racists or heartless monsters, although many were. They were operating on the basic principle of buying the cheapest labor on the market. Herein lies the reason for the poor record of bracero/grower relations.

The braceros, on the other hand, also saw the chance to contract their labor as a way of bettering their plight in Mexico. But once in the United States, they could not bid their labor at the highest price because of their contract and wage controls. It is likely that braceros would have labored as hard as they could or were expected to do provided that they had felt themselves to be receiving a fair wage. But in the Northwest, the men exercised their right to organize and struck in protest of low and discriminatory wages, often with the support of Mexican government officials. Judging from the strikes alone, the braceros were conscious of their predicament and for that reason violated their contracts and disrupted the farmers' production. When braceros did this, employers reasoned that the workers were impervious to any monetary incentive, and more strikes followed. The pattern of labor unrest among braceros in the Pacific Northwest must be seen in light of these circumstances, some of which were peculiar to the region.

It is clear that neither the federal government nor farmers were too intelligent with regard to labor. The government assumed that farmers would honor the workers' rights as spelled out in their contracts, although the past history of grower/employee relations indicated otherwise. Work stoppages had a multiplying effect that, without question, slowed national production. By extension, if growers had treated the braceros better, larger per capita output would have increased their profits. With rare exception, farmers could not see this. To them it was their right to keep their workers materially deprived and socially alienated.

In many ways, farmers and braceros played out Armageddon in the Northwest from 1943 until 1947. Farmers dehumanized the Mexican men and reduced them to a semicaptive labor force that resembled Latin American peonage. They did so with impunity, all the time hiding their transgressions behind the shield of patriotism and commitment to the war effort. Apparently, the pursuit of human rights, to which they were committed as American citizens, was an ideal not applicable on their farms.

5. Bracero Social Life

PERHAPS WORSE than being held under the thumb of their employers, the braceros were victims of terrible injustices stemming from inadequate camp facilities, inept officials, and racism. Their contracts prohibited racial discrimination, but it occurred because the employers disavowed the entire agreement as meaningless.

In the early years of the bracero program, the laborers lived in the FSA camp facilities since most farmers did not have private housing for their workers. Growers did not construct living quarters on their property, because during the 1930s, housing had not been necessary in order to secure labor. The construction of private labor camps to house the braceros was costly because the camps had to meet the standards of the WFA and pass inspection before anyone was allowed to stay in them. Finally, the federal government, not the employers, had undertaken the primary responsibility of providing shelter for farm workers through the FSA.

By the time the Mexican workers arrived the network of FSA camps had been placed under the WFA, where the philosophy and purpose of federal housing were altered dramatically. Camps were no longer seen as agencies of social rehabilitation and instead served as labor storehouses to meet the war shortage and nothing more. Accordingly, the WFA changed the designation from "farm family camps" to "farm labor supply centers." Along with the change in purpose, the spirit of democratic resident camp communities was replaced by a more centralized system of management.

Oddly, even after these changes the growers remained critical of the camps, which served as essential pools of farm labor. This stern opposition by farmers toward the camp system did not cease when the FSA relinquished the facilities to the WFA. Now growers perceived that the housing complexes existed solely to serve the farmer in providing much-needed labor for food production. Criticism went on because the WFA, like th FSA, exercised responsibility for maintaining standards of employment, wages, and housing for the foreign workers and the agency stood in the way of farmers having their way.

Physically, the permanent housing complexes had started to suffer from a shortage of upkeep, but otherwise they were ready for the Mexican men. When the temporary camps were used to house braceros some minor modifications to the initial design were necessary. The community tent was converted into a single mess hall to feed the single men. Also, as the wartime labor program took on an air of permanency concrete slab foundations replaced the wooden tent platforms. Much of the equipment, however, had deteriorated badly from repeated use and was in a very sorry state of disrepair when the Mexican workers moved in.[1]

As the use of braceros increased, the Office of Labor found that its permanent and temporary camp facilities were stretched to their maximum capacity with out-of-state and imported labor. Hence, the Extension Service, which was supposed to provide housing for interstate labor only, began to permit braceros in its camps when other housing could not be found. More often, however, the county extension agent assisted the farm labor associations in securing the necessary equipment, such as tents, bunks, and other items from the military, to set up private, makeshift camps. When the housing provided by the Extension Service, private facilities, and the Office of Labor are considered together, the volume of quarters available for the bracero program was impressive.[2]

As a rule, the braceros lived in camps set aside exclusively for them. At other times they were placed in the same facility with out-of-state workers but segregated in one section of the complex. In actuality few guidelines governed the conditions in the camps beyond the stipulation that housing should be "adequate." Other regulations specified that campsites could not be within twenty-five miles of each other, operate for a minimum of seventy-five days, and have fewer than one hundred residents.[3] Since the camps were only a precondition for obtaining the workers, the guidelines were seldom followed to the letter. For instance, corners were cut in the construction of the camp facilities and these actions were then easily justified as expedient since the housing was only temporary. In some instances, minicamps were established with as few as forty men despite the government mandate.[4]

Overall, the braceros' quarters provided little more than a rudimentary place to sleep. At first appearance these facilities looked to be no more spartan than the camps used to house interstate workers or even the military, but they were worse. Not only did growers retain a sour attitude toward the camp system but some insisted that, as Mexicans, braceros deserved nothing better than their own homes in Mexico. A letter to the *Northwest Farm News* asked, Why "send to Mexico for more men to partake—from a Mexican viewpoint—in the almost Heavenly standard of living of the American worker?"[5]

Between 1943 and 1947, most braceros were quartered in the mobile camps. One striking aspect of these camps was the poor appearance of the site. Some camps were erected on land that had only recently been plowed over from sage brush or otherwise idle acreage. Within a few days after the workers moved in, the foot and vehicle traffic created an intolerable dust problem that was harmful to the men and damaged the camp equipment as well.[6] It was worse when the wind blew, and when loose dirt was not a problem weeds and grass quickly reclaimed the open ground until narrow footpaths mapped out the activities of the men. Often deep ruts developed, and if an attempt was made to level the ground, the situation was only made worse because more dust was created and a ready supply of irrigation water was not available to improve the appearance. The most practical solution was to plant trees, lay gravel, or establish a grounds maintenance program. However, the transient nature of the mobile camp and the fact that looks were not important overrode these considerations.

In some instances, the braceros arrived and found that the camp was not ready for occupation. On one occasion, the men arrived as construction workers were pouring the concrete bases for the tents.[7] In another instance, a camp manager came to the camp ahead of the braceros and discovered that the tents were not ready and kitchen mess facilities and telephone service were not available.[8] Under these circumstances, the workers were returned to the nearest town for food and necessary lodging.

Even after the camp was in place there was no guarantee that the tents, flimsy and fragile against strong gusts of wind, would remain up. Long and sustained use weakened the tents further and made them susceptible to collapse. At one Oregon camp, a wind storm arrived and within minutes it was impossible to see more than a few feet due to the thick dust. Before the strong windstorm had passed, twenty-one tents had been leveled and their contents scattered about the countryside.[9]

When the Mexican workers were not quartered in the tent camps, they were placed in makeshift shelters where conditions were as bad if not worse. In Idaho, an abandoned Civilian Conservation Corps camp was used to accommodate the Mexican men.[10] The Oregon State Extension Service had the choice of placing the braceros at either the Hillsboro High School or the fairgrounds and opted for the latter.[11] In Washington, farmers placed army cots against the walls of main grandstand at the Whatcom County fairgrounds; this the braceros had to call home.[12] In some communities, farmers obtained permission to erect tents at the city ball park. In another instance some old aircraft hangers served as housing for the contracted workers.[13] Elsewhere, the braceros' kitchen facilities were an unused packing shed, and they dined on an adjacent loading platform.[14] Other farmers solved their housing needs by leasing a campsite from the Milwaukee Railroad, then obtaining the necessary portable equipment from the nearby Ephrata Military Air Base.[15] The list of improvisations were long and does not end here. As the war came to an end, former prisoner of war camps were appropriated from the military as quarters for braceros. These examples suggest that almost any type of facility and condition could qualify as a bracero camp.

As the first groups of braceros arrived in 1943, farmers were as unprepared to relate with them on a personal level as they were to house the men adequately. Very few farmers understood Spanish or were acquainted with Mexican culture and probably fewer even cared. Braceros were like-minded in that they brought with them a limited understanding as well as unreliable images of life in the United States. The evidence is clear, however, that they differed in their outlook. After they arrived braceros enrolled in evening English classes sponsored at local schools, when available, demonstrating an interest in the host culture. Beyond the obvious cultural differences, the expectations of the profit-conscious farmers and improverished Mexican men were also at odds, causing a wider chasm to develop between them.

In essence, the braceros lived in much physical discomfort and psychological distress while they were in the Northwest. This stemmed from the emergency nature of the braceros program and facility with which the farm labor associations could sidestep the workers' contracts. The absence of a friend and protector in the communities where they were assigned also made life difficult. In the following pages a detailed examination of the work experiences, camp life, and social activities of braceros is developed. Although some of the individual cases may appear overdrawn and inflammatory, they are nevertheless accurate.

Technically, the braceros were under the guardianship of the federal government, so camp managers were required to make monthly reports on daily feeding, sanitation, the camp governing council, maintenance, occupancy, and other activities to the WFA headquarters in Portland. The official record of the braceros' daily activities provides a close look, over several years, at a complex and unpleasant social experience filled with hard truths and clear meaning. However, much can never be known because the political sensitivity between Mexico and the United States over the MFLP compelled the Office of Labor to control the release of information to the public as well as what was placed in its own files.[16] The Mexican side, as told by the workers, is less frequently available in State Department and USDA records, because they were purged of the more embarrassing documents.[17] Much less is known from the federal records or other sources about the men in private camps, because the WFA had little jurisdiction unless some complaint was filed. Even than, most farmers considered their property as their own castle and closed it to all trespassers.

Life was difficult for the braceros because they were young men from the rural areas steeped in traditional Mexican culture. Typical were the eighty men housed at the Lyndon, Washington, camp, where the majority were between twenty and thirty years of age and only two were over forty.[18] For most, their sojourn to the United States marked the first separation from their immediate and extended families, which were (and are) important in Mexican culture. Thus they arrived ill-prepared to cope with the unfriendly and unfamiliar circumstances and tensions surrounding the war. Not surprisingly, many men became distraught and feigned illness or wrote to their families asking that they be recalled for reasons of supposed illness or death before the end of the contractual obligation. In one week alone at the Preston, Idaho, camp, twelve men went home before their contracts had expired.[19] Federal officials from Portland expressed concern that braceros in the Northwest would use any means to return early. They "definitely want to be sent home now," observed one official. "If there is a way to hasten their departure, they will find it . . . either by refusing to work or violation of the ceiling."[20] In 1945, the chief of operations at Portland reported that one in ten braceros contracted to the Pacific Northwest was either missing or had been granted an early repatriation.[21]

Some men did have genuine reasons for requesting an early return. A month after his wife died in Mexico, a bracero learned the tragic news and became so overcome with grief that he could not work and was repatriated.[22] Psychosomatic disorders among the men, stemming from despondency over camp life and absence of home and family, constituted legitimate reasons for wishing to return to Mexico. A writer with the *Northwest Farm News* empathized with the men living beneath the grandstands at the Lyndon, Washington, fairgrounds. He reported that they had little to do at night except huddle in their blankets and listen to the radio with little if any comprehension. "They sing a lot and whistle too," he wrote, "as they work in the fields or lounge about in the evenings. It helps dispel the homesickness which sometimes bothers them, even as it would afflict anyone so far from his native land."[23] One former bracero recalled that eight to ten days after they arrived from Mexico, nostalgia and hard work were "enough to make anybody cry."[24]

Upon arriving, the workers' first order of business was to check in with the manager. More than any other person, he was central to the bracero program and the difference between "good" and "bad" camps. Camp managers in the Northwest rarely received any special administrative training or classes in the Spanish language. One camp manager pointed out to the Portland office that he had requested and been promised an interpreter but never received one.[25] On occasion and in pressing situations, camp officials would enlist local residents into translation duty.

Compounding the language problem, the attitude, conscience, and resourcefulness of the camp director also shaped the braceros' camp life. Some managers honestly tried to improve the comfort and safety of the camp, but many others were indifferent to their charges. One manager so feared reprisals from alienated men that he had the local sheriff present at the camp as the men prepared to depart at the close of the work season.[26]

In the Northwest, the braceros lived in mobile tent camps designed to be erected where needed among the widely dispersed agricultural areas. As a rule, six workers lived together in a sixteen-by-sixteen-foot tent furnished with folding cots, one blanket per person, and stove heaters when available.[27] Although each worker was entitled to bring seventy-seven pounds of personal effects from Mexico, in reality most arrived with little more than a change of clothes. Within time, the workers scavenged for discarded crates or boxes and placed them inside the tents for storage and seating. These makeshift creations, along with personal pictures of loved ones, tokens of remembrance, or knickknacks purchased locally, completed the interior.

Under the terms of the work agreement, braceros were entitled to but rarely received adequate and equal housing to that offered the domestic workers. During the summer, the men were often driven from the tents by 100 degree temperatures, and in the fall and winter the fabric structures offered little protection from the inclement northwestern weather. Stoves, if provided, were virtually ineffective because the loose sides of the tent allowed heat to escape quite easily. Moreover, the frequent lack of adequate supplies of kerosene, coal, or dry wood meant that the stove heaters were often useless.[28] As early as October, the camp manager at Hazelton, Idaho, found it nearly impossible to keep the braceros inside their assigned quarters because insufficient fuel and the lack of stoves in some tents resulted in "unusually cold" lodgings.[29] Cement floors, frozen water pipes, absence of heat, and badly worn tents at the Caldwell, Idaho, camp exacerbated the already intolerable temperatures.[30]

The struggle to heat the tents was complicated by the federal bureaucracy. The camp manager at St. Anthony, Idaho, suggested that the tent walls should be insulated by three-foot-high wooden walls in order to lessen the loss of heat.[31] This and other recommendations went nowhere due to long bureaucratic delays. All decisions or modifications concerning the use of almost any critical material in the camps had to clear the Office of Labor and the War Production Board. Sometimes requests for changes were answered with rebukes, as in the following response to an Oregon camp manager: "It is up to the War Production Board and not the District Engineer to determine whether the savings of critical materials of one kind warrants the use of critical materials of another."[32]

Since the camp managers were restricted in what they could do to cope with the cold, ingenuity on the part of all concerned was an invaluable resource. Sometimes the men would pile their blankets together and sleep underneath them, often wearing every piece of clothing at their disposal. Workers commonly used cardboard to insulate their flimsy structures.

Although the specter of hypothermia was ever present, the braceros faced a more serious threat from fire as they struggled to keep warm with a combination of kerosene, old stoves, and highly flammable tents.[33] Besides frequent tent fires, there were also destructive explosions. In one instance in October 1944, some braceros living at Marsing, Idaho, barely escaped injury when an oil-burning water heater exploded and destroyed everything around it.[34] Careless use of cigarettes and matches, cooking facilities, or faulty electrical connections could just as easily ignite a fire that would engulf the entire camp.[35] Fire at one camp leveled the kitchen and dining area used to serve the braceros.[36] The following year the same camp suffered a worse blaze that destroyed the men's quarters and personal possessions.[37] The risk of fire and the danger it posed to the entire camp were very real. As was the case with other signs around the facilities, the fire notices, although printed in Spanish, were unreasonably complicated. At one camp a long horn signaled attention. A long horn followed by a short blast meant that the recreation area, the camp manager's house, and the health clinic were on fire. A long horn and two short ones indicated the braceros' quarters, kitchen, and restrooms. Two long horns meant the first twenty-five homes were on fire. Three long horns involved the last twenty-five homes and large storage buildings.[38]

When fires occurred in the mobile camps, the fire alerts served to do little more than to empty the tent camps because the entire water system was above ground and often frozen. Water barrels with hand-pumped fire extinguishers were also useless during freezing temperatures. "We have these 2-1/2 gallon water extinguishers which are no good in cold weather and our fire hydrants freeze up at night," complained a worried camp manager. "We try to keep the water faucets dripping at night but the Mexicans are taught to conserve water in Mexico and turn them off at night."[39] Worse yet, some towns had a limited water supply and would cut it off to the labor camps when it was needed by food-processing plants.[40]

The camp grounds, particularly at the temporary sites, were often covered with dry weeds and grass, making them potential tinderboxes. This was certainly the case in northeastern Oregon, where the natural vegetation consisted of waves of bush grass. When the braceros arrived in this area their camp was covered with dry and very combustible ankle-high grass. Faced with an obvious fire hazard, the camp manager approached the Blue Mountain Corporation as owners of the property and employers of the men and requested them to improve the grounds. The corporation promised to do some controlled burning and to bulldoze firebreaks around each tent, but months later nothing had been done to lessen the potential of a disastrous fire.[41]

Although the braceros complained strongly about their living accommodations, they grumbled most about the poor quality of food served in the camps. Under the terms of the worker agreement, each bracero was entitled to receive adequate food at cost in camp facilities. This not always possible, however, due to food shortages, administative loopholes, or indifference. The cost of meals in the camps varied—Washington braceros paid $1.30 per day in 1943.[42] By 1946, the braceros were charged $1.41 in Idaho and Washington and $1.45 in Oregon.[43] The sanitation and nutritional value of the food rested with the WFA regardless of whether the Office of Labor, Extension Service, growers associations, or private catering companies operated the food service. Food, a prerequisite to good morale and worker production, was costly, yet it is difficult to understand how the federal government and growers could allow it to become such a problem.

When the camps had been under the jurisdiction of the FSA, most of the residents were families who prepared food in their own homes. As the single Mexican workers were moved in, the Office of Labor, as well as the Extension Service and growers, had to scramble about for central kitchen equipment. Another problem was the procurement and preparation of food that would fit the taste and diet of the foreign workers. In light of wartime rationing, food of all types was hard to obtain, but it was particularly difficult to find Mexican specialty items. When this was not a problem, experienced Mexican cooks capable of preparing traditional dishes were hard to find in the Northwest. Finally, kitchen facilities were inadequate to prepare some types of Mexican food on a large scale. In 1944, federal officials ordered the camp manager at Wendell, Idaho, to suspend all food services because of a lack of refrigeration and a single vehicle to bring fresh provisions from town.[44] Some kitchens required the men to furnish their own makeshift containers for coffee or milk.[45] The kitchens themselves posed particular problems because they were usually housed in large tents. The mess tent at Wilder, Idaho, for example, measured 150 feet long.[46] Not only was such a large tent unstable in strong winds but dust entered easily and quickly blanketed the food. At other locations, the kitchen's capacity was simply inadequate to feed the number of workers living in the camp.[47] The two basic problems, food preparation and facilities, were never completely resolved in the Northwest during the entire period of PL-45. Office of Labor officials conceded, "It was difficult to prepare many of the Mexican type dishes on a mass production basis, even when the 'know how' existed and the ingredients were available."[48]

In the Northwest, as in California, meals were the source of more discontent and work stoppages than any other single aspect of camp life. In July 1943, Mexican workers at the Skagit County camp north of Seattle went on strike in order to call attention to the terrible kitchen services. Workers there started their daily routine with breakfast at 4:30 A.M. Seven and a half hours later, they stopped work to eat a noon lunch consisting of meat, egg salad, or jelly sandwiches. A sweet roll and one half a pint of milk were also provided. The camp, improvised at the county fairgrounds, had no refrigeration; therefore, by lunch time the sandwiches, prepared the day before, were unappetizing and the milk was "sour or blinky."[49] The type of sack lunches served in the Northwest were found in most bracero camps throughout the country. Three years after the start of the bracero program in the Northwest, the standard fare served to the men in the fields consisted of one meat sandwich, one jelly sandwich, one sweet roll, an orange, and half a pint of milk (in the workers' own containers).[50] Although the men had a strong dislike for white bread and lunch meats, cooks served such sandwiches because they were easy to prepare. In California, camp kitchens continued to serve sack lunches for many years after the war.[51]

The braceros' pattern of strikes related to food service is telling testimony that this aspect of the bracero program was poorly developed. Three months after they arrived in 1943, workers stopped work over the quality of meals.[52] Three years later, braceros at the Athena, Oregon, camp went on strike to demand better food.[53]

The braceros expressed their displeasure with the food in other ways. In one camp, the local sheriff was called to quell a "near riot" when the men dumped their evening meal on the floor in protest. After investigating the incident, the sheriff and other city officials concluded that there was little reason for the disturbance other than that the food "did not rate 100 per cent" with the Mexicans. Infuriated by the braceros' behavior, the sheriff issued an ultimatum to the workers—either clean up the mess, which they begrudgingly did, or go to jail.[54]

Contributing to the discontent over meals was wartime rationing, which meant that desirable quantities and varieties of food were not always available. The Agricultural Workers Health Association (AWHA), a government-sponsored cooperative which provided health care to farm workers in the Northwest, supported the complaints of the braceros. In 1945, it reported that the poor-quality, iron-deficient food was the main cause of nutritional anemia among the workers.[55] This disclosure prompted the Mexican embassy to take action that led to improvement in the quality of food served to northwestern braceros.[56] The Office of Labor in its own investigation failed to find a problem with the preparation of food, nutritional content of the diet, or the camp kitchens. Instead, the report concluded that the scarcity of commodities due to rationing was the root cause of the problem.[57]

Despite wartime shortages and other problems, sometimes the federal government adopted measures to try and provide more nutritious and appetizing food. Six months after the bracero program started, the State Department obtained permission from the Mexican government to allow braceros to volunteer as cooks.[58] As soon as the authorization was announced, Gregorio Rodríguez took over as head cook at the Burlington, Washington, camp—the scene of the first food strikes. In his first lunch menu, he replaced the jelly sandwiches with fried eggs, meatloaf, cold canned salmon, onion slices, lettuce salad, tortillas, milk, and chile salsa. To the workers' delight, this meal was followed by an overall marked improvement in the food services in the camp.[59] At Gooding, Idaho, the camp manager reported that "meals turned out with better success by the day" after bracero cooks were placed in the kitchen.[60]

Although Mexican cooks could prepare a variety of traditional food items, the problems of limited facilities and availability of supplies remained. These limitations made satisfying the workers well-nigh impossible, and the Mexican cooks soon learned this. In a turnabout of events, an obviously frustrated Mexican cook, instead of the workers, walked off his job during breakfast at one Oregon camp.[61]

At times, the federal government was compelled to take action and open the bottlenecks in procurement. When Idaho's congressman warned the USDA that braceros were "threatening to quit work because they could not get bread for sandwiches," the government quickly released two tons of flour a day.[62] Such quick results were unusual, since most recommendations to make more food available to the braceros were not acted upon by the federal government.[63]

The poor kitchen services were exacerbated by the camp managers, who were often inept and inexperienced supervisors. At Weiser, Idaho, a hopeless but outspoken manager described the workers' food as a "lamentable situation" because "any jam or jelly has soaked through the bread; cheese had begun to harden, and prepared meats run the chance of becoming spoiled before the sandwich is eaten."[64] On the other hand, a more resourceful manager at Milton-Freewater, Oregon, instructed the growers to return to the camp to pick up the sack lunches between 10:00 and 11:00 A.M so that the meals would be fresher and more appetizing.[65] The attitude of the camp official at Payette, Idaho, illustrates how managers could also worsen food-related problems. At the beginning of the work season, the camp kitchen had three hundred spoons. By the middle of the year, there were seven spoons left and in November a single spoon remained for 110 men. Though more were available, the camp manager refused to request them because he believed the workers were stealing or losing the spoons.[66]

Other camp supervisors did everything possible to improve the food services, including simple but important considerations designed to prevent health risks. The camp manager at Stanwood, Washington, translated signs reading "Wash Your Hands" into Spanish and recommended that similar safety regulations in other camps be translated. Otherwise, he stated, the signs amounted to little more than "wasted effort."[67] In 1944, workers staged a one-day strike in order to convince the manager to modify the time when the evening meal was served. At this particular camp, the braceros returned from the fields at 9:00 P.M.—two hours after the kitchen closed. Although the cook eventually extended the serving hours, it was done after the men resumed work because the growers refused to negotiate "as long as they [the braceros] were idle."[68] Many other problems nagged the food services program. Most braceros, even after spending some time in the United States, could not acquire a taste for non-Mexican dishes such as roast beef.[69] At other times, the braceros left corned beef untouched because they thought it was uncooked horsemeat.[70] At this same camp in Oregon, the camp manager was "flabbergasted" that the men preferred sack lunches over hot lunches during the noon meal.[71] Given the inadequacy of the food services, some workers exercised their right not to join the camp mess and ate elsewhere. Within time, however, they returned to the camp kitchens, given the high cost and unchanging menu at restaurants.

Kitchen services were lacking in other ways. At Preston, Idaho, a cook was dismissed because she tested positive for syphilis. Several days later, the camp manager was shocked to find the same woman back in the kitchen.[72] Although the cook was fired again, this incident illustrates the laxity in supervision of food preparation. Workers were not provided containers to carry coffee or milk, so they used anything that they could find without much thought to sanitation. This doubtlessly contributed to bracero camps in the Northwest having an unusually high incidence of food poisoning. The most serious outbreak of food poisoning occurred in 1943 on a hop ranch near Grants Pass, Oregon, where 500 of 511 fell sick and 300 required hospitalization.[73] The next year, five of eight men were hospitalized after eating sandwiches containing spoiled meat.[74] In 1946 in an eight-month period, there were five outbreaks of food poisoning.[75] The Pacific Northwest was not unusual in this respect, for elsewhere gastrointestinal disorders also developed as the most common health problem among Mexican workers.[76]

Growers tried various angles to reduce kitchen costs in their own camps. Food expenses in the grower-operated camps were a major concern to the growers because the braceros were entitled to free subsistence during the time that work was not possible or available. The Oregon Seed Growers League, the Washington State Peach Council, and other growers' groups complained that they had to assume the responsibility of providing free food during conditions that were beyond their control.[77] They pointed out to Congress:

> Our sponsoring committee must pay board on all Mexican nationals for everyday they do not work. Our committee just does not have the funds to pay this board for the hundreds of Mexicans we know will be idle for parts of that period. The situation

> is more or less the same throughout the state so they cannot be very well loaned. If we let them go we will not have them back for the fall's work of harvesting beets, hops, potatoes, apples, peaches, pears, hay, etc. If your committee could persuade some [branch] of the government to help us with the payment of this board during this slack period it would help to avoid food losses.[78]

The WFA responded that the farmers were ultimately responsible since they had accepted the workers' contracts. In 1946, farmers did achieve a small but significant victory when the WFA agreed to assume part of the expense for board during periods of inclement weather.[79] This was an important concession to northwestern sugar beet growers because harvest operations often ran well into the month of October when freezing temperatures kept the men from working.

From 1945 on, the Northwest division of the Office of Labor began to encourage the local sponsoring farmers' labor associations to assume the responsibility of feeding the men by contracting with private catering services. This move, not followed at the time in other parts of the country, had the advantage of relieving the division of the task of securing ample supplies of scarce foods and kitchen help and tedious paperwork. It did little, however, to improve the food services and in some instances the quality and amount of food served per worker generally lessened. "One complaint from the Mexican Nationals with regard to the food is that there is not enough of it," wrote a camp manager where the kitchen was operated privately. "It seems as though the workers are not given a second helping. As I recall when the Labor Branch operated kitchens we always permitted second helpings."[80]

The food program deteriorated further under the private companies because the federal government placed a limit on the amount that could be charged for food per worker. When the cost of providing the food to the workers exceeded that amount, the profit-motivated catering companies used ways of making up the difference. Cooks frequently prepared large quantities of one particular food and served it meal after meal until the workers tired of it. The favorite dish of the cooks but least appreciated by the workers was beef stew, because lesser-quality meats and an abundance of rice, beans, and potatoes could be used as ingredients. There were other problems with the catering companies that were contracted to feed the Mexican workers. Most of them were home based in California and their experience in providing food services to bracero camps in that state was not entirely applicable in the Northwest. In one instance, the Immigration and Naturalization Service workers reported that "in place of having a meat sandwich, a jelly sandwich, and a peanut butter sandwich for lunch" the workers "preferred to have a bean sandwich, and instead of having beef stew and other American foods, they wanted tortillas." The company made an effort to meet the workers' request, but tortillas made of flour were not satisfactory, and an effort to import corn or *masa* (corn dough) from Mexico was considered impractical.[81] At times, the out-of-state companies turned their individual operations over to local representatives that used every form of chiseling to lower costs in the mess halls. All things considered, the move to allow private commissary companies to contract for food services in the bracero camps turned out badly.

The end of the war and of food rationing, as well as greater availability of equipment, meant improved food services and fewer food-related complaints. In fact, by 1947 some of the Mexican-run kitchens at the camps were rated as "excellent."[82] Yet, until the end of the bracero program in the Northwest or elsewhere, the feeding services remained one of the most glaring weak spots of the bracero program.

Food services were a serious problem, but more critical was the braceros' exposure to toxic fumigants in the camps. During the summer, the tents provided little protection from insects, rodents, and snakes which infested the camps. The outdoor privies and open garbage pits and the common practice of disposing of waste water above ground served to attract these pests even more. To combat the nuisance and disease carried by these unwanted intruders, the camps had to be flooded with highly poisonous hydrocyanic acid. The fumigant was effective but not without posing a risk to the workers when they re-entered the camp.[83] Less toxic DDT mixed with kerosene was also sprayed at two-week intervals in the camps to combat fly infestations.[84] Judging from the ineptness of some camp managers, workers were doubtless exposed to these noxious fumigants.

Leisure time activities, a key to the physical and social well-being of most persons, was just as precious to the braceros, yet the men had little to do during their off hours. Sporting equipment was not provided to the bracero camps, although it was available to non-Mexican camps under the Lanham Act (1940). Left to their own resources, the men found ways to pass the time by fashioning rings out of scrap pieces of pipe or putting together suitcases and simple furniture out of crates and plywood ends.[85] In some camps, the workers pooled their resources and purchased radios out of curiosity and to break the monotony. Since there was no Spanish-language broadcasting, the braceros understood few words other than "hello" and "thank you." In the mobile camps, the braceros operated their radios as long as the motor-driven generator was in operation. At night, the heavy drain of power caused by lights and other equipment interfered with the radio's reception.

Since Mexican contracted workers were to be kept busy at work in order to maximize their potential, the WFA was not terribly concerned with the absence of leisure time activities in the camps. In 1945, the federal government recognized the detrimental effects on the workers and published the first issue of *El Mexicano,* a Spanish-language newsletter for braceros. *El Mexicano* carried general news from Mexico and about braceros in the different regions of the United States, but its main purpose was to exhort the men to work. The first issue described how five thousand nationals had harvested the largest crop of apples in the last twelve years in the Yakima and Wenatchee valleys, Washington, and in the Hood River Valley, Oregon. It went on to say that saving the pea crop in the Milton-Freewater area between Washington and Oregon was "owed to them."[86] The issue concluded with the "Corrido de los Trenes Especiales" (Ballad of the Special Trains), written by Enrique García. The following verses pinpoint the message and purpose of *El Mexicano:*

Well, what do you say, men?
Sir, we have nothing to say.
We are going to the United States
To help with the war.

Everybody at the border
Is very sad
Because they don't have permission
To enter the United States.

Friend, don't worry.
Answer [your critics] with pride.
It is a sacred responsibility
To defend democracy.

Don't fail at work,
Friends, please,
Because you cast a bad hue
On our tricolor banner.[87]

Notwithstanding the fact that *El Mexicano* was little more than a clever way of urging the braceros to press on by instilling in them a sense of purpose and pride in their work, the newsletter was well received by workers eager for news from home. With the exception of a *Guía de Inglés* (Guide to English) which was also distributed free by the WFA, *El Mexicano* was the federal government's only effort to provide news and information to the braceros across the nation. As far as can be determined, no other similar publication or piece of recreational equipment became standard government issue at the bracero labor camps.

The publication of *El Mexicano* so late in the bracero program illustrates the WFA's lack of attention to the overall needs of the Mexican men. Also, the concept of *El Mexicano* was not original since plans had been developed earlier in Washington State for a statewide bracero newspaper.[88] The *Guía de Inglés* was not new either; some camps developed a basic ten-page dictionary of Mexican-English vocabulary for the benefit of the men.[89]

The WFA did play a leading role in organizing camp celebrations to commemorate Mexican Independence Day, September 16, 1810. The Office of Labor sanctioned the festival because officials recognized it as an excellent way to sustain morale and a dedication to work among the imported work force. State farm labor officials also encouraged local communities to cooperate with the celebrations at the labor camps. In California, where Mexico's national holidays were also observed, Mexican government officials frequently delivered patriotic speeches, a practice described by Ernesto Galarza as "worn thin" and ineffective by 1944.[90] In California, Mexican American communities had traditionally celebrated the day in a festive manner that was more attractive and familiar to the braceros. Outside of some parts of eastern Idaho, the braceros in the Pacific Northwest lacked this community with which to identify and were limited to the activities planned by the WFA.

Independence Day festivities in most northwestern camps were largely improvised activities that included races, tugs-of-war, jumping contests, and watermelon busts. Films, boxing matches, and mock bullfights were also organized and provided a welcome break from the daily routine. The braceros decorated the camp tents with crepe paper in the colors of the Mexican flag. Cooks made a special effort to please the men during this day. Camp Prescott braceros at Medford, Oregon, were given the opportunity to choose the day's menu, so they requested and got cabrito (roasted kid and a Mexican favorite) served at the city park.[91] At Wilder, Idaho, the workers held an impromptu evening dance, but because "Mexican Señoritas" were not available, some men agreed to dress in women's clothes in order to provide partners for the camp population.[92] In a similar situation at Lincoln, Idaho, braceros were more fortunate, because growers agreed to transport "señoritas" from Pocatello's small Mexican American community.[93]

Another much-celebrated occasion in the camps was Cinco de Mayo, the 5th of May, the anniversary of the defeat of the French at Puebla by Mexican forces in 1862. At Medford, Oregon, in 1944 more than one thousand persons attended, including Senator Rufus Holman (a member of the Senate Appropriations Committee), the mayor of Medford, members of the chamber of commerce, students from local high school Spanish classes, many farmers and their wives and families, and "several of the local barmaids." The local radio station broadcast the day's activities while music from the camp jukebox and musicians from the camp population gave the day some authenticity. Guests at the camp entrance were greeted by an enormous welcome sign depicting a scene of a burro, serape, and cactus and five large Vs for victory in the national colors of Mexico and the United States. Three pigs were butchered for the noon meal and participants dined on two thousand handmade tortillas, enchiladas, fifty gallons of ice cream, and one thousand soft drinks. As a symbol of friendship, the flags of both countries were raised as bugles called the crowd to attention. In the evening, the camp hosted a dance, complete with orchestra, where the growers' wives and daughters danced with the Mexican workers.[94]

The Mexican men looked forward to the celebration of these national holidays and considered them as more than an opportunity for a day of rest because news was exchanged between camps. At the Medford celebration, each bracero paid $3.00 and raised an estimated $1,000.00 to cover the expenses for the day including the cost of the evening dance orchestra.[95] The farmers took these events less seriously and could have done without them; at the Medford camp, the employers' contribution to the camp fund amounted to $50.00. At Gooding, Idaho, the men were charged $1.00 to attend the day's celebration.[96] Even during the 4th of July, a holiday of more significance to the growers, work went on as usual but at time-and-a-half wages.[97] Neither the farmers nor the federal government should have been expected to foot the entire expense of these celebrations, since these parties were for the benefit of the workers. But in truth, the observance of Mexican national holidays gave the workers a feeling of self-worth and pride, and employers benefited in the form of sustained productivity.

The annual celebrations were no substitute for the WFA's and employers' indifference to the social needs of the braceros during the rest of the year. Soon, northwestern braceros, like their compatriots in California, recognized that the celebrations served the self-interests of the growers and voted to continue to work rather than celebrate the 16th of September.[98] For that reason, when Oregon Governor Earl Snell presented each worker with a specially prepared souvenir copy of a statement exalting Miguel Hidalgo, the liberator of Mexico, it probably meant little to them.

Among the workers, a strong and active camp council could function as a planning board for social and recreational activities. The camp council concept was inherited by the WFA when it took over the camp system. Under the FSA the camp council was a democratically elected body of residents that participated in the decision-making process at each camp. Mexican officials, as they did during labor disputes, encouraged the braceros to exercise their right to organize the camp council. Due to their sheer numbers in some camps they were easily elected to the camp council.[99] Still, a large Mexican majority did not ensure adequate representation on the council. At least one of the workers in the bracero camps had to understand English in order to make the council effective. Where they did serve, braceros sometimes made up the entire body, but often they shared power with Anglos or Jamaicans.[100] Bracero representation on the camp council resulted in activities familiar to the Mexican men, including soccer and baseball teams and organized competitions between camps.[101]

Catholicism is a powerful force in Mexico, and it was overlooked in the workers' contract. Therefore, the camp councils were responsible for asking local priests to attend to the spiritual needs of the camp. At the Burlington, Washington, camp, Sunday mass began at 5:30 A.M. for the benefit of the workers.[102] Throughout Idaho and Oregon, councils helped set up temporary altars on the camp grounds so mass could be said on a regular basis.[103] It is doubtful that every resident attended church services or would understand the English-speaking priests, but the fact that mass was regularly scheduled in the camps does indicate that a spiritual need existed among the Mexican men. At Wilder, Idaho, religious services at the camp were so well attended that mass for the Mexicans was scheduled twice a week.[104] Not to be outdone by the Catholics, the First Baptist Church, among several denominations, competed for the attention of the workers by handing out free Spanish-language Bibles to the camp population.[105] By the 1950s, Catholic leaders became concerned enough with the proselytizing efforts of other denominations that they initiated a missionary program that allowed Mexican priests to travel to the United States to work among the braceros.[106]

The camp councils organized recreational committees, such as the Club Recreativo Mexicano at Midway, Oregon, to plan social activities. A popular recreational project in many camps was the purchase of jukeboxes. The braceros stocked the players with Mexican records brought up from the Southwest by the workers themselves or else obtained directly for distributing companies in California or Mexico.[107] In any case, the selection of Mexican music was limited and the few records that were available were played repeatedly. The camp manager at Wilder, Idaho, soon tired of the repetitious and unintelligible songs, especially after the workers connected the jukebox to the camp's loudspeakers for added effect.[108] Fed up, the camp manager at Medford, Oregon, quipped that the jukebox and Mexican records were "getting plenty of use."[109]

Mexican movies projected outdoors on tent walls were a bright spot in an otherwise dull camp routine. At most camps, and as long as the camp manager consented, the camp councils obtained films from distributors located in California and Utah.[110] To cover the "prohibitive" cost of the films, all camp residents were expected to contribute to the camp council.[111] Where the cost of the films was shouldered equitably, sometimes enough money was raised to schedule two films per week or present double features. Camps held "movie night" inside the mess halls or outside on any suitable surface. At Hillsboro, Oregon, the camp population gathered at dusk to watch the evening's feature on the wall of the Boys and Girls Club Building at the Washington county fairgrounds.[112] In Idaho, eastern Oregon, and eastern Washington, October's "cool evenings" marked the end of the film schedule unless indoor facilities were available.[113]

Among the films making the rounds of the bracero camps and enjoying great popularity were *La Zandunga, Jalisco nunca pierde, Huapango, Dos mujeres y un don Juan, Ojos tapatíos*, and *El héroe de Nacozarí*."[114] These films and others were popular among the braceros because they starred the leading Mexican stars of the golden years of Mexican cinema: Pedro Infante, Arturo de Córdova, Pedro Armendariz, and Emma Roldán, to name a few. Another reason for their popularity were the themes emphasized by Mexican producers of the late 1930s and early 1940s: an exaltation of rural life in prerevolutionary Mexico, veneration and respect for family and authority, resignation to poverty and personal hardship. Simply stated, the films not only aroused nostalgia for the homeland but also appealed to the Mexicans with their conservative and nationalistic message.[115] The braceros cheered the underdog and empathized with the romanticized life portrayed on the screen, thereby temporarily forgetting the harsh conditions that had compelled them to come to the United States in the first place. Still others seemed to equate their experiences as braceros to life on the canvas walls and inspired them to persevere in spite of their adversities. The popularity of these films was so great that growers would occasionally transport several hundred men by truck to a camp where one of the movies was being featured.[116]

When films were not available, the camp council organized other activities to pass time during nonworking hours. In some camps, such as Walla Walla, the braceros could attend English-language classes at the YMCA or listen to the local high school band when it performed at the camp.[117] In 1945, the braceros at this camp hosted two Christmas parties in one week and invited the Whitman College Spanish class.[118] The men had been in Walla Walla since April, so the chance to sing and dance with "the college girls," together with the Christmas spirit, explains the festive mood at this camp.[119] That same year and nearby at Kennewick, the camp council also organized a gala Christmas Eve party where gifts were exchanged in the camp and Santa Claus handed out stockings filled with oranges, apples, candy, and nuts. That evening the workers feasted on a Christmas turkey dinner contributed by the Washington Egg and Poultry Cooperative.[120]

At Caldwell, Idaho, the bracero camp joined with the Boise League of Women Voters and presented "Mexican Serenade," a program of Mexican music at the Crystal Ballroom of the Hotel Boise. A talented quartet of workers presented songs such as "La chinita," "Allá en el Rancho Grande," and "Solamente una vez" during a three-hour public performance. In an impressive gesture of good will, a local radio station broadcast the program, allowing an estimated two thousand nationals in camps in the Boise and eastern Oregon areas to listen.[121] This broadcast may well have been the first Spanish-language broadcast in the Pacific Northwest. More important, it demonstrated the degree of meaningful cooperation that was possible between the community and the bracero camps. Unfortunately, this kind of mutual cooperation was rare.

Aside from the celebration of Mexican independence, religious services, the Mexican films, or sports, little else existed for the braceros to do during their off hours in camps. Except for the nurse and on special occasions described above, women were not allowed on the camp premises. In some camps, gambling was a popular pastime that would last the entire weekend. A former bracero recalled admonishing the younger men not to gamble their earnings away. "After all," he would tell them, "the sole reason they were in the United States was to take money back to Mexico."[122] Liquor was discouraged or banned outright in most camps, so to escape the boredom the workers would go to the nearest town.

Although the workers' contracts specified that personal items could be purchased at places of their own choosing, it said nothing about how the men were to get to business establishments several miles away. Since the camps were often five miles or more from the nearest community, the braceros had to provide their own means for reaching town. Few men, after working hard for most of the day, were in any mood to walk into town and back, so taxi cabs provided the most convenient means of transportation. In many communities, the braceros were an important source of income for the cab companies since they were busy shuttling workers to and from town. Braceros at Camp Marshall near Salem, Oregon, were issued special identification cards to show taxi drivers in order to insure their return to camp.[123] Even in taxis the Mexicans were under the watchful eye of the Office of Labor. There were unwritten restrictions in some communities, such as Nampa, Idaho, where cab drivers were advised not to allow the men to take liquor into the camp.[124]

When taxis were not used, the workers used other public transportation. At Marsing, Idaho, the local bus company would dispatch a vehicle to the camp on payday and every second Saturday of the month to bring the workers into town.[125] Otherwise, the men made arrangements with their employers for transportation, or business establishments often provided one-way rides. As a last resort, the men turned to hitchhiking, a practice that was dangerous. At night and along the narrow rural roads, men were often struck by passing traffic. Near Marsing, Idaho, a bracero traveling with a companion suffered a fractured skull when he was hit by a passing automobile.[126] A more serious accident occurred when Alejandro Simanacas and some friends climbed on top of a gravel truck going to Caldwell, Idaho. Simanacas, who had arrived from Mexico five days earlier, slipped and was fatally injured.[127] These were not exceptional or isolated cases. Carelessness on the part of drivers as well as the unfamiliarity of the Mexicans with the rules of traffic on American roads were reasons for these accidents. Braceros did not purchase automobiles because almost none could drive, automobiles were beyond their means, and vehicles of all kinds were hard to come by during the war.

Given the widespread anti-Mexican sentiment faced by the workers in many northwestern communities, it is surprising that the braceros left their camps in the first place. Other than Saturday evenings, the braceros' first opportunity to get to town was on Sunday, when most stores except for beer parlors and pool halls were closed. Yet taverns in some communities did not welcome the Mexicans. In fact, Marsing, Idaho, temporarily banned liquor sales on Sundays when braceros were in the area. The prohibition on the sale of beer was in the interest of good public relations and tranquility in the worker camp, according to the village board of trustees.[128] In Washington State such measures were unnecessary since the state's blue laws forbade the sale of liquor on Sundays. In effect, the workers had little else to do on Sunday except congregate on the street corners or public parks of many northwestern communities.

On Saturday evenings, the braceros found many establishments closed, except for theaters which discriminated against nonwhites, taverns, or bawdy houses. Perhaps mindful of the fact that Sunday was a day off and to forget their problems, many of the young men quickly got drunk. To cope with the nuisance of the intoxicated men, the Milton-Freewater Police Department did not even bother with the names of those involved in drunk cases; instead, the camp manager was asked to come and pick them up.[129] Ostracism led to drunkenness, and that became a problem among the braceros. The solution for the Saturday night disorders in many communities was to post "No Mexicans, White Trade Only," signs in beer parlors and pool halls.[130] The banning of Mexicans from taverns and the like was the start of more discriminating practices against the braceros.

In the Northwest, Idaho developed the most notorious reputation for discrimination. Prejudice became so common and deep-seated that in 1946 the Mexican government threatened to forbid its workers to go into the state and two years later made good on its threat.[131] Consequently, Idaho, like Texas, was blacklisted by the Mexican government for its mistreatment of braceros.[132] The action of the Mexican government was prompted by the blatant racism of some Nampa and Caldwell merchants and businesses who posted "No Japs or Mexicans Allowed" signs.[133] A Mexican labor inspector found that "signs in both Nampa and Caldwell business houses forbid the Mexicans to enter. Seven beer parlors in Caldwell and 11 in Nampa have such signs posted."[134] The members of the Notus Farm Labor Committee, which had contracted the braceros, denounced the Caldwell Chamber of Commerce for violating the provisions against discrimination in PL-45 and cautioned that the practice jeopardized their labor supply. The committee requested that certain stores remain open in the evening so workers could make necessary purchases without harassment.[135] "We have worked hard to get that labor in here and it is doing us a service," declared a committee spokesperson. "If by our discriminating signs we are to lose the labor it will be a blow to the farmers of this area."[136] The committee also asked the local camp councils to instruct the workers "to not congregate in too large of groups in any of the business houses at any one time" as a way of lessening the prejudice.[137] The chamber of commerce promised cooperation, but whether the request not to congregate made braceros less conspicuous and hence more acceptable is questionable. However, the farmers' pressure on the community did open the doors of some establishments to Mexican patrons.

Antipathy against the braceros developed outside Idaho as well. In Seattle, the Reverend U. G. Murphey, chairman of the Evacuees Service Counsel, which worked on behalf of Japanese Americans relocated in internment camps, was unsympathetic toward the Mexican men, and although PL-45 did not provide for permanent residency, he opposed the settlement of braceros.[138] Meanwhile, the superintendent of public schools at Boardman, Oregon, asked Senator Rufus C. Holman why the "15,000 Mexicans in Oregon" could not be conscripted into the military. Ignorant of the exclusion of braceros from military service, he reminded the senator that "the majority of the men [were] under 35 years of age and eligible."[139]

At Stanwood, Washington, braceros usually met to sing and play guitars at a soda fountain until some high school students and a local marshal decided they "were going to put a stop to their singing" and run them out of town. "We don't need these Mexicans here anyway, the town would be much better off without them," remarked the marshal. He promised to go to each merchant and make a list of establishments that wanted the Mexicans' patronage. The braceros would have to "stay away" from where they were not wanted.[140] Following a "near race riot" between the marshal and students and the braceros, the farmers association, city officials, and business owners met to discuss the risk of losing the workers on grounds of discrimination. The city threatened some arrests, but before long the incident and the concern over discrimination were forgotten.[141]

Not long thereafter, the camp manager at Medford, Oregon, reported that a Mexican national was attacked in public "without provocation" and severely injured by five young men. After the assault, the battered man was arrested on a charge of being intoxicated. During the arraignment, the judge acknowledged that "those who made the attack, should have been arrested instead." As it turned out, the bracero had been staggering and presumed drunk "due to the beating received and not due to alcoholism as claimed."[142]

The cases cited did not occur daily, but they did form a pattern of racial antipathy toward Mexicans. The Mexican government received repeated complaints from the workers, and communities were warned about condoning the practice. Still, the disregard for the civil rights of Mexican workers continued until braceros in Idaho asked Mexican consul Pesqueira to intercede on their behalf against the discriminatory practices. It was their protest, coming on the heels of earlier complaints about conditions in Idaho, that finally resulted in the state being placed off limits to Mexican laborers in October 1948. "I have been directed by my government," wired Pesqueira to Idaho growers, " . . . that employers in Idaho are hereby suspended from importation of nationals of my country for any purpose until further notice. This suspension is prompted by discrimination against our nationals on social and economic grounds and by violations of the international agreement and the individual workers' contracts."[143] Pesqueira and his attorney went on to say that although "Mexicans are not allowed in some taverns and eating houses, mainly in southern Idaho," the same "discrimination was found, too, in Eastern Oregon and Washington."[144]

Braceros experienced much animosity because the Northwest, as other states in the West, had a long history of racial antipathy against certain groups such as native Americans, Asians, and blacks. When braceros arrived in the area, this antipathy was easily transferred to the Mexicans. Especially during the war, the Mexican aliens were victims of the xenophobic and nationalistic upswell of the times. To what degree anti-Mexican sentiment in the Northwest was due to the notoriety of the "zoot suit" riots of 1943 in Los Angeles is difficult to ascertain. Certainly communities in the Northwest were aware of the riots, because the national press covered the violent racial disturbances between servicemen and Mexican American youths called pachucos. The Mexican government was deeply concerned about the effect of the Los Angeles riots on the treatment of braceros in California and the Northwest because it raised the issue with the WFA.[145]

As noted, blatant discriminatory acts against Mexicans were not everyday or so ingrained in the social fabric of the region that broadminded citizens were nonexistent. Townspeople in Twin Falls, Idaho, for one, invited the camp residents to various clubs and community gatherings.[146] When a carnival and rodeo show was held at Filer, Idaho, the community arranged for free entrance for all braceros.[147] At Weiser, Idaho, a bank president agreed to remain open on Monday nights as a courtesy to the workers.[148] Braceros did not experience discrimination in Preston, Idaho, according to the camp authorities.[149] In Ontario, Oregon, business establishments welcomed the patronage of the nationals, and relations between the community and the camp were "excellent."[150]

With the hope that her letter would "have a better chance of reaching the President," a woman wrote to Mrs. Roosevelt to express her concern over the ill-treatment of contracted workers.[151] "Something should be also done about the Nazi minded element, by that I mean the people who are persecuting these boys," she stated. In her mind this type of discrimination was "pure sabotage" because it jeopardized Idaho's labor supply.

> So long as these boys are here, helping on the home front, (and they are doing a good job of it) [*sic*]. It seems to me that they should enjoy the same rights and privileges as a United States citizen, and so long as they are not drunk and disorderly they should be able to go in any place that a white man can go, and be waited on in a like manner. Does not our Constitution demand liberty and justice for all?[152]

Labor officials agreed that intolerance was destructive since the efficiency of the Mexican workers was "hampered considerably through social discrimination."[153] In the opinion of a camp manager, the public did not really comprehend the nationals and their significant contribution to the war because the "difference in language is a bar to free conversation and exchange of ideas."[154]

Braceros faced another severe form of discrimination from health officials. Some hospitals refused to treat them, and this prompted the chief of operations of the Office of Labor in Portland to suggest that the federal government establish infirmaries in areas where Mexicans could not obtain medical care.[155] Sometimes the workers were denied treatment on racial grounds, while on other occasions health practitioners doubted the men's ability to pay their medical expenses and feared they would be left with outstanding bills. As the following instances illustrate, their apprehensions were sometimes justified. Early on the morning of May 9, 1946, the New West Asparagus Farms was transporting some braceros from Grandview, Washington, to its fields in Sunnyside when the bus in which they were riding was struck broadside by an automobile operated by Jesse Montgomery, an employee of the Yakima Golding Farms. Montgomery's automobile, since it was used in connection with his employment, was insured by his employer. Police authorities, after investigating the mishap, determined that Montgomery was negligent and fined him $25. The bus carrying the workers was insured by New West, but their insurance denied any medical liability on the grounds that New West's driver was not at fault. In the meantime, a legal firm representing the injured workers collected a fee of 33 percent of the amount of lost wages paid to the braceros of the Yakima Golding Farms. The attorneys also obtained a release from the workers for any further liability from both insurance companies, leaving the doctors with outstanding bills.[156] In another case, a bracero was injured while fighting forest fires and died before he could be hospitalized. The U.S. Forestry Service disclaimed any liability on the grounds that the farm labor association, which originally contracted the bracero from Mexico, was liable.[157]

In some communities, the braceros were held responsible for health problems over which they had little control. Since food poisoning was so prevalent, the men were thought to be naturally filthy. Tied to a lack of cleanliness, venereal disease among the camp population led communities to label the men as immoral and objectionable. Veneral disease was serious, especially in camps like the one at Blackfoot, Idaho, where seven men were treated for syphilis during September 1944.[158] In the Yakima Valley, gonorrhea and syphilis were particularly prevalent among the camp population.[159] At many camps, the men contracted venereal diseases from prostitution, which flourished on payday and the days following. Medical officials in the WFA noted that in many communities where bracero camps were located, "leading citizens will not lift a finger to do anything about juvenile delinquency, complete lack of hospitals, prostitution, gambling, etc., which has been existent for a number of years."[160] This was particularly true at Nampa, Idaho, where prostitution houses in Ontario and Nyssa, Oregon, and Marsing and Boise, Idaho, afflicted the Meridian camp with venereal disease.[161] The sweeping generalizations about the men's values obscured the public's ability to recognize that vice was already present and not introduced by the braceros. In fact, each worker was screened for venereal disease in Mexico as a precondition to entering the United States. But in the Northwest, the braceros faced tough social circumstances including few leisure activities, discrimination in most places except brothels, and an absence of their own women. For these reasons it is not surprising that the basic morality of some of the braceros did disintegrate. Yet they remained of sound moral character because there is not a single case of criminal activity listed in the records of the bracero program for the Northwest Division. When medical authorities and community hospitals treated the braceros, the workers usually received minimal attention, especially in hospitals that the WFA described as "not too satisfactory."[162] On one occasion in 1945, a Mexican worker received a gunshot wound in the abdomen (cause not stated) and later died. The Agricultural Workers Health Association, which worked with the braceros, strongly condemned the doctor who treated the victim. "Burial visually eliminates medical incompetence," stated a spokesperson for the association, and "it is indeed unfortunate in such cases that the physician cannot be given as the cause of death."[163] That same year in Idaho some braceros had been summoned to fight forest fires. On the third day a tree fell on one of them, Ramón Carrillo, and injured his leg. He was examined at the hospital in Grangeville, found fit, and returned to duty. Back fighting forest fires he continued to experience considerable pain in his leg. Six or seven days later Ramón was examined once more, but the doctors found no reason for his suffering. Finally, Ramón made his own way to a nearby War Food Administration office where he explained what had happened. Subsequent X-rays disclosed that Ramón's leg was fractured. Twice he wrote to Mexican Consul Carlos Grimm at Salt Lake City but did not succeed in receiving compensation for the time lost from work. Then in despair he sent a letter in Spanish to President Franklin D. Roosevelt. "They do as they please," he complained to the president, "because I cannot speak English."[164] Ramón was more fortunate than another worker, who failed to recover from anesthesia administered to set a fractured arm.[165]

The workers arrived in good health because medical examinations in Mexico excluded those with malfunctions, illnesses, or diseases. Once in the Northwest, they experienced respiratory and digestive illnesses and injuries related to a combination of poor diet, inadequate camp and working conditions, and accidents. These health problems were not life-threatening, but discrimination and the incompetence of private medical authorities made them so. In 1945, eleven of eighteen deaths among braceros in the Northwest were caused by accidents, four by pneumonia, and the remainder were due to heart attack, encephalitis, and uremia.[166] This prompted the U.S. Public Health Service to organize a four-day conference at Boise to discuss the health problems of the Mexican workers the following year.[167] Even as braceros and other farm workers received inadequate medical attention, they were called to support local medical facilities. In 1946, the Caldwell, Idaho, camp contributed $398 to the Caldwell Memorial Hospital Fund. During the same period, the camp surpassed the local Red Cross's quota of $50.00 and donated $87.55.[168]

Over the years, the braceros' experiences in the camps and with the local townspeople worsened. They were taken for granted, and as far as the federal government was concerned, the growers' constant outcry over the terms of the workers' contract was reason to water down its provisions. Two years after the start of the bracero program, the Oregon State Extension Service noted "rapid deterioration" of the mobile camp equipment.[169] Following the end of the war, the men were moved out of the dilapidated tent quarters and into the former German prisoner of war farm labor camps at Nyssa, Oregon, Nampa, Idaho, and Wapato, Washington.[170] Although these permanent camps were an improvement over the mobile quarters, the workers were hardly impressed with the prisonerlike layout of the camps.

In most camps, the cooks continued to serve unappetizing meals lacking in nutrition. For the most part, the braceros had few organized social activities. The fact that the men worked long hours often was a convenient excuse for not providing some camp recreation. "There has been no organized recreational activity," explained a camp manager in 1944, "because the men leave to work shortly after day-light; and it is dark when they return home."[171] Where social functions were organized, the braceros were expected to continue to pay the expense.[172]

In a noted improvement in camp sanitation, camp managers began to use hydrogen peroxide in scrubbing water and chloride of lime in the toilets by 1946.[173] In a spirit of cooperation, the camp manager at Medford, Oregon, installed blackboards and helped the workers order books from Mexico so they could learn to read and write Spanish.[174] Relations between the Mexicans and northwestern communities remained poor. One camp official pointed out that relations tended to improve when "the money earned by the workers, both Mexican and domestic alike, has been spent downtown," because it put the merchants "in a good frame of mind."[175]

The braceros experienced loneliness and estrangement but to what degree cannot be measured. "These workers are separated from their homes and families by thousands of miles," wrote an employee of the WFA. "They have had to adapt themselves to habits, customs, and climatic conditions that differ considerably from their own. Yet, these workers have shown an admirable spirit of cooperation and generally have conducted themselves in a way that is a credit to their people."[176] Another sympathetic manager summarized what others missed by their insensitivity toward the braceros: "I have learned much from these men and have a deep respect for the honesty and ambition of many of them."[177]

Amazingly, most Northwesterners failed to understand the strained social circumstances endured by the braceros. Worse yet, neither the farmers nor the communities, both desperately in need of the services of these men, understood that the ill-treatment lowered worker productivity and actually came close to endangering essential war food production.

6. From Braceros to Chicano Farm Migrant Workers

PL-45, WHICH had sanctioned the wartime phase of the bracero program, expired in April 1947 and was superceded by PL-40, ending a two-year debate on the continued use of Mexican contracted workers. The new legislation contained major administrative changes and conditions that, when coupled with the protests of the braceros, were reason enough for northwestern growers to stop contracting braceros.

By 1947, northwestern growers felt that control over the bracero program, and the workers themselves, had slipped away from them. Earlier, in June 1945, over the objections of the American Farm Bureau and the National Council of Farmer Cooperatives, which wanted the bracero program under the Extension Service, the administrative control of the program was transferred from the WFA to the Department of Agriculture.[1] Since 1945, northwestern bracero employer representatives had worked hard to ensure that the program would continue after the war. That year at a regional farm labor conference held in Salt Lake City, representatives from the Northwest helped draft recommendations for future farm labor legislation. They recommended that Congress should continue to provide funds for recruitment and transportation of all farm workers, including braceros. The federal government, together with state agencies, should provide growers and workers with statistical information on crops and farm labor shortages or surpluses. Conditions of employment would be entirely a matter between employer and worker, and employers should be given the authority to operate existing government farm labor camps. No additional government camps would be constructed unless requested by a majority of growers in the district and if built not to exceed a capacity for one hundred families.[2]

Following the Salt Lake City conference, representatives of farm labor employers met with President Truman to urge that farm labor remain in the USDA instead of transferring it to the Labor Department. They asked that farm labor not be "subjected to the red tape and complicated handling of the Labor Department, NLRB [National Labor Relations Board] and other agencies connected with same" but rather "considered by people who think in terms of agriculture both perishable and non-perishable, and not in terms of steel, lumber, cement and brick."[3] Despite the objections of the farm lobby, the president transferred the farm labor program to the Department of Labor by 1947.

PL-40 did not give growers all the conditions outlined at the Salt Lake City conference. However, it provided for temporary annual binational labor agreements between 1948 and 1951 and until PL-78 continued the bracero program through 1964. During the first binational agreement, the federal government continued to furnish braceros to growers as before. This decision went against the wishes of National Extension Service officials, who asked Congress to make employers, which had become "spoiled" during the war, bear the cost of providing their own labor.[4] The USDA's Bureau of Agricultural Economics agreed that farmers could afford to cover the cost of their own labor because they now had the highest cash reserves in history. Record incomes during the war, restricted expenditures, and the availability of federally sponsored credit had resulted in general farm prosperity, reported the bureau. Moreover, during the war overall production costs had been out-distanced by gross farm income due to the low cost of labor.[5]

The announcement of the terms of the second binational agreement in 1948 brought shock and dismay to Pacific Northwest farmers. Until now, the federal government had shouldered all the expense of contracting the workers: screening, selection, and round-trip transportation of the braceros from Mexico to the Northwest. Hereafter, the workers' contracts would be negotiated directly between employer and bracero. Neither the USES nor the Immigration and Naturalization Service would participate in or subsidize recruitment, transportation, supervision, or compliance on behalf of either party. Under these new terms, growers were required to go to Mexico at their own expense, select the men, transport them to the Northwest, as well as return them to their homes at the end of the contract period.

Excepting the basic language of the workers' contract, which was left to the Mexican and U.S. negotiators, the USES outlined all new procedures for employers to follow. Each farmer's request for foreign workers had to be certified by the Bureau of Employment Security, as an agency of the USES, along with the state Farm Placement Service. The secretary of labor gave final approval of the requests for braceros, and only then were growers free to travel to predesignated recruitment sites in Mexico.

Pacific Northwest growers were especially upset over the fact that Congress and the Mexican government, in revamping the bracero program, had allowed Mexico unilaterally to select the recruitment areas. Regardless of the location of the recruitment sites, transportation costs were greater to the Northwest than to the Southwest. For this reason, northwestern growers charged discrimination unless they would be allowed to recruit directly across the U.S.-Mexican border.

In pure economic terms, northwestern growers had a point. In 1945, the federal government's cost in transporting braceros to Washington was greater than to any other state. The round-trip railraod fare from the U.S.-Mexican border to Washington amounted to $90, Oregon $78, and Idaho $76, compared to Montana $80, Utah $60, Wyoming $58, or Colorado $40.[6] Transporation costs from the border to the southwestern states were considerably lower. Travel expenses per bracero from the recruitment center to the U.S.-Mexican border and back was an additional $57.20. Seven days of travel were required to reach the Northwest, and en route the federal government furnished each worker with three meals per day at a cost of $2.25 in the United States and $.90 in Mexico. All told, the round-trip expenses per worker to Washington farms amounted to $162.95.[7] Considering that some farms used many workers, this was a considerable labor expense.

By 1948, northwestern employers sought ways of lowering travel expenses from Mexico if they were to continue to employ braceros. The Amalgamated Sugar Company proposed to contract five hundred braceros in Tampico, transport them to the U.S. border by bus, then fly the men to Idaho on converted army transport planes.[8] A Seattle corporation had a similar plan to fly directly to Mexico and pick up men contracted with the Holly Sugar Company and Great Western Sugar Company.[9] When air charters did not work out, farmers considered other alternatives such as the use of public carriers. This idea was impractical because it was costly and slow, and the Mexicans faced segregation in public places as they traveled through Texas and other states.

As soon as growers realized that transportation was a fixed cost, they cast about to locate domestic workers. As before the war, the larger agricultural interests paved the way for the smaller farmers.

The Amalgamated Sugar Company, even as it was considering the use of bus and air transportation to move Mexican labor, announced that it would recruit Mexican American beet workers from California "at a considerably lower cost than that anticipated for Mexican Nationals."[10] In May, the *Idaho Daily Statesman* reported that 650 "California Mexicans" had arrived in the Nampa-Caldwell area to work on sugar beet farms associated with the U & I Sugar Company.[11] The shift from braceros to migrant workers was significant because it marked the beginning of the end of the bracero program in the Pacific Northwest. After 1948, northwestern farms used fewer braceros as they stepped up the recruitment of Mexican Americans from the Southwest.

Unlike in the Southwest, PL-40 had made it economically unfeasible for northwestern farmers to continue to contract Mexican workers. Yet even if growers had elected to continue with the braceros, cost what it may, other factors connected with this program argued against that decision. Local labor continued to protest the need to import the Mexican nationals even as they refused agricultural employment. The braceros were seen as real threats to the well-being of local workers because contracted workers worked for cheaper wages. Protests over food services were still a problem at some bracero camps. Strikes and work stoppages over conditions of employment among the Mexican workers also played on the minds of the farmers. Mexico's internal politics and concern over the treatment of the braceros in the United States were added considerations because several times a cut-off of the labor supply had been threatened. Threats by the Mexican government to withhold braceros from the Pacific Northwest, especially Idaho, over the issue of racial discrimination were real concerns. The *Northwest Farm News* took all this into account and advised growers:

> No industry can long afford to remain dependent on the seasonal importation of foreign labor. The experience this spring when it required the concerted efforts and influence of many agencies to overcome the original decision of the Mexican government that workers would not be supplied to Montana, Wyoming and other western states [Idaho included] is an example of the difficulties that are continually encountered in arranging for an adequate supply of workers.[12]

On top of the tranportation costs, the Mexican government had negotiated new terms which raised the minimum wage from $.30 to $.37 per hour and guaranteed each worker a minimum of $33.60 in earnings every two weeks.[13] After five years' experience with the braceros, northwestern employers considered the entire farm labor program as too much bureaucratic red tape and "boondoggling."

Mexican Americans, the replacements for the braceros, were an ideal work force since they did not require any preconditions of employment. Being free wage earners, growers could hire and treat them as they saw fit without any federal agency caring the least. They were also plentiful. During the war, some migrant farm laborers had traveled along the West Coast on transportation provided by sugar companies and canneries. Others came of their own volition, especially after 1942, when the secretary of agriculture issued special identification cards to migrant workers entitling them to gasoline, tires, and automobile parts. In this way, migrants continued their sojourns to the Northwest during the war.

The war's end witnessed substantial increases in the number of migrant farm workers seeking employment, more than at any time since 1942. Washington State farm labor officials noted more migratory farm workers registering for jobs than in the previous years. The Extension Service was surprised to learn that some farmers did not want to house braceros in the government labor camps in order to free the shelters for seasonal Mexican American workers.[14]

The following year saw an even greater influx of Mexican American migratory laborers. In April, the Blue Mountain Canning Company brought one hundred "domestic Mexicans" to Walla Walla to harvest asparagus and speculated that their orders for Mexican nationals would be cancelled.[15] The *Northwest Farm News* commented that braceros were no longer in heavy demand and those already in the area could be transferred to some other state where they were needed.[16] The camp manager for the Yakima Farm Labor Camp reported a "big surplus of domestic labor" and considered it "shameful" to bring in transported workers.[17] During July, the Washington State Extension Service said that all counties had practically discontinued trying to recruit workers due to the increasing abundance of migrants.[18] The next month, the Walla Walla camp manager wrote, "It appears to us that there is the largest number of migrants on the road now than there has been at any time since the war."[19]

The war's end also solved the problem of a shortage of transportation facilities. Throughout the war, this was a major problem that often delayed the arrival and departure of braceros. The scarcity became worse after the surrender of Japan, when POWs, war brides, and returning soldiers and sailors had priority to travel on the railroads while braceros under government sponsorship and migrants traveling on their own had no priority on this or other means of transportation. By 1946, however, the *Idaho Daily Statesman* noted that the flow of migrants had increased, since private cars were readily available.[20] But it was more than automobiles; gasoline and tires were no longer hard to obtain. All these factors accounted for the greater mobility of migrants traveling outside the Southwest. They were attracted to the Pacific Northwest by higher wages and expanding job opportunities and encouraged to leave the Southwest because the continued flood of braceros was depressing the postwar farm wage economy.

The termination of the war and the administrative reorganization of the entire federal farm labor program forced northwestern farmers to rethink their dependence on braceros. This did not mean, however, that growers could return to the prewar method of obtaining farm help, because too much had changed between 1941 and 1945.

During the war, new canneries and packing companies had been established in the Northwest, resulting in expanded acreage of row crops. Before the war, Oregon had raised 21,000 acres of processing peas, and by 1946 the acreage increased to 50,000. At the start of the war, 22,000 acres were devoted to snap bean production, but by 1946 44,000 acres were planted. Washington and Idaho experienced similar increases. Between 1945 and 1946 alone, Washington farmers expanded the pea cultivation from 68,000 to 80,000 acres.[21] Although growth was irregular among different crops, an aggregate expansion of farm production meant that the demand for hand labor remained high if not greater than during the war.

The slow rate of mechanization of agriculture during the war and after was still another factor that shaped the demand for labor. From the start, the war had practically halted all production of farm machinery, as steel was set aside for war munitions. In 1942, the chief of civilian supply of the War Production Board addressed the Western Farmers Machinery Conference to explain that the release of 540,000 tons of steel from civilian to war production would result in 34,000 light, 14,000 medium, and 7,000 heavy tanks and 1.7 million machine guns.[22] The following year, the War Production Board set the manufacture of farm implements at 83 percent of 1940 levels; one year later, it was reduced to 20 percent.[23] This meant that for the duration of the war, farm machinery and parts were hard to come by if they could be found at all.

After the war, many farmers were in a position to purchase new labor-saving equipment but found that little was available on the market. Farmers in the Northwest were especially affected. The use of newer farm implements was one way to remain competitive. However, they required specialized farm machinery which had not been improved since the thirties, and some crops were not mechanized at all.

Sugar beet production exemplifies the uneven rate of mechanization. From 1943 on, new plant thinning and digging equipment was not available, making hand labor indispensable to the industry. The war's end brought some hope to sugar beet farmers. A vice-president of the U & I Sugar company was optimistic before a conference of farmers. "I have recently returned from a meeting of sugar beet manufacturers of this country and it will be of interest to all sugar beet growers to know that the processors are setting up a united organization to bring about as quickly as possible a complete mechanization of beet growing." "The war," he continued, "has made it difficult to proceed with mechanization but this year will see hundreds of beet harvesters in use."[24] Total mechanization of beet cultivation was difficult to envision. Harvesting was mechanized but the spring and summer operations—thinning and seeding—did not yield to machines until years later.

Potato farmers experienced similar problems with mechanization. Although harvesting machines had been developed to dig and sack potatoes long before the war, hand labor was still the rule in 1945.[25] The problem was not only that machines were expensive and unavailable during the war; farmers did not mechanize for marketing reasons. The Oregon State College Agricultural Experiment Station found that some growers resisted machine harvesters because "potatoes handled in this way are usually not so attractive and the attractiveness of the Klamath crop is its big selling point."[26]

Rising expectations of a better life among the local work force was another reason that growers faced continued labor shortages after the war. On the balance, the hardship of the Depression was a distant memory, as most people were thrust into a new peacetime society shaped by the momentum and prosperity of war. Wrote a historian, "there could be no returning to the farm and the small town; there would be no exodus from major metropolitan areas; there would be no backward movement from West Coast to Eastern Seaboard."[27]

This change in the pace of life, aspiration, and forward vision did not bypass the Northwest. In 1945, growers were told not to expect a return to prewar labor conditions. "The trend back to farm work hasn't started as yet and there is no sign it is going to begin in anything like a big way," warned the Oregon State Extension Service. "Workers just laid off from easier jobs, shorter hours and better pay seem to want something more to their newly educated taste than 'going back to a farm job again' . . . some are looking at farm work but 'they're choosy.'"[28]

In 1946, a plan to give veteran and local labor preference in obtaining agricultural jobs fell flat because neither former farm workers nor returning veterans in Washington or Idaho were much interested in farm labor.[29] By 1947, farm labor officials sounded discouraged: "the need for farm labor instead of diminishing as we had expected in 1946 is continuing to grow. With the closing of our war plants and the return of servicemen, the demand for year around men had lessened somewhat, but the need for seasonal workers is increasing almost alarmingly."[30] Added to the reluctance of veterans and war workers to accept farm employment, the Washington State Farm Labor Committee reported, "Youth and women, who have contributed so much in the past in harvesting and processing food, have lost their enthusiasm and apparently are making no effort to return again this year to the fields and food processing plants where their help is so vitally needed."[31]

In 1947, remarkable change had transpired in agriculture. Even as farmers faced expanded production, limited mechanization, and an uncooperative local work force, PL-40 discouraged further dependency on bracero laborers. Hereafter, farm workers in northwestern communities would not come from Mexico. Mexican Americans would be called north from the Southwest to replace the braceros. Guided by promises of higher earnings than they were accustomed to in the Southwest, they came north in hopes of grasping a share of the momentum of World War II which had bypassed them. They would migrate by the hundreds to the Pacific Northwest only to realize that their expectations would turn to disillusionment. As they left communities, scattered from Texas to California, vacancies in the ranks of southwestern farm laborers would be filled by an ongoing but regionally more limited bracero work force.

Conclusion

DURING THE 1920S and at the height of immigration from Mexico to the United States, Mexicans migrated north into Idaho, Oregon, and Washington. Agricultural expansion and railroad construction, the same factors that stimulated Mexican immigration to the Southwest, created the jobs filled by these laborers in the Pacific Northwest. The Great Depression halted the flow of Mexican people across the border and even reversed it. Yet in spite of the faltering economy and a corresponding idle work force, farmers continued to recruit Mexican workers to northwestern farms at dirt-cheap wages. While the status of many citizens improved under the various federally sponsored relief programs, the condition of Depression-era Mexican agricultural workers worsened in the Northwest because they were denied the same opportunity. Poverty-stricken already, Mexicans emerged no less poor after the New Deal.

World War II lifted the nation out of the Depression and once again provided unparalleled opportunities for economic advancement to everyone. Industry boomed and so did agriculture. As one northwestern farm owner recalled, "During the Depression, I had less than nothing and during the war, I accumulated a little bit."[1] Most of the work force, including women, gained much from the rapid expansion of economic activity. As far as Mexican farm laborers were concerned, the circumstances were distinct. When the rural work force went into war-related industrial jobs, many Mexican seasonal migrants were frozen in low-paying unskilled agricultural employment.

As labor shortages intensified and threatened crop production, agribusiness turned to Mexico for help under PL-45. By agreeing to come to the Northwest, braceros guaranteed food production. Growers benefited as much from their ability to meet the demand for farm products as they profited from low-cost Mexican labor. To a degree, braceros in the Northwest also made it possible for other workers to be employed in higher-paying nonfarm jobs. Had farmers gotten their way and frozen local workers on the farms, many more Americans would have emerged from the war in a similar state of semiservitude as the Mexicans and Chicanos. Herein lies the contribution of the thousands of braceros who entered the United States: they replaced the work force that went into industry and made agricultural expansion and sustained high levels of farm production possible.

Despite this signifcant contribution, the braceros were generally treated worse than Italian and German prisoners of war held in northwestern farm labor camps. The latter, one historian has written, in many cases received more and better food, drinks, and cigaretts than American civilians.[2] Protected by the Geneva Convention, they were better treated by their guards than employers treated the braceros.

Although the workers had contracts guaranteeing minimum job standards, their employers unilaterally established rock bottom and discriminatory wage rates. In doing so, growers reduced the workers to a state of peonage similar to that in many parts of Latin America. In addition, the farmers' reckless abandon of human considerations was shocking and led to numerous job-related accidents. In sum, while other war workers made good in the new economic order, the Mexicans arrived unskilled and stayed that way.

Yet in spite of what has been written on this topic, braceros were not powerless to act. When work and living conditions became unbearable, they went on strike. These work stoppages were not along class lines but over bread and butter issues defined by the workers' own intolerable status. In the end, the link between the federal government and the growers made the one-sided relationship between employer and bracero difficult to change. In the long run, the braceros' pattern of striking was one reason that growers ended their reliance on contracted laborers and turned to migrant workers. The federal government and the farmers were not alone in their mistreatment of the Mexican men. Through the Extension Service, the land grant colleges and their faculty defined the working and living conditions of contracted agricultural labor.

Bracero-assisted record agricultural production translated into economic prosperity in many rural northwestern communities. Even so, the civil and human rights of the braceros were seldom considered by many of the residents of these towns. Braceros were the victims of much social and physical discrimination, which further limited their upward mobility. As in the case of work conditions and when social pressures became unbearable, they responded by requesting the Mexican consuls to intercede on their behalf. The consuls, contrary to what has been written, did not turn their backs on their countrymen. They faced up to the growers to the extent that they could.

The transition to a peacetime economy was accompanied by administrative changes to the bracero program. To northwestern employers, these changes were enough to cast about for another source of labor. By 1947, Chicano migrant seasonal workers began to stand in for the Mexican nationals. Therefore, while the bracero program continued until 1964 in other areas, it ended in the Northwest right after the war.

This study is important for several reasons. In the same way that World War II pushed the nation's concern over the Depression-era farm migrants into the background, forty years after the end of the war few persons are fully aware of the role of Mexican labor during this critical juncture of our history. Second, some important lessons can be learned from the social and work experiences of the braceros. Their struggle is significant for what it reveals about agriculture's access to and the workers' isolation from the centers of power. These lessons deserve to be restated because in many respects the ongoing powerlessness of agricultural wage earners stems from public ignorance of the political and economic reality of the industry.

Third, in 1971 Richard B. Craig suggested that the bracero program was a system of labor and simultaneously a composite of interrelated parts that needed to be studied in its own environmental context.[3] Forty years after the end of World War II, the full history of the bracero program remains to be written. Most historians of the war slight the bracero's role in national agricultural production and characterize these years as the last true example of the "can do" spirit of the American people. On the other hand, most studies of Mexican labor and immigration focus largely on the southwest during the periods preceding or following the war. Outside of California and Texas, the bracero program in other parts of the country is poorly understood. This study is an initial contribution, and perhaps it will stimulate a more detailed and comparative study of the full effect of the wartime bracero program.

Finally, in the minds of many people, the bracero program of World War II, the postwar period until 1964, and the present guest worker provision of the 1985 Immigration and Reform Act mean little more than a temporary foreign worker program. But many of the braceros who first immigrated to the United States at the invitation and encouragement of the federal government returned as free laborers. When the bracero program was terminated in the Pacific Northwest and elsewhere later, the men did not stop coming north from Mexico. Substantial numbers of former braceros, many times accompanied by their families and friends, continued to migrate for seasonal work. One study of a rural Mexican town discovered that 64.3 percent of the 1942 to 1944 braceros and 62.5 percent of those contracted between 1945 to 1949 eventually obtained visas to enter the United States.[4] In short, the current population of Chicanos in the Pacific Northwest, as well as in many other parts of the nation, had its genesis in the U.S.-conceived and -sponsored bracero program of World War II. In this respect, the bracero of World War II functioned as a conduit of Mexican immigrants to many Chicano communities throughout the United States. Given the new guest worker provision, probably many more contracted workers will become immigrants in the future.

World War II clearly marks a watershed in Mexican and Chicano migration into the Pacific Northwest. This was not the aim of the bracero program. Agriculture rejoiced in the fact that the braceros would enter the country temporarily as cheap laborers and then be ordered back to Mexico. But it was illogical to assume that former braceros would give up a livelihood upon which they depended and not continue to come into the United States. As a result, Mexican Americans constitute one of the largest minority communities in the region.

There are some hard lessons in this history of the bracero program. Agribusiness's wish for a return to a national bracero or guest worker program has never completely gone away. This study should serve as a forceful reminder of the gulf between paper agreements and the reality of the contracted workers themselves. For much of the twentieth century, when the United States called on the Mexican people for their labor, they came. Their experiences demonstrate society's attitudes toward farm workers and foreigners. Many stayed and others returned later as immigrant workers to this country. As such, the history of these men is an important part of U.S. and Chicano social and labor history. It deserves to be told and understood.

Notes

Introduction

1. In Spanish, the term *bracero* means a worker who works with his hands or arms, especially in the United States. The male workers contracted to enter the United States under the terms of the binational labor agreement were popularly called braceros. The farm labor program itself was also known as the bracero program. During the same period many undocumented Mexicans left Mexico under their own accord to work in agriculture—they were not legally braceros.

2. Several book-length monographs as well as numerous articles have examined the bracero agricultural workers in the Southwest. See, for example, Scruggs, "Evolution," "Texas and the Bracero Program," and "The Bracero Program"; Smith, "Farm Workers"; and Rasmussen, *A History.* The politics of the binational agreement are the subject of Craig, *The Bracero Program;* and Hawley, "Politics." The exploitive nature of the bracero program in California is discussed by Galarza, *Merchants of Labor;* and Anderson, "The Bracero Program." The more recent studies of the war labor program include Kirstein, *Anglo over Bracero;* and McCain, "Texas and the Mexican Labor Question."

For the relatively few studies of braceros in the Pacific Northwest, see Gamboa, "Mexican Migration," "Mexican Labor," and "Braceros in the Pacific Northwest." The Mexican perspective is found in Tellez, *La migración de braceros;* and Topete, *Aventuras de un bracero.*

3. In this study, the term *Mexican* refers to immigrants from Mexico and is used synonymously with the term *bracero.* Mexican American and Chicano refer to persons of Mexican ancestry in the United States without regard to place of birth.

4. Two worthwhile publications that examine Mexican and Chicano immigration within theoretical frameworks are Portes and Bach, *Latin Journey;* and Valdez, Camarillo, and Almaguer, *The State of Chicano Research.*

1. Agribusiness and Mexican Migration

1. Menig, *The Great Columbia Plain,* pp. 509, 511.

2. Henry A. Wallace, Secretary of Agriculture, to Harold L. Ickes, Sec-

retary of Interior (n.d., [1935?]), Records of the Office of Secretary of Agriculture, File: Correspondence 1935, Record Group 16, National Archives, Washington, D.C. (Records of Secretary of Agriculture, National Archives, hereafter cited as RG16, NA.)

3. Hurd and Hollands, "Economic Conditions," p. 5.
4. Ibid.
5. Gamboa, "Mexican Migration," p. 123.
6. Hurd and Hollands, "Economic Conditions," p. 36.
7. The trend to large commercial farms was beginning to develop. In 1936, a sample of farms noted that only 9 percent exceeded sixty acres. See Landis and Brooks, "Farm Labor," p. 6.
8. Ibid., p. 24.
9. Ibid., p. 26; Hurd and Hollands, "Economic Conditions," pp. 78, 79.
10. Landis and Brooks, "Farm Labor," p. 29.
11. Hollands, Hurd, and Pubols, "Economic Conditions," p. 14.
12. Davis and Mumford, "Farm Organization," p. 2.
13. DeLoach and Sutton, "Marketing Central Oregon," p. 11.
14. "The Farming Business in Idaho," p. 32.
15. See Cardoso, *Mexican Emigration*, pp. 1–17.
16. Ibid., 38. The conditions which compelled emigrants to leave for the United States are discussed succinctly by Romo, *East Los Angeles*, pp. 30–59.
17. Romo, *East Los Angeles*, p. 42.
18. Recent studies of Mexican immigration into areas outside the Southwest are being developed. For a skillful treatment of migration into Oklahoma, see Smith, *The Mexicans in Oklahoma*. A short history of Mexicans in Illinois is found in Kerr, "Chicano Settlements."
19. Broadbent, "The Distribution of Mexican Population," pp. 12–13.
20. Recorded interview with Juan R. Salinas, Toppenish, Washington, Aug. 6, 1972.
21. During the 1920s, Mexico City's newspaper *El Universal* wrote that Mexican workers were traveling to the Alaskan salmon canneries. See Bulnes, *Los grandes problemas*, p. 8.
22. *Yakima Herald Republic*, Oct. 7, 1972. Salinas had been preceded by other Mexicans traveling through the area as early as the 1800s.
23. Cardoso, *Mexican Emigration*, p. 26.
24. The dispersal patterns of immigration are discussed in Martínez, "Mexican Immigration," pp. 28–29.
25. U.S. Congress, Senate, *Report of the Immigration Commission, Part 25*, pp. 1114, 1116.
26. Interview with Geraldo Cárdenas, Sept. 15, 1972.
27. Idaho Migrants, *Chicano Studies*, p. 4.
28. Broadbent, "The Distribution of Mexican Population," pp. 12, 31; "The Farming Business in Idaho," p. 38.
29. The lifting of the restriction on Mexico is discussed in Reisler, *By the Sweat of Their Brow*, pp. 24–42.

30. García, *Desert Immigrants*, p. 59.

31. McWilliams, *Ill Fares the Land*, p. 249; García, *Desert Immigrants*, p. 59.

32. *Idaho Daily Statesman*, Apr. 14, 1924, p. 8.

33. Ibid., May 16, 1927, p. 10.

34. Gamboa, "A History of Chicanos," p. 38; Arrington, *Beet Sugar in the West*, p. 196.

35. Cardoso, *Mexican Emigration*, pp. 88–89.

36. Interview with Gunn Supply Company, Apr. 24, 1928, Paul S. Taylor Papers, File: Labor Contractors, Bancroft Library, University of California, Berkeley, p. 1.

37. Ibid.; Pomeroy, *The Pacific Slope*, p. 281.

38. Taylor, "Increases of Mexican Labor," p. 82.

39. Ourada, *Migrant Workers in Idaho*, p. 17.

40. Ibid., p. 4.

41. Bulnes, *Los grandes problemas*, p. 8.

42. For the best history on Mexican repatriation, see Hoffman, *Unwanted Mexican Americans.*

43. Repatriation from the Midwest is discussed in Betten and Mohl, "From Discrimination to Repatriation."

44. Hollands, Hurd, and Pubols, "Economic Conditions," p. 37.

45. Winther, *The Great Northwest*, p. 338.

46. Johnson and Vogel, "Types of Farming in Idaho," p. 33.

47. Young, "Index Number," p. 9.

48. Bowden, "Wartime Wages," p. 1119.

49. Ibid., p. 1115.

50. Ibid.

51. The issue of parity is discussed in Albertson, *Roosevelt's Farmer*, chap. 10.

52. The powerlessness of agricultural workers is discussed by Daniel, *Bitter Harvest*, pp. 40–70.

53. Saloutos, "The Immigrant."

54. In northeastern Colorado, for example, the German Russian beet growers increased in numbers from 665 to 2,590 between 1909 and 1927. See Taylor, "Migratory Farm Labor," p. 544.

55. Arrington, *Beet Sugar in the West*, pp. 123–132; and Cottrell, *Beet Sugar Economics*, pp. 30–31, 268–271.

56. *Manual of Sugar Companies, 1942*, p. 158.

57. Arrington, *Beet Sugar in the West*, p. 132.

58. Ibid., p. 127.

59. Webb, *The Migratory Casual Worker*, pp. 95–96.

60. Interview with Chuck Martínez, July 14, 1982.

61. *Idaho Daily Statesman*, Sept. 9, 1931.

62. Ibid., Sept. 28, 1935, p. 6.

63. Gamboa, "A History of Chicanos," p. 38.

64. Paul S. Taylor, "The Migrants and California's Future," mimeographed

copy by Resettlement Administration of speech delivered Sept. 13, 1935, U.S. Government Documents Center, University of Washington Library, Seattle, Washington, p. 5.

65. Taylor, "Migratory Farm Labor."

66. *Manual of Sugar Companies, 1942,* pp. 155–157.

67. *Idaho Daily Statesman,* May 11, 1935.

68. Ibid., May 25, 1936. An example of the handbills used in the recruitment is found in Gamboa, "Mexican Migration" p. 128.

69. U.S. Congress, House of Representatives, *Interstate Migration Hearings,* p. 2532 (hereafter cited as the Tolan Committee).

70. Ibid., p. 2218.

71. Ibid., p. 1815.

72. Ibid., p. 1861.

73. Ibid., parts 4–5, p. 1800.

74. *Idaho Daily Statesman,* Sept. 28, 1935.

75. Ibid., May 11, 1935.

76. Ibid., May 25, 1936.

77. Ibid., Oct. 23, 1935.

78. Ibid.

79. Ibid., May 14, 1937.

80. The view of the federal government toward these migrants is discussed in Stein, *California and the Dust Bowl Migration,* chap. 5. For a discussion of the politics surrounding the New Deal and the vacillation of the Roosevelt administration toward farm labor, see Daniel, *Bitter Harvest,* pp. 258–285. A different view of the New Deal is presented by Cohen, *The Roosevelt New Deal,* pp. 201–219.

81. Tolan Committee, part 6, pp. 2652–2655.

82. *Idaho Daily Statesman,* Sept. 7, 1931.

83. Landis and Wakefield, "The Drought Farmer," p. 40.

84. Tolan Committee, part 6, p. 2636. This figure is extrapolated from the FSA estimate of 450,000 persons in the region.

85. Ibid., p. 2589.

86. Ibid.

87. Ibid.

88. Ibid., p. 2660.

89. FSA resettlement areas in the Pacific Northwest included Vale-Owhyee, east-central Oregon, near the Snake River, 90,000 acres; Black Canyon, southwest Idaho, near the Snake River, 56,000 acres; Roza, central Washington, near Yakima, 72,000 acres. At the time, the Columbia Basin project was expected to bring in an additional 1,000,000 acres for resettlement. See ibid., p. 2637.

90. Under this program in the Northwest region, William Chastin was the first to achieve ownership of a 145-acre farm in the Willamette Valley in 1938. See "Farm Security Information Division Report."

91. Tolan Committee, part 6, p. 2593.

92. Ibid., p. 2661.

93. Correspondence Concerning Migratory Labor Camps, 1935–1943,

Records of Farm Security Administration, File: Housing, Record Group 96, National Archives, Washington, D.C. (Records of Farm Security Administration, National Archives, hereafter cited as RG96, NA.)

94. Winston Phelps, "Uncle Sam Has His Own Refugee Problem, the Thousands of Homeless Farm Families" (May 1939), mimeograph of Farm Security Administration copy located at University of Washington Library, Seattle, Washington, p. 4.

95. "Yakima Civic Leader Reports on California Farm Family Labor Camps," report reproduced by Farm Security Administration, Aug. 8, 1938, Carey McWilliams Papers, UCLA Library, Los Angeles, California.

96. Letter, May 3, 1940, Dan A. West to Carey McWilliams, Carey McWilliams Papers.

2. World War II and the Farm Labor Crisis

1. Rasmussen, *A History,* p. 15.

2. A discussion of the effect of World War II on the West is found in Nash, *The American West Transformed;* also see Pomeroy, *The Pacific Slope,* pp. 297–300.

3. "Employment and Earnings of Agricultural Workers Living in FSA Migratory Labor Camps in Oregon, Washington, and Idaho in 1940," Correspondence Concerning Migratory Labor Camps, 1935–1943, RG96, NA, p. 8.

4. "Migratory Labor Camp Program, September 1941," ibid., p. 15.

5. Ibid.

6. "Labor Situation in Sugar Beet Malheur County, Oregon and Vicinity," Bureau of Agricultural Economics, General Correspondence, File: Farm Labor Sugar Beet Areas, Record Group 83, National Archives, Washington, D.C., p. 2. (hereafter cited as "Labor Situation in Sugar Beets, Malheur County"; Bureau of Agricultural Economics, National Archives hereafter cited as RG83, NA).

7. *Yakima Daily Republic,* Aug. 20, 1941.

8. Ibid., Aug. 6–7, 1941.

9. *Toppenish Review,* Sept. 5, 1941.

10. *Yakima Daily Republic,* Aug. 15, 1941.

11. Ibid., Aug. 19, 1941.

12. *Toppenish Review,* Sept. 18, 1941.

13. *Yakima Daily Repbulic,* Aug. 18, 1941.

14. "Labor Situation in Sugar Beets, Malheur County," p. 2.

15. Ibid.

16. Ibid., p. 5.

17. *Oregonian,* Dec. 14, 1941.

18. Ibid.

19. *Idaho Daily Statesman,* Apr. 30, 1941.

20. *Proceedings of the Thirty-third Annual Report,* p. 53.

21. Arrington, *Beet Sugar in the West,* p. 141.

22. "Labor Situation in Sugar Beets, Malheur County," p. 6.

23. Ibid.

24. *Idaho Daily Statesman,* June 21, 1941; "Labor Situation in Sugar Beets, Malheur County," p. 6.

25. Memorandum, September 29, 1941, Assistant Representative, State Bureau of Agricultural Economics to Division of State and Local Planning, General Correspondence, 1941–1946, File: Farm Labor, RG83, NA, p. 5.

26. *Proceedings of Fifty-sixth Annual Meeting,* p. 22.

27. Memorandum, September 29, 1941, Assistant Representative, State Bureau of Agricultural Economics to Division of State and Local Planning, General Correspondence, 1941–1946, File: Farm Labor Tex-Wyo, RG83, NA.

28. "Labor Situation in Sugar Beets, Malheur County," p. 3.

29. Ibid., p. 4.

30. Ibid.

31. *Idaho Daily Statesman,* June 9–14, 1941.

32. Letters from Pacific Northwest farmers to their Congressmen were common by 1941. See Walter Pierce Papers, File: Agriculture and Labor, University of Oregon Library, Eugene.

33. Winther, *The Great Northwest,* pp. 309–311.

34. For example, water from the Roza Project first flowed ninety-five miles from Kittitas through Yakima and Benton counties on Apr. 19, 1941, *Yakima Sunday Herald,* Mar. 4, 1951.

35. Albertson, *Roosevelt's Farmer,* p. 277. In 1933, one farm in ten had electric service, and by 1941 35 percent of all farms had electric power. See Cohen, *The Roosevelt New Deal,* p. 211.

36. See Sims, "The Japanese American Experience in Idaho."

37. Bollinger, "Demand, Labor, Prices, Income," p. 2.

38. *Northwest Farm News,* Jan. 8, 1942.

39. Ibid., Feb. 19, 1942.

40. Ibid., Jan. 29, Feb. 12, 1942.

41. Ibid., Mar. 26, 1942.

42. Ibid., May 14, 1942.

43. Ibid., June 4, 1942.

44. Ibid.

45. Ibid., July 9, 1942.

46. Ibid., June 25, 1942.

47. Ibid., July 2, 1942.

48. Ibid., Aug. 6, 1942.

49. "The 1942 Farm Labor Program in the Wenatchee and Okanogan Fruit Areas," General Correspondence, 1943, Reports: Regulatory Work, Secretary of Agriculture, Record Group 16, National Archives, p. 13 (Secretary of Agriculture, General Correspondence hereafter cited as GCRG16, NA).

50. *Northwest Farm News,* Oct. 8, 22, 1942.

51. Taylor, *Labor on the Land,* p. 243.

52. *Idaho Daily Statesman,* July 4, Aug. 4, 1942.

53. Ibid., Aug. 6, 1942.

54. Ibid., Aug. 25, 1942.

55. Ibid., July 9, 1942.

56. Sims, "The Japanese American Experience in Idaho," p. 5. Also see *Idaho Daily Statesman*, Mar. 14, 15, 1942.

57. *Idaho Daily Statesman*, Sept. 1, 1942.

58. Ibid., July 25, 1942.

59. Sims, "The Japanese American Experience in Idaho," p. 8; *Northwest Farm News*, Oct. 15, 1942.

60. *Northwest Farm News*, Oct. 8, 1942.

61. *Idaho Daily Statesman*, June 6, 7, 24, 1942.

62. Ibid., June 3, 4, 1942. A discussion of businessmen as farm laborers is found in *Business Week*, Oct. 10, 1942, p. 78.

63. *Idaho Daily Statesman*, June 4, 1942.

64. Smith, "Preacher Leads Labor Gang."

65. Reider, "School Children Mobilized," p. 147.

66. Sasuly, "Camps Guide Farm Labor," p. 20.

67. *Northwest Farm News*, May 21, 1942.

68. Reider, "School Children Mobilized," p. 146.

69. *Northwest Farm News*, May 21, 1942, June 11, 1942.

70. "Labor Situation in Sugar Beets, Malheur County," p. 7.

71. Ibid., pp. 6–9.

72. Ibid., p. 9.

73. *Northwest Farm News*, Oct. 15, 1942.

74. Brodell and Cooper, "Agriculture in a Gasoline Age," p. 13.

75. Gamboa, "Mexican Migration," p. 124.

76. "Potatoes are King," p. 15.

77. Letter, May 21, 1943, H. Gordon Chute to Chester Davis, Office of Labor, General Correspondence, Farm Labor Problems: Farm Labor, Record Group 51, National Archives (Office of Labor, General Correspondence hereafter cited as GCRG51, NA).

78. Letter, Dec. 9, 1942, Mary A. Metzer to Claude Wickard, Office of Labor of the War Food Administration, General Correspondence, Farm Labor Problems: Farm Labor, Record Group 224, National Archives (Office of Labor of the War Food Administration, General Correspondence hereafter cited as GCRG224, NA).

79. Albertson, *Roosevelt's Farmer*, p. 245.

80. Flynn, *The Mess in Washington Manpower Mobilization*, p. 135.

81. Albertson, *Roosevelt's Farmer*, p. 134; Flynn, *The Mess in Washington Manpower Mobilization*, p. 133.

82. Flynn, *The Mess in Washington Manpower Mobilization*, p. 132.

83. Nash, *The American West*, p. 41.

84. Albertson, *Roosevelt's Farmer*, p. 122.

85. Flynn, *The Mess in Washington Manpower Mobilization*, p. 139.

86. Albertson, *Roosevelt's Farmer*, pp. 365, 372–374.

87. U.S. Congress, Senate, *Farm Labor Program Hearings*, pp. 16, 50.

88. Rasmussen, *A History*, p. 11.

89. "Labor Branch Farm Labor Program in the Northwest Division from Inception to January, 1947," Department of Agriculture, Production and Marketing Administration, Labor Branch, Portland, 1942, p. 6.

90. Flynn, *The Mess in Washington Manpower Mobilization,* p. 134.

91. Rasmussen, *A History,* p. 31.

92. Ibid.

93. U.S. Congress, Senate, *Farm Labor Program Hearings,* p. 231.

94. Ibid., p. 175.

95. *Northwest Farm News,* Feb. 25, 1943.

96. Proceedings of the Thirty-third Annual Report, p. 53.

97. U.S. Congress, Senate, *Farm Labor Program Hearings,* p. 121.

98. *Northwest Farm News,* Feb. 11, 1943.

99. Ibid., July 30, 1942.

100. Ibid., July 9, 1942.

101. Letter, Mar. 1943, Governor C. A. Bottolfsen to Paul V. McNutt, C. A. Bottolfsen Papers, File: "War Manpower Commission and Production Board," Idaho State Library, Boise, Idaho.

102. *Northwest Farm News,* Aug. 20, 1942.

103. Ibid., Sept. 17, 1942.

104. Ibid., Feb. 11, 1943.

105. Ibid., Mar. 4, 1943.

106. Ibid.

107. *Oregonian,* May 4, 1941.

108. *Idaho Daily Statesman,* Aug. 4, 1942.

109. *Northwest Farm News,* July 13, 1943.

110. Rasmussen, *A History,* p. 202.

111. Nash, *The American West,* p. 79.

112. Martínez, "Mexican Immigration," p. 18.

113. *Northwest Farm News,* May 14, 1942.

114. *Idaho Daily Statesman,* June 9, 1942.

115. Ibid.

116. Flynn, *The Mess in Washington Manpower Mobilization,* pp. 133, 135.

117. Herbert B. Peterson, "Twentieth-Century Search for Cíbola: Post-World War I Mexican Labor Exploitation in Arizona," in Servin, *An Awakening Minority,* pp. 113–132. This essay offers an outstanding view of the tragic consequences of the temporary admission program in the Salt River Valley, Arizona.

118. Reisler, *By the Sweat of Their Brow,* p. 260.

119. The anti-Mexican sentiment which was present is southwestern communities is analyzed in Mirandé, *Gringo Justice,* pp. 156–173.

120. Ibid., p. 161.

121. *Northwest Farm News,* Apr. 30, 1942.

122. *Idaho Daily Statesman,* June 11, 1942.

123. Scruggs, "Evolution," pp. 140–144. Also see Rasmussen, *A History,* p. 205.

124. Galarza, *Merchants of Labor,* p. 47; Rasmussen, *A History,* p. 205.

125. Rasmussen, *A History,* p. 206.

126. *Northwest Farm News,* Aug. 13, 1942.

127. *Toppenish Review,* Sept. 11, 1942.

128. Galarza, *Merchants of Labor,* pp. 47, 48.

129. Rasmussen, *A History,* p. 208.

130. Craig, *The Bracero Program,* p. 43.

131. Rasmussen, *A History,* p. 64.

132. *Northwest Farm News,* Feb. 4, 1943.

133. U.S. Congress, Senate, *Farm Labor Program Hearings,* p. 81.

134. *Idaho Daily Statesman,* Apr. 8, 1943.

135. U.S. State Department, "Foreign Consular Offices."

136. Albertson, *Roosevelt's Farmer,* p. 358.

137. Townsend, "Farm Mobilization Campaign," p. 10.

138. Letter, Jan. 14, 1943, Paul V. McNutt to Secretary of Agriculture, File: Agriculture.138, GCRG16, NA.

139. "Farm Outlook," p. 4.

140. Tolley, "Agricultural Production," p. 18.

141. Labor Supervisor Annual Report 1943, Records of Extension, Record Group 33, Extension Service Farm Labor Program 1943, Box Oklahoma–South Carolina, File: Oregon, p. 1, National Archives (Records of Extension hereafter cited as RG33, NA).

142. Idaho Farm Labor Supervisor Annual Report, Farm Labor Program Annual Narrative and Statistical Reports, Box Colorado-Idaho, File: Idaho, p. 1, RG33, NA.

143. *Northwest Farm News,* Mar. 25, 1943.

144. Ibid., Feb. 4, 1943.

145. Letter, Mar. 10, 1943, S. A. Moffett Company to Agricultural Division Bureau of Placement Office, Box 16, File: Farm Labor Recruitment, GCRG224, NA.

146. *Northwest Farm News,* May 27, 1943.

147. Telegram, Mar. 3, 1943, Claude R. Wickard to Governor C. A. Bottolfsen, C. A. Bottolfsen Papers, File: Farm Committee, Idaho State Library, Boise.

148. Letter, Mar. 8, 1943, Secretary Wickard to Governor C. A. Bottolfsen, Box 297, File: Agriculture, GCRG16, NA.

149. Letter, Mar. 6, 1943, Governor Arthur Langlie to Secretary Wickard; Letter, Mar. 8, 1943, C. A. Bottolfsen to Secretary Wickard; Letter, Mar. 4, 1943, Governor Snell to Secretary Wickard, all in Box 13, Farm Labor, File: Release of School Children from School, GCRG224, NA.

150. *Northwest Farm News,* Sept. 16, 1943.

151. *University of Washington Daily,* Oct. 8, 9, 13–16, 1942.

152. Minutes of State Farm Advisory Committee Meeting at Boise, Idaho, Nov. 26, 1943, C. A. Bottolfsen Papers.

153. *Northwest Farm News,* May 14, 1942.

154. Memorandum to County Farm Labor Committee, Minutes of State

Farm Advisory Committee Meeting at Boise, Idaho, Nov. 26, 1943, C. A. Bottolfsen Papers.

155. Rasmussen, *A History,* p. 148.

156. Plan of Work, Arthur F. Kulin, Mar. 1943–July 1944, Annual Reports, Director of Extension and Assistants, 1943, Emergency Farm Labor Reports Extension Service, Washington State University Archives, Washington State University at Pullman, p. 8 (hereafter cited as EFLR, WSUA).

157. "Annual Narrative Report of Arthur F. Kulin, Feb. 1–Dec. 31, 1943," Annual Reports, Director of Extension and Assistance, 1943, EFLR, WSUA.

158. State Farm Advisory Committee Meeting, Boise, Idaho, Nov. 26, 1943, C. A. Bottolfsen Papers.

159. James W. Doddington to Governor Langlie, Apr. 28, 1943, Box 16, File: Farm Labor Prisoners, GCRG224, NA. Similar letters to the other state governors are found in this file together with the responses.

160. Ibid.

161. Rasmussen, *A History,* p. 97.

162. "Recruitment," Box 16, File: Farm Labor, GCRG224, NA.

163. Emergency Farm Labor Reports, Sept. 1943, p. 5. EFLR, WSUA.

3. The Bracero Worker

1. Galarza, *Merchants of Labor,* p. 53. The precise figure was 46,954 and it was compiled from a series of mimeographed monthly farm labor reports issued between June 30, 1943, and Dec. 31, 1947, by the U.S. Department of Agriculture. These reports were organized by state and included the total number of imported farm workers, including Mexicans, Canadians, Jamaicans, and Bahamians. These reports were issued by the Department of Agriculture's Bureau of Agricultural Economics until Feb. 1946, when they were prepared by the department's Office of Production and Management Administration.

2. Farm Labor Supervisor Annual Report, 1944, Farm Labor Program, Box 23, Idaho-Iowa, p. 13, RG33, NA.

3. *Northwest Farm News,* May 16, 1944.

4. Arthur Kulin, Specialist, Record of County Visit, Yakima, King, Aug. 11, 1943, EFLR, WSUA (Specialist, Record of County Visit hereafter cited as Visitation Report, followed by name, location, date).

5. "Mexican National Transportation Orders, Workers Delivered and Prospective Delivery Schedule for Mexican Workers by Employing Groups as of November 30, 1943," Department of State General Records, Record Group 59, State Decimal File, 1943–1944, Folder: 263, National Archives (Department of State General Records hereafter cited as RG59, NA).

6. *Northwest Farm News,* Feb. 3, 1944.

7. Smith, "Farm Workers from Mexico," p. 12.

8. *Yakima Daily Republic,* Apr. 27, 1943.

9. Letter, Mar. 26, 1943, R. L. Webster, Assistant to Secretary of Agriculture, to Charles C. Teague, Box 927, File: Agriculture, GCRG16, NA.

10. Letter, July 29, 1948, W. F. Kelley, Assistant Commissioner, Immi-

gration and Naturalization Service, to Paul J. Reveley, Chief, Division of Mexican Affairs, Department of State, Box 4826, File: Mexico, RG59, NA.

11. Memorandum, April 24, 1945, Harry Brown to William Anglian, File: Laborer Reports, GCRG224, NA.

12. Letter, August 10, 1943, Robert G. McGregor, Jr., American Embassy, to William G. McLean, State Department, Box 3348, File: Mexico, RG59, NA.

13. Ibid.

14. Ibid.

15. Ibid.; *Idaho Daily Statesman,* Sept. 16, 1945.

16. Narrative, June 1943, Hood River, Oregon, Box 52, File: Oregon, GCRG224, NA.

17. Plan of Work 1944, Extension Farm Labor Program State of Washington, p. 3, EFLR, WSUA.

18. *Idaho Daily Statesman,* May 6, 1945.

19. *Northwest Farm News,* May 14, 1942.

20. Ibid., Feb. 21, 1946.

21. "Annual Report of Emergency Farm Labor Program 1947," Extension Service, Oregon State College, OSUA, Corvallis, Oregon, p. 1 (Oregon State College hereafter cited as OSC).

22. *Idaho Daily Statesman,* May 26, 1946.

23. Visitation Reports, Arthur F. Kulin, Yakima County, July 7, 1943, p. 1. EFLR, WSUA.

24. Visitation Reports, Arthur F. Kulin, Walla Walla, July 10, 1943, p. 1. EFLR, WSUA.

25. Visitation Report, Walter E. Zuger, Kittitas, Oct. 8, 1943, p. 4. EFLR, WSUA.

26. Specialist Monthly Report, Arthur F. Kulin, July 1945, EFLR, WSUA.

27. Visitation Reports, Walter E. Zuger, Walla Walla, June 25–26, 1945, EFLR, WSUA.

28. "Farm Labor News Notes, Annual Report Emergency Farm Labor 1944," Extension Service, p. 1. OSUA, OSU.

29. *Idaho Daily Statesman,* July 10, Sept. 28, 1945.

30. Visitation Reports, Walter E. Zuger, Kittitas, Aug. 28, 1943, EFLR, WSUA.

31. "Monthly Field Operations Report July 1944," Records of U.S. Employment Service, Record Group 183, Box 414, File: Washington, Records of United States Employment Service (hereafter cited as RG183).

32. Visitation Reports, Walter E. Zuger, Snohomish, Apr. 16, 1945, EFLR, WSUA.

33. *Northwest Farm News,* Feb. 8, 1945.

34. *Idaho Daily Statesman,* July 10, 1945.

35. Letter, July 27, 1945, Clinton P. Anderson to Fred J. Martin, Box 1165, File: Agriculture, GCRG16, NA.

36. Labor Branch Farm Labor Program in the Northwest Division, pp. 26–29.

37. Ibid., p. 27.

38. Visitation Reports, Arthur F. Kulin, Pacific County, Oct. 26, 1944, EFLR, WSUA.

39. Visitation Reports, Arthur F. Kulin, Pierce County, Feb. 22, 1945, Visitation Reports, Arthur F. Kulin, Yakima County, Apr. 30–May 1, 1946, EFLR, WSUA.

40. *Northwest Farm News*, July 13, 1944.

41. Letter, July 18, 1944, Henry Walsh to Rt. Magelby, Box 61, File: Mexicans 1944, GCRG224, NA.

42. Narrative, Aug. 1944, Meridian, Idaho, Box 52, File: Idaho, GCRG 224, NA.

43. *Idaho Daily Statesman*, Aug. 24, 1945.

44. Ibid., Aug. 18, 1946.

45. Ibid., May 22, 1945.

46. Letter, Mar. 28, 1946, J. W. Williams to Senator Wayne L. Morse, Box 1348, File: Employment, GCRG16, NA.

47. Narrative, Dec. 1946, Midway, Oregon, Box 101, File: Camps, Midway, Oregon, GCRG224, NA.

48. "Conference Called by Governor Walgren of Washington at Yakima on Feb. 6, 1945," Box 88, File: Yakima Farm Labor Conference, p. 1, GCRG224, NA.

49. Ibid.

50. "Labor Utilization Activities: Excerpts from Reports of State Extension Services," U.S. Department of Agriculture, Extension Service Farm Labor Circular no. 34, Aug. 1946, WSUA. The following titles represent the type of training brochures available for the farmers' use; "Ganar más dinero pizcando papa/Earn More Money Picking Potatoes," "Sugestiones para la pizca de durazno/Suggestions for Picking Peaches," "Instrucciones para el desaije y espacio de betabeles de azucar/Instructions for Thinning and Spacing Sugar Beets," "Lista de preguntas ventajosas para los pepenadores de papas/List of Worthwhile Questions for Potato Pickers" (English translation by author, Spanish titles appear as they were printed).

51. Cumberland, *Mexico*, p. 29. Braceros were exempt from all literary requirements since they were not immigrants.

52. Visitation Reports, James E. Jensen, Yakima County, Apr. 20, 1945, EFLR, WSUA.

53. Ibid.

54. Jones, *Mexican War Workers*, p. 25.

55. "Labor Market Development Reports, Idaho Falls, May 15, 1943," Area Labor Market Survey Reports, Box 82, Idaho, File: General, p. 1, RG183, NA.

56. *Northwest Farm News*, July 13, 1943.

57. Visitation Reports, Arthur F. Kulin, Skagit County, July 21, 1943, p. 1, EFLR, WSUA.

58. Ibid.

59. Ibid.

60. *Northwest Farm News*, July 15, 1943.

61. Ibid., July 29, 1943.

62. Ibid.

63. "Farm Labor 1943–47," Extension Service Series I, p. 72, OSUA.

64. Ibid., p. 60.

65. *Northwest Farm News,* July 13, 1943.

66. Ibid., Apr. 27, 1944.

67. Visitation Reports, Arthur F. Kulin, Whatcom County, Mar. 22, 1944, p. 1, EFLR, WSUA.

68. *Northwest Farm News,* Dec. 7, 1944.

69. Ibid., June 28, 1945.

70. Letter, Oct. 25, 1945, D. L. Fourt to Roy D. LaRue, Governor Charles C. Gossett Papers, Box 5, Idaho State Library, Boise. This observation is corroborated by a recent preliminary study on POW farm workers' productivity, *Seattle Times,* Jan. 8, 1984.

71. *Idaho Daily Statesman,* Oct. 18, 1945.

72. "Annual Report of Arthur F. Kulin, Feb. 1–Dec. 31, 1943," p. 8, EFLR, WSUA.

73. State Farm Labor Committee Meeting, Mar. 30, 1943, C. A. Bottolfsen Papers.

74. "Plan of Work 1944," Emergency Farm Labor Program, State of Washington, p. 4, EFLR, WSUA.

75. Ibid., p. 7.

76. Visitation Reports, Arthur F. Kulin, Chelan County, Oct. 12, 1944, p. 4, EFLR, WSUA.

77. "Annual Report," Arthur F. Kulin, Specialist Reports, 1945, p. 4, EFLR, WSUA.

78. Ibid., p. 4.

79. Narrative, Oct. 1944, Twin Falls, Idaho, Box 52, File: Idaho, GCRG224, NA.

80. *Idaho Daily Statesman,* Oct. 29, 1945.

81. Ibid.

82. *Oregonian,* Sept. 29, 1943.

83. "Monthly Labor Market Development Report, October 1943," Area Labor Market Survey Reports, Box 83, Idaho, File: Blackfoot, p. 3, RG183, NA.

84. "Regulatory Work," Box 985, File: Reports, p. 25, GCRG16, NA.

85. Letter, Feb. 28, 1946, Secretary of Agriculture to Senator Wayne Morse, Box 1348, File: Employment, Agriculture, GCRG16, NA.

86. Visitation Reports, Robert H. Pelley, Snohomish County, Feb. 13, 1946, p. 1, EFLR, WSUA.

87. Ibid.

88. *Idaho Daily Statesman,* June 1, 1946.

89. Ibid., May 12, 1946.

90. Narrative, Sept. 1946, Stanwood, Washington, Box 102, File: Stanwood, GCRG224, NA.

91. Visitation Reports, Arthur F. Kulin, Yakima, April 30–May 1, 1946, EFLR, WSUA.

92. Letter, Feb. 21, 1946, Northwest Canners Association to Secretary of

Agriculture, Box 107, File: Public Relations–Commendation, Endorsement of the Program, GCRG224, NA.

93. Visitation Reports, Arthur F. Kulin, Kittitas, Sept. 15, 1943, p. 1, EFLR, WSUA.

94. "Conference Called by Governor Walgren of Washington at Yakima on Feb. 6, 1945," Box 88, File: Yakima Farm Labor Conference, p. 7, GCRG224, NA.

95. Narrative, July 1943, Milton-Freewater, Oregon, Box 52, File: Oregon, GCRG224, NA.

96. *Northwest Farm News*, Apr. 27, 1944.

97. Letter, Sept. 20, 1943, Abrahan Martínez Frausto to Congress of United States, Box 60, File: Mexicans, GCRG224, NA.

98. Narrative, May 1944, Medford, Oregon, Box 52, File: Oregon, GCRG224, NA.

99. Letter, Dec. 1, 1946, Paul Hinchiff to O. B. Hardy, Box 101, File: Camps Oregon, Midway, GCRG224, NA.

100. Ibid.

101. Ibid.

102. Narrative, Aug. 1944, Hillsboro, Oregon, Box 52, File: Oregon, GCRG224, NA.

103. Visitation Reports, Arthur F. Kulin, Okanagon, Oct. 12, 1944, p. 1, EFLR, WSUA.

104. Narrative, July 1946, Dixie, Washington, Box 101, File: Camps, Washington, Dixie, GCRG224, NA.

105. Specialist Monthly Report, Arthur F. Kulin, July 1945, EFLR, WSUA.

106. Narrative, Aug. 1946, Milton-Freewater, Oregon, Box 101, File: Camps Oregon, Athena, GCRG224, NA; Arthur F. Kulin, Specialist, Monthly Report, July 1945, p. 1, EFLR, WSUA.

107. Letter, June 25, 1946, Paul Hinchliff to D. B. Hardy, Box 101, File: Oregon, Milton-Freewater, GCRG224, NA.

108. Ibid.

109. Letter, Oct. 22, 1943, Charles F. Miller to Col. Phillip G. Burton, Box 60, File: Mexicans, GCRG224, NA.

110. "Admission of Alien Farm Workers," p. 124.

111. Narrative, June 1944, Nampa, Idaho, File: Idaho; Narrative, Apr. 1944, Kennewick, Washington, File: Washington; Narrative, May 1944, Medford, Oregon, File: Oregon; all in Box 52, GCRG224, NA.

112. "Labor Branch Farm Labor Program," pp. 25, 26.

113. Letter, May 14, 1944, William A. Anglim to Col. Philip G. Burton, Box 61, File: Mexicans, GCRG224, NA.

114. Ibid.

115. Memorandum, Dec. 3, 1945, Tolbert, Chief of Operations, Portland, to Director of Labor, Washington, D.C., Box 87, File: Laborer Reports, GCRG224, NA.

116. Walter E. Zuger, Visitation Report, Berkeley, California, Conference, July 25, 26, 1945, EFLR, WSUA. Puerto Ricans had the highest rates of ab-

senteeism among all contracted laborers. In 1944, the rate was as high as 60 percent. See Maldonado, "Contract Labor," p. 111.

117. Narrative, July 1944, Vale, Oregon, Box 52, File: Oregon, GCRG 224, NA.

118. Ibid. Perhaps the worst case of braceros working in cold temperatures was reported at Missoula, Montana. Here the men arrived in "Palm Beach suits" as the temperature hovered at −18°F. See *Northwest Farm News,* Mar. 1, 1945.

119. Narrative, Dec. 1946, Idaho Falls, Idaho, Box 100, File: Idaho, GCRG224, NA.

120. Ibid.

121. In spite of health tests and screening in Mexico some of the men did arrive ill. Narrative, May 1947, Nyssa, Oregon, Box 111, File: Camps, Oregon, GCRG224, NA. On accidents, see Narrative, Sept. 1944, Payette, Idaho, Box 52, File: Idaho; Narrative, Apr. 1945, Kennewick, Washington, Box 79, File: Camps; Narrative, May 1946, Idaho Falls, Idaho, Box 99, File: Camps; Narrative, Apr. 1945, Kennewick, Washington, Box 79, File: Camps; all in GCRG224, NA.

122. Narrative, Apr. 1945, Kennewick, Washington, Box 79, File: Camps, GCRG224, NA.

123. Narrative, May 1944, Kennewick, Washington, Box 53, File: Washington, GCRG224, NA.

124. Shields, "Labor Conditions," p. 14.

125. Reports, April to June, Box 85, File: Health Services Reports, GCRG224, NA.

126. Ibid.

127. Narrative, Oct. 1944, Weiser, Idaho, Box 52, File: Idaho, GCRG224, NA.

128. Ibid.

129. Narrative, Aug. 1944, Hillboro, Oregon, Box 52, File: Oregon, GCRG224, NA.

130. Ibid.

131. Narrative, June, August, 1944, Kennewick, Washington, Box 53, File: Washington, GCRG224, NA.

132. *Northwest Farm News,* May 13, 1943.

133. Ibid., July 13, 1944.

134. Narrative, Aug. 1946, Weiser, Idaho, Box 100, File: Camps, GCRG224, NA.

135. Narrative, Oct. 1944, Weiser, Idaho, Box 52, File: Idaho, GCRG224, NA.

136. Letter, Oct. 13, 1943, J. R. Beck to Certain County Agents, Extension Service, Box 24, Farm Labor 1943–47, OSUA.

137. Ibid.

138. Narrative, Aug. 1944, Hillsboro, Oregon, Box 52, File: Oregon, GCRG224, NA.

139. Narrative, Aug. 1944, Nampa, Idaho, Box 52, File: Idaho, GCRG224, NA.

140. Narrative, Sept. 1944, Payette, Idaho, Box 52, File: Idaho, GCRG224, NA.

141. Report of Surgeon, Office of Labor Medical Officer, Northwest Division, August 1945, Box 85, File: Health Services Reports, June, August, p. 6, GCRG224, NA.

142. Ibid.

143. Narrative, Aug. 1946, Weiser, Idaho, Box 100, File: Camps, GCRG224, NA.

144. Narrative, June 1946, Weiser, Idaho, Box 100, File: Camps, GCRG224, NA.

145. Narrative, Aug. 1946, Weiser, Idaho, Box 100, File: Camps, GCRG224, NA.

146. Memorandum, Aug. 22, 1946, Wilson Buie to Production Management Administration Portland Office, Box 107, File: Organizations-Plans Safety, GCRG224, NA.

147. Narrative, Aug. 1946, Payette, Idaho, Box 100, File: Camps, GCRG224, NA.

148. Narrative, Aug. 1946, Stanwood, Washington, Box 102, File: Camps, GCRG224, NA.

149. Narrative, June 1946, Homedale, Idaho, Box 111, File: Camps, GCRG224, NA.

150. Narrative, Apr. 1947, Wapato, Washington, Box 111, File: Camps, GCRG224, NA.

4. *Huelgas:* Bracero Strikes

1. Ernesto Galarza, "Personal and Confidential Memorandum on Mexican Contract Workers in the United States, August 28, 1944," Box 4821, File: Mexico, pp. 1–10, RG59, NA.

2. Scruggs, "Texas and the Bracero Program," p. 258.

3. This strike was followed and reported in detail by the *Idaho Daily Statesman,* June 18, 20, 25, 26, 1946.

4. Ibid., June 18, 1946.

5. Galarza, "Personal and Confidential Memorandum," pp. 8–9.

6. The concern over communists within the ranks of California agriculture is discussed in Daniel, *Bitter Harvest,* pp. 105–140.

7. *Northwest Farm News,* Jan. 13, 1938.

8. In this and other similar cases, the State Highway Patrol was ordered to assist farmers during labor unrest. See *Idaho Falls Post Register,* Sept. 12, 1938; *Yakima Daily Republic,* Aug. 25, 1933.

9. "Recent State Legislation," p. 942.

10. *Northwest Farm News,* Jan. 20, 1938.

11. Balderrama, *In Defense of La Raza,* p. 115.

12. Montejano, *Anglos and Mexicans,* pp. 268–269.

13. Galarza, *Merchants of Labor,* p. 232.

14. U.S. State Department, "Foreign Consular Offices."

15. Ibid.

16. Liss, "Farm Wage Boards," p. 107. I have made extensive use of this and the following articles by Liss on farm wages during the war: "The Concept and Determination of Prevailing Wages" "Farm Wage Boards under the Wage Stabilization Program."

17. Liss, "Farm Wage Boards," p. 107.

18. Ibid.

19. Ibid.

20. Liss, "Farm Wage Boards under the Wage Stabilization Program," p. 128; Wilcox, "The Wartime Use of Manpower," p. 737.

21. "Ceiling Wage Rates for Farm Labor" (poster), Office of General Counsel, Office of Solicitor, U.S. Department of Agriculture, RG16, Box 11, File: Wage Stabilization, Oregon, Federal Records and Archives Center, Seattle, Washington (Office of General Counsel, Office of Solicitor, U.S. Department of Agriculture, Federal Records and Archives Center, Seattle, Washington hereafter cited as RG16, FRAC).

22. *Northwest Farm News,* June 22, 1944.

23. Ira A. Alvord to C. E. Herrington, Memorandum, Aug. 23, 1945, Box 11, File: Wage Stabilization, Idaho, RG16, FRAC.

24. Report of Operation of Specific Wage Ceiling Regulation 27, Harvesting Apples and Pears in Hood River County, Oregon—1945, Box 94, File: Wage Stabilization Oregon, p. 10, GCRG224, NA.

25. *Northwest Farm News,* Feb. 3, 1944.

26. Ibid., July 29, 1943.

27. Minutes of Idaho State Farm Labor Advisory Committee meeting, Nov. 26, 1943, C. A. Bottolfsen Papers, File: Farm Labor Committee, Idaho State Library, Boise, Idaho.

28. Ibid.

29. Plan of Work, Arthur F. Kulin, Mar. 1943, July 1944, p. 5, EFLR, WSUA.

30. Ronald W. Purcell to War Food Administration, Telegram, May 29, 1943, Box 18, File: Farm Labor, GCRG224, NA.

31. Minutes of Idaho Farm Labor Advisory Committee Meeting, June 29, 1943, C. A. Bottolfsen Papers, File: Farm Labor Committee, Idaho State Library, Boise, Idaho.

32. Visitation Reports, Arthur F. Kulin, Grant County, July 24, 25, 1944, EFLR, WSUA.

33. Ibid.

34. Narrative, June 1944, Preston, Idaho, Box 52, File: Idaho, GCRG224, NA.

35. Ibid.

36. Narrative, July 1944, Rupert, Idaho, Box 52, File: Idaho; Narrative, Oct. 1944, Wilder, Idaho; all in GCRG224, NA.

37. Narrative, Oct. 1944, Sugar City, Idaho, Box 52, File: Idaho; Narrative, Oct. 1944, Lincoln, Idaho; all in GCRG224, NA.

38. Narrative, Oct. 1944, Marsing, Idaho, Box 52, File: Idaho, GCRG224, NA.

39. Narrative, Oct. 1944, Preston, Idaho, Box 52, File: Idaho, GCRG224, NA.

40. *Idaho Daily Statesman,* Oct. 5, 1945.

41. Annual Report of State Supervisor of Emergency Farm Labor Program 1945, Extension Service, p. 56, OSUA.

42. Letter, Sept. 25, 1945, Secretary of Agriculture to Senator Guy Gordon, Box 1165, File: Employment, Farms, GCRG16, NA.

43. *Northwest Farm News,* Aug. 23, 1945.

44. Ibid.

45. Minutes of Wage Board Meeting, Nov. 6, 1946, Box 11, File: Wage Stabilization Oregon, RG16, FRAC.

46. *Northwest Farm News,* Apr. 19, 1945.

47. Ibid.

48. Transcript of Hearing of Washington State USDA Wage Board, Aug. 20, 1945, Box 126, File: Wage Stabilization Board 1942–46 Green Houses, Labor, GCRG224, NA. The absence of worker representation was common. See Transcript of Hearing of Wage Board, Feb. 8, 1945, Box 119, File: Wage Stabilization Board 1942–46, Apples, Cherries.

49. Annual Narrative Report Emergency Farm Labor Program 1946, p. 7, EFLR, WSUA.

50. *Idaho Daily Statesman,* May 1, 1945.

51. Visitation Reports, Walter E. Zuger, Walla Walla County, June 12, 1945, EFLR, WSUA.

52. Ibid.

53. Ibid.; Visitation Reports, Arthur F. Kulin, Walla Walla County, July 5, 1945, EFLR, WSUA.

54. *Idaho Daily Statesman,* June 8, 1945.

55. Ibid., June 29, 1945.

56. Ibid., July 11, 14, 1945.

57. Ibid., Sept. 7, 11, 14, 1945.

58. Ibid., Sept. 1, 1945.

59. Ibid., Sept. 11, 1945.

60. Conference called by Governor Walgren of Washington at Yakima on Feb. 6, 1945, Box 88, File: Yakima Farm Labor Conference, GCRG224, NA.

61. Letter, Oct. 26, 1945, C. E. Herrington to D. R. Bush, Box 11, File: Wage Stabilization Idaho, RG16, FRAC.

62. Ibid.

63. Letter, Nov. 6, 1945, Ivan Blume to C. E. Herrington, Box 11, File: Wage Stabilization Idaho, RG16, FRAC.

64. Letter, Nov. 6, 1945, Walter E. Davidson to C. E. Herrington, Box 11, File: Wage Stabilization Idaho, RG16, FRAC.

65. Letter, Nov. 8, 1945. I. R. Area Supervisor to C. E. Herrington, Box 11, File: Wage Stabilization Idaho, RG16, FRAC.

66. The names of the braceros identified by the camp managers are contained in the camp files. Report of Operation of Specific Wage Ceiling Regulation 27, Harvesting Apples and Pears in Hood River County, Oregon, 1945, Box 94, File: Wage Stabilization Oregon, p. 7, GCRG224, NA.

67. *Idaho Daily Statesman*, July 16, 1945.

68. Walter E. Davidson to C. E. Herrington, Office of Solicitor, Box 11, File: Wage Stabilization Idaho, RG16, FRAC.

69. Ibid.

70. Ibid.

71. Letter, Feb. 21, 1946, Ben Davidson to Secretary of Agriculture, Box 1349, File: Employment, GCRG16, NA.

72. *Idaho Daily Statesman*, June 20, 1946. This strike was followed in detail by the *Idaho Daily Statesman*, June 18, 20, 25, 26, 1946.

73. Ibid., June 20, 1946.

74. Ibid.

75. Ibid.

76. Narrative, June 1946, Nampa, Idaho, Box 100, File: Nampa, Idaho, GCRG224, NA; *Idaho Daily Statesman*, June 18, 1944.

77. *Idaho Daily Statesman*, June 18, 1946.

78. Ibid., June 22, 1946.

79. Ibid., June 26, 1946.

80. Ibid.

81. Ibid., June 29, 1946.

82. Ibid., July 12, 1946.

83. Telegram, July 22, 1946, Carl G. Izett to Wilson R. Buie, Box 108, File: Mexican Collaborators, GCRG224, NA.

84. Carl G. Izett to Wilson R. Buie, July 22, 1946, Box 108, File: Mexican Collaborators, GCRG224, NA.

85. Letter, July 18, 1946, Carl G. Izett to Wilson Buie, Box 108, File: Wage Stabilization, GCRG224, NA.

86. Narrative, Aug. 1946, Caldwell, Idaho, Box 100, File: Idaho, GCRG224, NA. Other strike activity was reported in the *Idaho Daily Statesman*, Sept. 11, 1946, and Narrative, Aug. 1946, Weiser, Idaho, Box 100, Folder: Idaho.

87. Visitation Reports, Walter E. Zuger, Walla Walla County, June 28, 29, 1946, EFLR, WSUA.

88. Visitation Reports, Arthur F. Kulin, Skagit County, July 2, 1946, EFLR, WSUA.

89. Visitation Reports, Walter E. Zuger, Skagit County, July 13, 1946, EFLR, WSUA.

90. Narrative, Aug. 1946, Burlington, Washington, Box 101, File: Washington, GCRG224, NA.

91. Ibid.

92. Washington Farm Labor Supervisor Annual Report 1946, Records of Federal Extension Service, Record Group 33, Box 40, File: Washington, National Archives (Records of Federal Extension Record Group 33, National Archives hereafter cited as RG33, NA).

93. Wage Violations, Jan. 1946–Dec. 1946, Box 108, File: Wage Stabilization, GCRG224, NA.

94. *Northwest Farm News*, Jan. 23, 1947.

95. Ibid.

96. Narrative, May 1947, Walla Walla, Washington, Box 111, File: Camps, Washington, GCRG224, NA.

97. Narrative, May 1947, Idaho Falls, Idaho, Box 111, File: Camps, Idaho, GCRG224, NA.

98. Ibid.

99. Narrative, Aug. 1947, Nyssa, Oregon, Box 111, File: Camps, Oregon, GCRG224, NA.

100. *Northwest Farm News,* June 1, 1944.

5. Bracero Social Life

1. Three permanent camps in Washington, one in Oregon, and two in Idaho were used to house braceros. The remainder of the men were placed in mobile camps. See "Labor Branch Farm Labor Program," p. 18.

2. "Projects, Extension Specialists," Oregon State Extension Service, Farm Labor Emergency, July 1946 through Aug. 1947, Oregon State University Archives, Corvallis, Oregon, pp. 14–16 (Oregon State University Archives, Corvallis, Oregon, hereafter cited as OSUA, Corvallis). In December 1941, the FSA operated seventy-four camps across the country capable of housing thirteen thousand families at any time. Cohen, *The Roosevelt New Deal,* p. 207.

3. "Conference Called by Governor Walgren of Washington at Yakima on February 6, 1945," Box 79, File: Laborers-Military: Yakima Valley Farm Labor Conference, pp. 9, 10, RG224, NA.

4. Ibid.

5. *Northwest Farm News,* July 27, 1944.

6. Monthly Narrative Report, May 1945, Kennewick, Washington, Box 79, File: Camps, Washington Farm Labor Supply Centers, 1945, GCRG224, NA (Monthly Narrative Report is hereafter cited as Narrative, followed by date, place).

7. Narrative, May 1946, Grandview, Washington, Box 102, Folder: Camp-Cooperation, GCRG224, NA.

8. Narrative, May 1947, Athena, Oregon, Box 110, File: Camps, GCRG224, NA.

9. Narrative, July 1947, Milton-Freewater, Oregon, Box 110, File: Camps, GCRG224, NA.

10. Narrative, November 1946, Rupert, Idaho, Box 100, File: Camps, GCRG224, NA.

11. "Farm Labor 1943–1947," Oregon Extension Services, p. 51, OSUA, Corvallis.

12. *Northwest Farm News,* Apr. 27, 1944.

13. Visitation Report, Arthur F. Kulin, King County, July 5, 1944, p. 4, EFLR, WSUA, Pullman.

14. "Annual Report of Emergency Farm Labor Program 1944," p. 16, EFLR, WSUA, Pullman.

15. Visitation Report, Mar. 28, 29, 1945, Robert H. Pelley, Kittitas County, EFLR, WSUA, Pullman.

16. Memorandum, Apr. 30, 1946, Box 107, File: Public Relations, Organizational Safety, GCRG224, NA.

17. Some folders in the Mexican Farm Labor Program are empty. The fact that the folders exist and are labeled suggests that they contained records at some point. At times reports are marked "personal and confidential," indicating that they were not intended for public scrutiny.

18. *Northwest Farm News*, Apr. 27, 1944.

19. Narrative, Oct. 1944, Preston, Idaho, Box 52, File: Idaho, GCRG224, NA.

20. Letter, Nov. 6, 1945, Ivan Blume, Area Supervisor Wage Stabilization Board, to C. E. Herrington, Box 11, File: Wage Stabilization Idaho, Oregon, and Washington: Stabilization Forms, RG16, FRAC.

21. Letter, Dec. 3, 1945, Chief of Operations, Portland, to Director of Labor, Washington, D.C., Box 87, File: Labor Reports, GCRG224, NA.

22. Narrative, Oct. 1944, Lincoln, Idaho, Box 52, File: Idaho, GCRG224, NA.

23. *Northwest Farm News*, Apr. 27, 1944.

24. Interview with Arturo Aguirre.

25. Narrative, Dec. 15, 1944, Nampa, Idaho, Box 52, File: Idaho, GCRG224, NA.

26. Report, June 16, 1948, District Director, Immigration and Naturalization Service, Spokane, Washington, Box 4826, File: Mexico 7-148-9-3048, p. 5, RG59, NA.

27. In 1946, the Office of Labor instructed that each worker was to receive a blanket. It could either be sold to the worker and deducted over time or a deposit was required for its use. See Telegram, Feb. 13, 1946, Office of Solicitor, USDA, to Jessie R. Farr, Box 10, File: Lodging, RG16, FRAC.

28. Narrative, Oct. 1944, Homedale, Idaho, Box 52, File: Idaho, GCRG224, NA.

29. Narrative, Oct. 1944, Hazelton, Idaho, Box 52, File: Idaho, GCRG224, NA.

30. Narrative, Dec. 1946, Caldwell, Idaho, Box 52, File: Idaho, GCRG224, NA.

31. Narrative, Oct. 1944, St. Anthony, Idaho, Box 52, File: Idaho, GCRG224, NA.

32. Memorandum, Nov. 12, 1942, Office of General Counsel, U.S. Department of Agriculture, Box 6, File: Instruction, RG16, FRAC.

33. Narrative, Oct. 1944, Marsing, Idaho, Box 52, File: Idaho, GCRG224, NA.

34. Ibid.

35. Narrative, Sept. 1946, Scappose, Oregon, Box 101, File: Oregon, GCRG224, NA.

36. Narrative, Apr. 1945, Kennewick, Washington, Box 79, File: Camps, Washington Farm Labor Supply Center, 1945, GCRG224, NA.

37. Specialist County Visitation Report, Apr. 29, 1946, EFLR, WSUA.

38. Translated from the Spanish by the author, Box 79, File: Camps, GCRG224, NA.

39. Narrative, Oct. 1946, Nampa, Idaho, Box 52, File: Camps, Idaho, Nampa, GCRG224, NA.

40. Narrative, Sept. 1946, Wilder, Idaho, Box 100, File: Camps, GCRG224, NA.

41. Narrative, July 1944, Milton, Oregon, Box 52, File: Oregon, GCRG224, NA.

42. *Northwest Farm News*, July 29, 1943.

43. "Labor Branch Farm Labor Program," p. 20.

44. Memorandum, Aug. 15, 1944, Box 51, File: Reports, GCRG224, NA.

45. Narrative, July 1944, Blackfoot, Idaho, Box 52, File: Idaho; Narrative, Sept. 1946, Grandview, Washington, Box 102, File: Camps; all in GCRG224, NA.

46. Narrative, Apr. 1944, Caldwell, Idaho, Box 52, File: Idaho; Narrative, Apr. 1944, Wilder, Idaho; all in GCRG224, NA.

47. Specialist Monthly Report, July 1945, EFLR, WSUA.

48. Ibid.

49. *Northwest Farm News*, July 22, 1943.

50. Narrative, Aug. 1946, Grandview, Washington, Box 102, File: Camps, GCRG224, NA.

51. Anderson, "The Bracero Program," pp. 94–96.

52. *Northwest Farm News*, July 29, 1943.

53. Specialist Monthly Report, July 1945, EFLR, WSUA; Narrative, Aug. 1946, Burlington, Washington, Box 101, File: Camps, GCRG224, NA; *Northwest Farm News*, July 25, Aug. 15, 1946.

54. *Idaho Daily Statesman*, Oct. 16, 1945.

55. "Report of Surgeon, Office of Labor, Medical Officer, Northwest Division, August, 1945," Box 85, File: Health Services Reports, GCRG224, NA.

56. Memorandum, No. 6800, Aug. 21, 1945, Mexican Embassy, Box 4821, File: Mexico, RG59, NA.

57. Letter, No. 0-1045, Oct. 10, 1945, Box 4822, File: Mexico, RG59, NA.

58. Rasmussen, *A History*, p. 229.

59. *Northwest Farm News*, July 22, 1943.

60. Narrative, Dec. 1944, Gooding, Idaho, Box 52, File: Idaho, GCRG224, NA.

61. Narrative, Aug. 1944, Hillsboro, Oregon, Box 52, File: Oregon, GCRG224, NA.

62. *Northwest Farm News*, June 13, 1946.

63. Narrative, Sept. 1946, Grandview, Washington, Box 102, File: Camps, Grandview, Washington, GCRG224, NA.

64. Narrative, July 1944, Weiser, Idaho, Box 52, File: Idaho, GCRG224, NA.

65. Narrative, Aug. 1946, Milton-Freewater, Oregon, Box 101, File: Camps, Milton-Freewater, Oregon, GCRG224, NA.

66. Narrative, Nov. 1944, Payette, Idaho, Box 52, File: Idaho, GCRG224, NA.

67. Narrative, Sept. 1946, Stanwood, Washington, Box 103, File: Camps, Stanwood, Washington, GCRG224, NA.

68. *Northwest Farm News,* Apr. 13, 1933.

69. Narrative, May 1947, Nyssa, Oregon, Box 111, File: Camps, Nyssa, Oregon, GCRG224, NA.

70. Narrative, July 1944, Milton-Freewater, Washington, Box 52, File: Oregon, GCRG224, NA.

71. Ibid.

72. Narrative, June 1944, Preston, Idaho, Box 52, File: Idaho, GCRG224, NA.

73. *Yakima Daily Republic,* Aug. 20, 1943.

74. Ibid.

75. See Rasmussen, *A History,* p. 189.

76. Galarza, *Merchants of Labor,* 187.

77. *Northwest Farm News,* Feb. 3, 1944, Report of Sept. 1945–Jan. 1946, Box 86, File: Laborers, Whatcom County Employment Association, GCRG224, NA.

78. Letter, June 21, 1945, Representative Hal Holmes to Lt. Col. Wilson Buie, Box 86, File: Laborers Rent on Feeding Collection, GCRG224, NA.

79. Rasmussen, *A History,* p. 211.

80. Narrative, May 1947, Nyssa, Oregon, Box 111, File: Camps, Nyssa, Oregon, GCRG224, NA.

81. Memorandum, No. 100-15933-R, June 16, 1948, Box 4826, File: Mexico, RG59, NA.

82. Narrative, June 1947, Twin Falls, Idaho, Box 111, File: Idaho, Twin Falls, GCRG224, NA.

83. Memorandum, Mar. 10, 1944, FSA Correspondence, 1943–44, Box 75, File: Office of Labor, GCRG224, NA.

84. Narrative, May 1946, Twin Falls, Idaho, Box 100, File: Camps, Twin Falls, Idaho, GCRG224, NA.

85. Narrative, Sept. 1944, Moses Lake, Washington, Box 53, File: Washington, GCRG224, NA.

86. *El Mexicano,* Jan. 1945, Box 4821, File: Mexico, p. 1, RG59, NA.

87. Ibid., pp. 1–4, my translation.

88. Visitation Reports, June 16, 1944, Washington State Extension Service Reports, 1944, vol. 5, EFLR, WSUA.

89. *Northwest Farm News,* July 20, 1944.

90. Galarza, "Personal and Confidential Memorandum," p. 9.

91. *Medford Mail Tribune,* Sept. 16, 1943.

92. Narrative, Oct. 1944, Wilder, Idaho, Box 52, File: Idaho, GCRG224, NA.

93. Narrative, Sept. 1944, Lincoln, Preston, Idaho, Box 52, File: Idaho; Narrative, Oct. 1944, Filer, Weiser, Idaho, Box 52, File: Idaho; all in GCRG224, NA.

94. Narrative, May 1944, Medford, Oregon, Box 52, File: Oregon, GCRG224, NA.

95. Narrative, May 1944, Medford, Oregon, Box 52, File: Oregon, GCRG224, NA; "Labor Branch Farm Labor Program," p. 19.

96. Narrative, Sept. 1944, Gooding, Idaho, Box 52, File: Idaho, GCRG224, NA.

97. Narrative, July 1944, Hillsboro, Oregon, Box 52, File: Oregon, GCRG224, NA.

98. *Idaho Daily Statesman,* Sept. 18, 1945.

99. Narrative, Oct. 1944, Nyssa, Oregon, Box 52, File: Oregon, GCRG224, NA.

100. Narrative, July 1947, Preston, Idaho, Box 111, File: Camps, Preston, Idaho; Narrative, Aug. 1944, Wilder, Idaho, Box 52, File: Idaho; Narrative, Jan. 1945, Kennewick, Washington, Box 53, File: Washington; all in GCRG224, NA.

101. Narrative, Nov. 1946, Homedale, Idaho, Box 100, File: Homedale, Idaho, GCRG224, NA.

102. Narrative, July 1946, Burlington, Washington, Box 101, File: Burlington, Washington, GCRG224, NA.

103. Narrative, July 1947, Preston, Idaho, Box 111, File: Preston, Idaho; Narrative, June 1947, Marsing, Idaho, Box 111, File: Marsing, Idaho; all in GCRG224, NA.

104. Narrative, May 1946, Wilder, Idaho, Box 99, File: Camps, Wilder, Idaho, GCRG224, NA. By the 1950s, the Catholic Church arranged for Mexican missionaries to provide services to the braceros in the United States. See Hancock, "The Role of the Bracero," p. 39.

105. Narrative, Oct. 1946, Wilder, Idaho, Box 99, File: Camps, Payette, Idaho, GCRG224, NA.

106. Hancock, "The Role of the Bracero," p. 39.

107. Narrative, Aug. 1946, Medford, Oregon, Box 101, File: Camps, Midway, Oregon; Narrative, May 1946, Wilder, Idaho, Box 100, File: Camps; all in GCRG224, NA.

108. Narrative, May 1946, Wilder, Idaho, Box 100, File: Camps, GCRG224, NA.

109. Narrative, Aug. 1946, Medford, Oregon, Box 101, File: Camps, Medford, Oregon, GCRG224, NA.

110. Narrative, July 1947, Preston, Idaho, Camps, Box 111, File: Preston, Idaho, GCRG224, NA.

111. Narrative, Sept. 1944, Moses Lake, Washington, Box 53, File: Washington, GCRG224, NA.

112. Narrative, Aug. 1944, Hillsboro, Oregon, Box 52, File: Oregon, GCRG224, NA.

113. Narrative, Oct. 1944, Wilder, Idaho, Box 52, File: Idaho, GCRG224, NA.

114. Narrative, Aug. 1944, Hillsboro, Oregon, Box 52, File: Oregon, GCRG224, NA. A description of these and other films of that era are found in Riera and Macotela, *La guía del cine mexicano.*

115. Monsavaís, "No te me muevas"; and Saragoza, "Mexican Cinema," pp. 107–124.

116. Narrative, June 1947, Marsing, Idaho, Box 110, File: Marsing, Idaho, GCRG224, NA.

117. Narrative, Apr. 1944, May 1944, Walla Walla, Washington, Box 53, File: Washington, GCRG224, NA.

118. Narrative, Dec. 1945, Walla Walla, Washington, Box 53, File: Washington, GCRG224, NA.

119. Ibid.

120. Narrative, Jan. 1945, Kennewick, Washington, Box 53, File: Washington, GCRG224, NA.

121. *Idaho Daily Statesman*, July 22, 1945.

122. Interview with Arturo Aguirre.

123. Narrative, July 1946, Camp Marshall, Box 101, File: Camps, Salem, Oregon, GCRG224, NA.

124. Narrative, June 1947, Nampa, Idaho, Box 111, File: Camps, Nampa, Idaho, GCRG224, NA.

125. Narrative, Sept. 1944, Marsing, Idaho, Box 52, File: Idaho, GCRG224, NA.

126. Narrative, June 1946, Marsing, Idaho, Box 100, File: Idaho, GCRG224, NA.

127. *Idaho Daily Statesman*, May 1, 1943.

128. Narrative, July–Sept. 1944, Marsing, Idaho, Box 52, File: Idaho, GCRG224, NA.

129. Narrative, July 1944, Milton-Freewater, Oregon, Box 52, File: Oregon, GCRG224, NA.

130. Narrative, May 1946, Nampa, Idaho, Box 100, File: Camps, Caldwell, Idaho, GCRG224, NA.

131. *Idaho Daily Statesman*, May 30, 1946, Oct. 13, 1948.

132. On the blacklisting of Texas, see Scruggs, "Texas and the Bracero Program," p. 254.

133. Narrative, May 1936, Caldwell, Idaho, Box 100, File: Camps, Caldwell, Idaho, GCRG224, NA.

134. Ibid.

135. Narrative, May 1946, Caldwell, Idaho, Box 100, File: Caldwell, Idaho, GCRG224, NA.

136. *Idaho Daily Statesman*, May 30, 1946.

137. Narrative, May 1936, Nampa, Idaho, Box 100, File: Nampa, Idaho, GCRG224, NA.

138. Letter, Dec. 29, 1945, Rev. U. G. Murphey to James F. Byrnes, Secretary of State, Box 4822, File: Mexico, RG59, NA.

139. Letter, Mar. 8, 1944, F. W. Harter to Senator Rufus C. Holman, Box 3349, File: 349, RG59, NA.

140. Narrative, Nov. 1946, Stanwood, Washington, Box 102, File: Camps, Stanwood, Washington, GCRG224, NA.

141. Ibid.

142. Narrative, Jan. 1947, Medford, Oregon, Box 111, File: Camps, Midway, Oregon, GCRG224, NA.

143. *Idaho Daily Statesman*, Oct. 13, 1948.

144. Ibid.

145. Letter, June 11, 1943, Rafael de la Colima, Mexican Embassy, to

Chester C. Davis, WFA, Box 14, File: Mexican Farm Labor, GCRG224, NA. The State Department files contain many clippings from the Mexican newspapers such as *Novedades, Excelsior, El Nacional, El Popular,* and *La Prensa.* These articles give much publicity and cover discrimination and other abuses against Mexicans in the United States. See Box 3348, File: Mexico, RG59, NA.

146. Narrative, Sept. 1944, Twin Falls, Idaho, Box 52, File: Idaho, GCRG224, NA.

147. Narrative, Sept. 1944, Filer, Idaho, Box 52, File: Idaho, GCRG224, NA.

148. Narrative, Oct. 1944, Weiser, Idaho, Box 52, File: Idaho, GCRG224, NA.

149. Narrative, Nov. 1946, Preston, Idaho, Box 100, File: Camps, Preston, Idaho, GCRG224, NA.

150. Narrative, Jan. 1946, Ontario, Oregon, Box 101, File: Camp, Ontario, Oregon, GCRG224, NA.

151. Letter, Aug. 21, 1943, Mrs. William D. Hall to Mrs. Roosevelt, Records of the War Manpower Commission, National Archives, Record Group 211, Box 16894, File: Special File (Records of the War Manpower Commission, National Archives hereafter cited as RG211, NA).

152. Ibid.

153. "Labor Utilization Activities."

154. Narrative, Sept. 1946, Rupert, Idaho, Box 100, File: Camps, Rupert, Idaho, GCRG224, NA.

155. Memorandum, Feb. 12, 1946, R. T. Magleby to Phillip B. Bruton, Box 86, File: Health Sciences, Hospitals, Clinics, GCRG224, NA.

156. Letter, Jan. 15, 1947, Regional Attorney to John C. Gabwell, Box 10, File: General, RG16, FRAC.

157. Letter, Sept. 13, 1946, Jesse R. Fran to F. V. Patterson, Box 10, File: General, RG16, FRAC.

158. Narrative, Sept. 1944, Blackfoot, Idaho, Box 52, File: Idaho, GCRG224, NA.

159. Narrative, Apr. 1945, Kennewick, Washington, Box 79, File: Camps; "Report of Surgeon, Office of Labor, Medical Officer, Northwest Division, August, 1945," Box 85, File: Health Services Reports, p. 1; all in GCRG224, NA.

160. "Report of Surgeon, Office of Labor, Medical Officer, Northwest Division, August, 1945," p. 1.

161. Narrative, June 1946, Meridian, Idaho, Box 100, File: Meridian, Idaho, GCRG224, NA.

162. Memorandum, Feb. 12, 1946, R. T. Magelby to Phillip B. Bruton, Box 86, File: Health Services, Hospitals, Clinics, GCRG224, NA.

163. "Report of Surgeon, Office of Labor, Medical Officer, Northwest Division, August 1945," p. 2.

164. Translator's Summary of Communication dated Aug. 21, 1945, Box 4821, Folder: Mexico, RG59, NA.

165. "Report of Surgeon, Office of Labor, Medical Officer, Northwest Division, August, 1945," p. 6.

166. Ibid.

167. *Idaho Daily Statesman*, July 7, 1946.

168. Narrative, Feb. 1946, Caldwell, Idaho, Box 100, File: Camps, Caldwell, Idaho, GCRG224, NA.

169. "Annual Report of State Supervisor, Emergency Farm Labor, Jan. 1, 1945–Dec. 31, 1945," Oregon State Extension Service, p. 145, OSUA.

170. Narrative, Jan. 1946, Nyssa, Oregon, Box 101, File: Camps, Nyssa, Oregon; Narrative, Apr. 1947, Wapato, Washington, Box 111, File: Camps, Wapato, Washington; all in GCRG224, NA; *Idaho Daily Statesman*, Sept. 24, 1946.

171. Narrative, Oct. 1944, Homedale, Idaho, Box 52, File: Homedale, Idaho, GCRG224, NA.

172. Narrative, Aug. 1946, Medford, Oregon, Box 101, File: Camps, Medford, Oregon, GCRG224, NA.

173. "Annual Report of Emergency Farm Labor Program, 1946," Oregon State Extension Service, p. 38, OSUA.

174. Narrative, Aug. 1946, Medford, Oregon, Box 101, File: Camps, Medford, Oregon, GCRG224, NA.

175. Narrative, Dec. 1946, Caldwell, Idaho, Box 99, File: Camps, Medford, Idaho, GCRG224, NA.

176. *Northwest Farm News*, Sept. 9, 1943.

177. Narrative, Nov. 1944, Blackfoot, Idaho, Box 52, File: Blackfoot, Idaho, GCRG224, NA.

6. From Braceros to Chicano Farm Migrant Workers

1. Already W. H. Martin, chairman of the Land Grant College Committee, had declined any further administrative responsibility for the farm labor program. Memorandum, Sept. 10, 1945, M. L. Wilson to J. B. Hutton, Secretary of Agriculture, Box 1165, File: Agriculture, GCRG16, NA. The National Grange urged that the farm labor program be removed from the jurisdiction of the Extension Service because it was controlled by the Farm Bureau. See the *Oregonian*, Nov. 21, 1946.

2. *Northwest Farm News*, Sept. 5, 1946.

3. Memorandum, Oct. 14, 1946, K. A. Butler to Secretary Clinton Anderson, Box 107, File: Organizational-Safety, GCRG224, NA.

4. Memorandum, July 28, 1945, Meridith C. Wilson to J. B. Hutton, Box 1165, File: Agriculture, GCRG16, NA.

5. "Impact of the War," pp. 1–9.

6. "Labor Branch Farm Labor Program," p. 16.

7. Ibid.

8. *Idaho Daily Statesman*, May 16, 1948.

9. Memorandum, Dec. 12, 1949, John J. Klak to Department of State, Box 4827, File: Mexico, RG59, NA.

10. Labor Market Development Reports, Idaho, Mar. 1948, Box 82, File: General, p. 1, RG183, NA.
11. *Idaho Daily Statesman,* May 16, 1948.
12. *Northwest Farm News,* June 20, 1946.
13. Rasmussen, *A History,* p. 211.
14. Visitation Report, Sept. 1945, Arthur F. Kulin, Okanogan County, EFLR, WSUA.
15. *Northwest Farm News,* Apr. 25, 1946; Visitation Report, Apr. 1946, Walter E. Zuger, Walla Walla County, EFLR, WSUA.
16. *Northwest Farm News,* May 2, 1946.
17. Visitation Report, May 1946, Walter E. Zuger, Yakima County, EFLR, WSUA.
18. Monthly Specialist Report, Jan. 1946, Arthur F. Kulin, p. 1, EFLR, WSUA.
19. Narrative, Aug. 1946, Walla Walla, Washington, Box 101, File: Walla Walla, GCRG224, NA.
20. *Idaho Daily Statesman,* June 15, 1946.
21. *Northwest Farm News,* Mar. 28, 1946.
22. Twenty-fourth Annual Report, p. 114.
23. "Farm Machinery," p. 7; "Farm Outlook," p. 4.
24. *Northwest Farm News,* Mar. 22, 1945.
25. "Potatoes Are King," p. 16.
26. Blosser, Franklin, and Manford, "Man Labor Requirements," p. 12.
27. Hacker, *The End of the American Era,* pp. 13, 14.
28. "Annual Report of State Supervisor Emergency Farm Labor Jan. 1, 1945–Dec. 31, 1945," Extension Service, OSUA.
29. *Northwest Farm News,* Oct. 11, 1945, Mar. 7, 1946.
30. Plan of Work Extension Farm Labor 1947, Specialist Reports vol. 3, p. 1, EFLR, WSUA.
31. *Northwest Farm News,* June 14, 1945.

Conclusion

1. *Yakima Daily Republic,* July 1, 1951.
2. *Seattle Times,* Jan. 8, 1984.
3. Craig, *Bracero Program,* p. xi.
4. Reichert and Massey, "History and Trends," p. 481.

Bibliography

Manuscripts and Archival Sources

Baptismal Records of Yakima Catholic Diocese. Yakima, Washington.

Bottolfsen, C. A. Papers. Idaho State Library, Boise.

Emergency Farm Labor Program, Extension Service. Record Group 111. Oregon State University Archives, Corvallis.

Emergency Farm Labor Report, Extension Service. Record Group 81. Washington State University Archives, Pullman.

General Records of the Department of State. Record Group 59. National Archives, Washington, D.C.

McWilliams, Carey. Papers. Archives and Manuscripts. University of California at Los Angeles Library.

Ourada, Patricia K. Papers. Boise State University Library.

Pierce, Walter. Papers. University of Oregon Archives, Eugene.

Records of the Agricultural Marketing Service. Record Group 136. National Archives, Washington, D.C.

Records of the Bureau of Agricultural Economics. Record Group 83. National Archives, Washington, D.C.

Records of the Farmers Home Administration. Record Group 96. National Archives, Washington, D.C.

Records of the Farm Security Administration. Record Group 96. National Archives, Washington, D.C.

Records of the Farm Security Administration. Region 11. U.S. Government Documents Center. University of Washington Library, Seattle.

Records of the Federal Extension Service. Record Group 33. National Archives, Washington, D.C.

Records of the General Counsel. Record Group 16. U.S. Department of Agriculture, 1937–1952. Federal Archives and Record Center, Seattle.

Records of the Office of Labor of the War Food Administration. Record Group 224. National Archives, Washington, D.C.

Records of the Office of Secretary of Agriculture. General Correspondence 1935. National Archives, Washington, D.C.

Records of the Office of the Secretary of Agriculture. Record Group 16. National Archives, Washington, D.C.

Records of the Office of War Mobilization and Reconversion. Record Group 250. National Archives, Washington, D.C.

Records of the President's Commission on Migratory Labor. Harry S. Truman Library. National Archives and Records Service, Independence, Missouri.

Records of Sunnyside School District 201. Sunnyside, Washington.

Records of the U.S. Employment Service. Record Group 183. National Archives, Washington, D.C.

Records of the War Manpower Commission. Record Group 211. National Archives, Washington, D.C.

State Bureau of Agricultural Economics. Record Group 83. General Correspondence 1941–1946. National Archives, Washington, D.C.

Taylor, Paul S. Papers. Bancroft Library, University of California, Berkeley.

Books

Albertson, Dean. *Roosevelt's Farmer: Claude R. Wickard in the New Deal.* New York: Columbia University Press, 1961.

Arrington, Leonard J. *Beet Sugar in the West: A History of the Utah-Idaho Sugar Company, 1891–1966.* Seattle: University of Washington Press, 1966.

Association for Chicano Studies, Editorial Committee. *History, Culture and Society: Chicano Studies in the 1980s.* Ypsilanti: Bilingual Press, 1983.

Balderrama, Francisco E. *In Defense of La Raza: The Los Angeles–Mexican Consulate and the Mexican Community, 1929 to 1936.* Tucson: University of Arizona Press, 1982.

Bookmap of the Rio Grande Valley. San Antonio: Bookmap, 1973.

Bulnes, Francisco. *Los grandes problemas de México.* Mexico City: Editorial Nacional, 1965.

Cardoso, Lawrence A. *Mexican Emigration to the United States, 1897–1931: Socio-Economic Patterns.* Tucson: University of Arizona Press, 1980.

Clinchy, Everett Ross, Jr. *Equality of Opportunity for Latin-Americans in Texas.* New York: Arno Press, 1974.

Cockcroft, James D. *Outlaws in the Promised Land: Mexican Immigrant Workers and America's Future.* New York: Grove Press, 1986.

Cohen, Wilber S. *The Roosevelt New Deal: A Program Assessment Fifty Years After.* Richmond: Virginia Commonwealth University, 1986.

Cortés, Carlos E., Rodolfo Acuña, Juan Gómez-Quiñones, and George F. Rivera, Jr. *The Mexican Experience in Texas.* New York: Arno Press, 1976.

Cottrell, R. H. *Beet Sugar Economics.* Caldwell: Caxton Printers, 1952.

Craig, Richard B. *The Bracero Program: Interest Groups and Foreign Policy.* Austin: University of Texas Press, 1971.

Cumberland, Charles C. *Mexico: The Struggle for Modernity.* New York: Oxford University Press, 1968.

Daniel, Cletus E. *Bitter Harvest: A History of California Farmworkers, 1870–1941.* Berkeley: University of California Press, 1981.

Easterlin, Richard A., David Ward, William S. Bernard, and Reed Ueda. *Immigration.* Cambridge: Harvard University Press, 1982.

Elac, John C. *Employment of Mexican Workers in U.S. Agriculture 1900–1960*. San Francisco: R. and E. Associates, 1972.

Flynn, George Q. *The Mess in Washington Manpower Mobilization in World War I*. Westport: Greenwood Press, 1979.

Galarza, Ernesto. *Merchants of Labor: The Mexican Bracero Story*. Santa Barbara: McNally Loftin Publisher, 1964.

———. *Strangers in Our Fields*. Washington, D.C.: Joint U.S. Mexico Trade Union Committee, 1956.

———. *Tragedy at Chular: El crucero de las treinta y dos cruces*. Santa Barbara: McNally and Loftin, 1977.

García, Juan Ramón. *Operation Wetback: The Mass Deportation of Mexican Undocumented Workers in 1954*. Westport: Greenwood Press, 1980.

García, Mario T. *Desert Immigrants: The Mexicans of El Paso 1880–1920*. New Haven: Yale University Press, 1981.

Granger Library. *Granger: The Town, the Land, the People*. Saxum Publications, 1975.

Hacker, Andrew. *The End of the American Era*. New York: Atheneum, 1974.

Hancock, Richard H. *The Role of the Bracero in the Economic and Cultural Dynamics of Mexico: A Case Study of Chihuahua*. Stanford: Hispanic American Society, 1959.

Hoffman, Abraham. *Unwanted Mexican Americans in the Great Depression: Repatriation Pressures 1929–1939*. Tucson: University of Arizona Press, 1974.

Hundley, Norris. *The Chicano*. 1st edition. Santa Barbara: Clio Books, 1975.

Idaho Migrants. *Chicano Studies: Its Relationship to a Developing Political Awareness among Migrants*.

Washington, D.C.: Montal Systems, 1971.

Johansen, Dorothy O. *Empire of the Columbia*. 2nd edition. New York: Harper and Row, 1967.

Jones, Robert C. *Mexican War Workers in the United States*. Washington, D.C.: Pan American Union, 1945.

Kirstein, Peter N. *Anglo over Bracero: A History of the Mexican Worker in the United States from Roosevelt to Nixon*. San Francisco: R. and E. Associates, 1977.

Leuchtenburg, William E. *Franklin E. Roosevelt and the New Deal 1932–1940*. New York: Harper and Row, 1963.

Loera, Francisco, José Romero, and Mario Alvarez. *Education: Emerging Opportunities for Chicanos in Oregon*. Washington, D.C.: Montal Systems, 1971.

McWilliams, Carey. *Ill Fares the Land: Migrants and Migratory Labor in the United States*. Boston: Little, Brown and Company, 1942.

Manual of Sugar Companies, 1942. New York: Farr and Company, 1942.

Martínez, John R. *Mexican Emigration to the U.S., 1910–1930*. San Francisco: Rand E. Associates, 1971.

Menig, D. W. *The Great Columbia Plain: A Historical Geography 1805–1910*. Seattle: University of Washington Press, 1968.

Mirandé, Alfredo. *Gringo Justice.* Notre Dame: University of Notre Dame Press, 1987.

Montejano, David. *Anglos and Mexicans in the Making of Texas, 1836–1986.* Austin: University of Texas Press, 1987.

Nash, Gerald. *The American West Transformed: The Impact of the Second World War.* Bloomington: Indiana University Press, 1985.

Ourada, Patricia K. *Migrant Workers in Idaho.* Boise: Boise State University, 1979.

Paredes, Américo. *A Texas-Mexican Cancionero: Folksongs of the Lower Border.* Chicago: University of Illinois Press, 1976.

Pedraza-Bailey, Silvia. *Political and Economic Migrants in America: Cubans and Mexicans.* Austin: University of Texas Press, 1985.

Perales, Alonso J. *Are We Good Neighbors?* New York: Arno Press, 1974.

Peterson, H. C., and Gilbert C. Fite. *Opponents of War 1917–1918.* Madison: University of Wisconsin Press, 1957.

Polenburg, Richard. *War and Society: The U.S. 1941–1955.* New York: J. B. Lippincott Company, 1972.

Pomeroy, Earl. *The Pacific Slope: A History of California, Oregon, Washington, Idaho, Utah, and Nevada.* Seattle: University of Washington Press, 1973.

Portes, Alejandro, and Robert L. Bach. *Latin Journey: Cuban and Mexican Immigrants in the United States.* Berkeley: University of California Press, 1985.

Reisler, Mark. *By the Sweat of Their Brow: Mexican Immigrant Labor in the United States 1900–1940.* Westport: Greenwood Press, 1976.

Riera, Emilio García, and Fernando Macotela. *La guía del cine mexicano: De la pantalla grande a la televisión.* Mexico City: Editorial Patría, 1984.

Romo, Ricardo. *East Los Angeles: History of a Barrio.* Austin: University of Texas Press, 1983.

Samora, Julian. *Los Mojados: The Wetback Story.* Notre Dame: University of Notre Dame Press, 1971.

Schwartz, Harry. *Seasonal Farm Labor in the United States.* New York: Columbia University Press, 1945.

Servín, Manuel. *An Awakening Minority: The Mexican American.* 2d edition. Beverly Hills: Glencoe Press, 1974.

Sobek, María Herrera. *The Bracero Experience: Elitelore versus Folklore.* Berkeley and Los Angeles: University of California Press, 1979.

Smith, Micheal M. *The Mexicans in Oklahoma.* Norman: University of Oklahoma Press, 1980.

Stein, Walter J. *California and the Dust Bowl Migration.* Westport: Greenwood Press, 1973.

Taylor, Fred G. *A Saga of Sugar.* Utah-Idaho Sugar Company, 1944.

Taylor, Paul S. *Labor on the Land: Collected Writings 1930–1970.* New York: Arno Press, 1981.

Tellez, Ignacio García. *La migración de braceros a los Estados Unidos a Norte América.* Mexico City: Hemeroteca Nacional, 1955.

Topete, Jesús. *Aventuras de un bracero.* 2d edition. Mexico City: Editora Gráfica Moderna, 1961.

Valdez, Armando, Albert Camarillo, and Tomás Almaguer, eds. *The State of Chicano Research on Family, Labor and Migration.* Proceedings of the First Stanford Symposium on Chicano Research and Public Policy. Stanford: Stanford Center for Chicano Research, 1983.

Webb, John. *The Migratory Casual Worker.* Washington, D.C.: U.S. Government Printing Office, 1937.

Whetten, Nathan L. *Rural Mexico.* Chicago: University of Chicago Press, 1948.

Winther, Oscar Osburn. *The Great Northwest: A History.* 2nd edition. New York: Alfred A. Knopf, 1956.

Articles

"Admission of Alien Farm Workers into the United States." *Monthly Labor Review* 57, no. 1 (July 1943): 124–125.

Betten, Neil, and Raymond A. Mohl. "From Discrimination to Repatriation: Mexican Life in Gary, Indiana, during the Great Depression." *Pacific Historical Review* 42 (August 1973): 370–388.

Blosser, John H., Earl R. Franklin, and Manford D. Curtis. "Man Labor Requirements for Potatoes in Klamath County, Oregon." *Agricultural Experiment Station Bulletin* No. 421, Oregon State College (July 1944): 1–15.

Bollinger, P. H. "Demand, Labor, Prices, Income." *Agricultural Situation* 25, no. 8 (August 1941): 1–2.

Bowden, Witt. "Wartime Wages and Manpower in Farming." *Monthly Labor Review* (December 1942): 1111–1124.

Brodell, A. P., and M. P. Cooper. "Agriculture in a Gasoline Age." *Agricultural Situation* 26, no. 7 (July 1942): 1–13.

Davis, G. B., and C. D. Mumford. "Farm Organization and Financial Progress in the Willamette Valley." *Circular of Information* No. 444, Agricultural Experiment Station, Oregon State College (February 1947): 1–75.

DeLoach, D. B., and Gordon R. Sutton. "Marketing Central Oregon and Klamath Basin Late Crop Potatoes." *Agricultural Experiment Station Bulletin* No. 400, Oregon State College (December 1941): 1–36.

"Farm Machinery." *Agricultural Situation* 26, no. 2 (February 1942): 7–8.

"Farm Outlook." *Agricultural Situation* 26, no. 11 (November 1943): 1–24.

"The Farming Business in Idaho: Part I." *Agricultural Experiment Station Bulletin* No. 151, University of Idaho (July 1927): 1–125.

Gamboa, Erasmo. "Braceros in the Pacific Northwest: Labors on the Domestic Front, 1942–1947." *Pacific Historical Review* 56, no. 3 (August 1986): 378–398.

———. "Chicanos in the Northwest: An Historical Perspective." *El Grito* 6, no. 4 (Summer 1973): 57–70.

———. "Mexican Labor in the Pacific Northwest 1943–1947: A Photographic Essay." *Pacific Northwest Quarterly* 73, no. 4 (October 1982): 175–181.

———. "Mexican Migration into Washington State: A History 1940–1950." *Pacific Northwest Quarterly* 72, no. 3 (July 1981): 123–131.

Glaser, David. "Migration in Idaho's History." *Idaho Yesterdays* 11, no. 3 (Fall 1967): 22–31.

Hawley, Ellis W. "The Politics of the Mexican Labor Issue, 1950–1965." *Agricultural History* 40 (1966): 157–176.

Hollands, Harold F., Edgar B. Hurd, and Ben H. Dubols. "Economic Conditions and Problems of Agriculture in the Yakima Valley, Washington: Part IV, Hop Farming." *Agricultural Experiment Station Bulletin* No. 414, Washington State College (July 1942).

Hurd, Edgar B., and Harold F. Hollands. "Economic Conditions and the Problems of Agriculture in the Yakima Valley, Washington: The Agriculture and Its Setting." *State College of Washington Agricultural Experiment Station Bulletin* No. 377, State College of Washington (July 1939): 1–82.

Johnson, Neil W., and Harold A. Vogel. "Types of Farming in Idaho: Part II, the Farming Areas." *University of Idaho Agricultural Experiment Station Bulletin* No. 208, University of Idaho (June 1934): 3–26.

Kerr, Louise Año Nuevo de. "Chicano Settlements in Chicago: A Brief History." *Journal of Ethnic Studies* 2 (Winter 1975): 22–32.

Landis, Paul H., and Melvin S. Brooks. "Farm Labor in the Yakima Valley, Washington." *State College of Washington Agricultural Experiment Station Bulletin* No. 343, State College of Washington (December 1936): 1–74.

Landis, Paul H., and Richard Wakefield. "The Drought Farmer Adjusts to the West." *State College of Washington Agricultural Experiment Station Bulletin* No. 378, State College of Washington (June 1939): 1–52.

Liss, Samuel. "The Concept and Determination of Prevailing Wages in Agriculture during World War II." *Agricultural History* 24, no. 1 (January 1950): 4–18.

———. "Farm Wage Boards under the Cooperative Extension Service during World War II." *Agricultural History* 27, no. 1 (January 1953): 103–108.

———. "Farm Wage Boards under the Wage Stabilization Program during World War II." *Agricultural History* 30, no. 3 (January 1956): 128–137.

McCain, Johnny M. "Texas and the Mexican Labor Question 1942–1947." *Southern Historical Quarterly* 85 no. 1 (July 1981): 45–64.

Maldonado, Edwin. "Contract Labor and the Origin of Puerto Rican Communities in the United States." *International Migration Review* 13, no. 1 (Spring 1979): 103–121.

Miller, Michael V., and Lee Robert Maril. "Poverty in the Lower Rio Grande Valley of Texas: Historical and Contemporary Dimensions." *Department of Rural Sociology Technical Report* No. 78, Texas A & M University (February 1979): 1–83.

Miller, Paul B. "The Role of Farm Labor Market Situations in the Lower Rio Grande Valley of Texas." *Department of Economics Wright State University* (December 1971): 1–176.

Monsavaís, Carlos. "No te me muevas paisaje (Sobre el cincuentenario del cine sonoro en México)." *Aztlán* 4, no. 1 (Spring 1983): 1–19.

"Potatoes Are King in Three Areas." *Agricultural Bulletin* 143 (September 1944): 15–17.

"Recent State Legislation Labor Relations." *Monthly Labor Review* 56, no. 5 (May 1943): 941–944.

Reichert, Josh, and Douglas S. Massey. "History and Trends in U.S.-Bound Migration from a Mexican Town." *International Migration Review* 14, no. 4 (Winter 1980): 475–491.

———. "Pattern of U.S. Migration from a Mexican Sending Community: A Comparison of Legal and Illegal Migrants." *International Migration Review* 13, no. 4 (Winter 1979): 599–623.

Reider, Robert. "School Children Mobilized and Trained in Farm Work." *Extension Service Review* 13, no. 10 (October 1942): 146–147.

Reyna, José R. "Notes on Tejano Music." *Aztlán* 13, nos. 1–2 (Spring/Fall 1982): 81–94.

Saloutos, Theodore. "The Immigrant in Pacific Coast Agriculture." *Agricultural History* 49, no. 1 (January 1975): 200–201.

Sasuly, Richard. "Camps Guide Farm Labor." *Agricultural Situation* 26, no. 5 (May 1942): 20–21.

Schorr, Daniel L. "Reconverting Mexican Americans." *New Republic* 114, no. 28 (September 1946): 412–413.

Scruggs, Otey M. "Evolution of the Mexican Farm Labor Agreement of 1942." *Agricultural History* 34, no. 3 (July 1960): 140–144.

———. "The First Farm Labor Program, 1917–1920." *Arizona and the West* 1, no. 4 (Winter 1965): 321–326.

Shields, Louis F. "Labor Conditions during the 1926 Apple Harvest in the Wenatchee Valley." *Monthly Labor Review* 24, no. 4 (April 1927): 13–17.

Sims, Robert C. "The Japanese American Experience in Idaho." *Idaho Yesterdays* 22, no. 1 (Spring 1978): 2–10.

Slatta, Richard W. "Chicanos in the Pacific Northwest: A Demographic and Socio-economic Portrait." *Pacific Northwest Quarterly* 70, no. 4 (October 1979): 155–162.

———. "Chicanos in the Pacific Northwest: An Historical Overview of Oregon Chicanos." *Aztlán* 6, no. 3 (Fall 1975): 327–340.

Smith, Bess F. "Preacher Leads Labor Gang." *Extension Service Review* 13, no. 9 (September 1942): 129–144.

Smith, Charles M. "Farm Workers from Mexico." *Agricultural Situation* 27, no. 6 (June 1943): 12–14.

Taylor, Paul S. "Increases of Mexican Labor in Certain Industries in the United States." *Monthly Labor Review* 32, no. 1 (January 1931): 83–89.

———. "Migratory Farm Labor in the United States." *Monthly Labor Review* 44, no. 3 (March 1937): 537–547.

Tolley, H. R. "Agricultural Production in 1943." *Agricultural Situation* 26, no. 10 (October 1942): 18.

Townsend, Clifford M. "Farm Mobilization Campaign." *Agricultural Situation* 27, no. 1 (January 1943): 10–11.

Wilcox, Walter W. "The Wartime Use of Manpower on Farms." *Journal of Farm Economics* 27, no. 3 (August 1946): 737–741.

Young, C. O. "Index Number of Idaho Farm Prices." *University of Idaho Agricultural Experiment Station Bulletin* No. 210, University of Idaho (June 1935): 1–35.

Dissertations, Theses, and Unpublished Papers

Anderson, Harry P. "The Bracero Program in California with Particular Reference to Health Status, Attitudes, and Practices." Ph.D. dissertation, School of Public Health, University of California, March 1961.

Broadbent, Elizabeth. "The Distribution of Mexican Population in the United States." Ph.D. dissertation, University of Chicago, 1941.

Driscoll, Barbara. "The Railroad Bracero Program of World War II." Ph.D. dissertation, University of Notre Dame, 1980.

Gamboa, Erasmo. "A History of Chicanos in the Yakima Valley, Washington and the Historical Development of Agriculture." M.A. thesis, University of Washington, 1973.

———. "Under the Thumb of Agriculture: Bracero and Mexican American Workers in the Pacific Northwest, 1940–1950." Ph.D. dissertation, University of Washington, 1984.

Houtz, Randal. "Social and Economic Conditions of Spanish Americans in Washington." Northwest Rural Opportunities, February 1977.

Koehler, Paul P. "Integration of the Mexican People in Woodburn, Oregon." Senior thesis, University of Oregon, 1982.

Lemos, Jesús. "A History of the Chicano Political Involvement and the Organizational Effects of the United Farm Worker's Union in the Yakima Valley, Washington." M.A. thesis, University of Washington, 1974.

Sameth, Sheli. "Struggles for an Agricultural Union: A Study with Specific Reference to the Farmworker's Effort in the Yakima Valley, Washington." B.A. thesis, Pitzer College, 1982.

Government Publications

"Agricultural Worker Health Associations Report of Activities." Washington, D.C.: Production and Marketing Administration, U.S. Department of Agriculture, 1946–1947.

Employment and Earning of Agricultural Workers Living in FSA Migratory Labor Camps in Oregon, Washington and Idaho. Farm Security Division Report. Farm Security Administration, U.S. Department of Agriculture, Region XI. June 1938.

Extension Service. *Guía para trabajadores de agricultura a lo largo de las carreteras occidentales.* Washington, D.C.: U.S. Department of Agriculture, 1948.

Farm Labor Fact Book. Washington, D.C.: U.S. Government Printing Office, 1959.

Farm Labor Report. Bureau of Agricultural Economics, U.S. Department of Agriculture. Washington, D.C.: U.S. Government Printing Office, 1943–1947.

"Farm Security Information Division Report." Farm Security Administration, U.S. Department of Agriculture, Region XI. Mimeographed June 1, 1938. U.S. Government Documents Center, University of Washington Library.

Flower, Robert, Jr. *Guiding Migratory Workers to Western Farm Jobs: An Operational Report for the Year 1947.* U.S. Department of Agriculture, Extension Farm Labor Service, 1948.

"Impact of the War and the Financial Structure of Agriculture." Bureau of Agricultural Economics, U.S. Department of Agriculture. Miscellaneous Publications No. 567. August 1945.

Jones, Robert C. *Mexican War Workers in the United States.* Division of Labor and Social Transformation. Pan American Union, 1945.

"Labor Branch Farm Labor Program." U.S. Department of Agriculture, Production and Marketing Administration Labor Branch. Portland, Oregon, 1942.

"Labor Utilization Activities: Excerpts from Reports of State Extension Services." U.S. Department of Agriculture, Extension Service, Farm Labor Circular No. 34. August 1946.

"Mobile Camps for Migrant Farm Families." U.S. Department of Agriculture, Farm Security Administration. Mimeographed. U.S. Government Documents Center, University of Washington Library.

1980 Census: A Statistical Abstract Supplement County and City Data Book 1983. Washington, D.C.: U.S. Government Printing Office, 1983.

Phelps, Winston. "Uncle Sam Has His Own Problem, the Thousands of Homeless Farm Families." U.S. Department of Agriculture, Farm Security Administration, May 1939.

Rasmussen, Wayne D. *A History of the Emergency Farm Labor Supply Program 1943–1947.* Agriculture Monograph No. 13. U.S. Department of Agriculture, Bureau of Agricultural Economics, September 1951.

Report of President's Commission on Migratory Labor. Migratory Labor in Government Agriculture. Washington, D.C.: U.S. Government Printing Office, 1951.

Taylor, Paul S. "The Migrant and California's Future." U.S. Resettlement Administration, 1935. U.S. Government Documents Center, University of Washington Library.

"Texas Mexicans in Sugar Beets, Vegetables, and Fruits: A Report on Improved Relations between Migratory Farm Workers and Agricultural Employers in North, Central and Great Plains States, 1943–1947." Extension Service, U.S. Department of Agriculture, 1948. Washington, D.C.: U.S. Government Printing Office.

U.S. Congress, House of Representatives. Interstate Migration Hearings before the Select Committee to Investigate the Migration of Destitute Citizens. House of Representatives, 76th Congress, Third Session, Parts 4–6. Washington, D.C.: U.S. Government Printing Office.

U.S. Congress, Senate. Farm Labor Program Hearings, Subcommittee of the Committee of Appropriations. U.S. Senate, 78th Congress, First Session of HJ Resolution 96. Washington, D.C.: U.S. Government Printing Office, 1943.

U.S. Congress, Senate. *Report of the Immigration Commissions, Part 25: Japanese and Other Immigrant Races in the Pacific Coast and Rocky Mountain States.* Vol. II, *Agriculture.* Washington, D.C.: U.S. Government Printing Office, 1911.

U.S. State Department. "Foreign Consular Offices in the United States, 1937–1948." Washington, D.C.: U.S. Government Printing Office.

Webb, John. *The Migratory Casual Worker.* Washington, D.C.: U.S. Government Printing Office, 1937.

Newspapers and Periodicals

Business Week, 1942.

Idaho Daily Statesman, Boise, Idaho, 1900–1947.

Idaho Falls Post Register, Idaho Falls, Idaho, 1919–1925.

Medford Mail Tribune, Medford, Oregon, 1942–1945.

Northwest Farm News, Bellingham, Washington, 1940–1947.

Oregonian, Portland, Oregon, 1940–1950.

Seattle Times, Seattle, Washington, 1940–1985.

Sunnyside Sun, Sunnyside, Washington, 1940–1950.

Toppenish Review, Toppenish, Washington, 1940–1950.

Tri-City Herald, 1960–1975.

Washington Post, Washington, D.C., 1945–1947.

Yakima Daily Republic, Yakima, Washington, 1920–1950.

Yakima Valley Mirror, Zillah, Washington, 1940–1950.

Interviews

Arturo Aquirre, Seattle, Washington, May 15, 1985.

Geraldo Cárdenas, Wapato, Washington, September 15, 1972.

Joe Eiqueren, Boise, Idaho, June 1980, tape recording in Ourada Papers, Boise University, Boise, Idaho.

Gumecindo Gamboa, Hawaiian Gardens, California, January 1981.

Salomón Gómez, Lovelock, Nevada, April 10, 1982, tape recording in Boise State Library, Boise, Idaho.

Luís Hernández, Mabton, Washington, May 1983.

Chuck Martínez, Boise, Idaho, July 14, 1982.

Hipólito Méndez, Jr., Sunnyside, Washington, March 1980.

Eusebio Pardo, Ganger, Washington, May 17, 1983.

Santiago Pérez, Grandview, Washington, May 18, 1983.

Leobardo Ramírez, Seattle, Washington, April 9, 1983.

Ilaria R. Salazar, Seattle, Washington, November 26, 1982.

Juan R. Salinas, Toppenish, Washington, July 26, 1972.

Conventions and Proceedings.

"President's Commission on Migratory Labor Stenographic Report of Proceedings Held at Portland, Oregon, Hearings on Migratory Labor." Washington, D.C.: Ward and Paul (Official Reporters, 1950).

Proceedings of the Thirty-third Annual Report Fifty-fifth Annual Meeting of the Oregon State Horticultural Society, December 10–11, 1941. Corvallis: Gazette-Times, 1941.

Twenty-fourth Annual Report, Fifty-seventh Annual Meeting, Oregon State Horticultural Society. Corvallis: Gazette-Times, 1941.

Index